# We move only
## forward

# We move only forward

## Canada, the United States and the First Special Service Force 1942–1944

## James A. Wood

**Vanwell Publishing Limited**

St. Catharines, Ontario

Vanwell Publishing acknowledges the financial support of the Government of Canada through the Book Publishing Industry Development Program for our publishing activities.

Vanwell Publishing Limited
1 Northrup Crescent
P.O. Box 2131
St. Catharines, Ontario L2R 7S2
sales@vanwell.com
tel: 905-937-3100
fax: 905-937-1760

Cover and book design: Renée Giguère
Cover photo:             First Special Service Force Ski Assault Training in Montana hills, 1943.
                         *(9820091-001 M-5 CWM)*
Back cover photo:        Parachute training at Fort William Henry Harrison, Montana, Summer 1942.
                         *(19900261-018 CWM)*

Printed in Canada


Library and Archives Canada Cataloguing in Publication

Wood, James A., 1978-
        We move only forward : Canada, the United States and the First Special
Service Force, 1942-1945 / James A. Wood.

Includes bibliographical references and index.
ISBN 1-55125-112-4

        1. First Special Service Force--History.   2. World War, 1939-1945--
Regimental histories--Canada.   3. World War, 1939-1945--Regimental histories--
United States.   4. World War, 1939-1945--Campaigns--Italy.   I. Title.

D794.5.W65 2006              940.54'1271              C2006-903684-5

# TABLE OF CONTENTS

## LIST OF MAPS AND TABLES

# ACKNOWLEDGEMENTS

An earlier version of this book received generous support from the Military and Strategic Studies program at the University of New Brunswick and the Canadian Department of National Defence through a Security and Defence Forum Scholarship. I am honoured to acknowledge the assistance of both organizations, whose funding supported the research and writing of the 2003 Master's thesis upon which much of the present work is based. I have also benefited greatly from the guidance and advice of my thesis supervisor, Dr Marc Milner, as well as my graduate student colleagues at the University of New Brunswick. Carol Leadenham and the staff of the Hoover Institution Archives at Stanford University were enormously helpful, as were the archivists at the US National Archives (College Park, Maryland), Library and Archives Canada, Ottawa (LAC) and Dr Steve Harris at the Department of National Defence's Directorate of History and Heritage in Ottawa. US Army Signal Corps (SC) photographs are from the US National Archives. Those noted as "George Ronald Collection" are courtesy of the Canadian War Museum Archives, Ottawa (CWM/MCG Archives 1982 0091-001 M-5 and PHOFILM File T4.8 Land Operations Canada. Canadian Army). Individual photographers have been noted where possible. I am grateful to Ben and Simon Kooter of Vanwell Publishing for their support and encouragement, as well as to their editor, Angela Dobler, for her assistance in bringing this book into print. Angela Wingfield edited the final manuscript and provided many valuable corrections. My deepest thanks are also due to two Force veterans, Charles Mann of Kincardine Ontario and Bill Story of Moneta Virginia for sharing their recollections of this remarkable US–Canadian outfit and for their comments on the manuscript.

Finally, my family has given me all manner of support and encouragement. My brother Lyle drew the maps and my parents read through drafts of every chapter, as did Natalie, who also shouldered the burden of keeping me on track throughout the year when it was being researched and written—allowing our excursions to Kouchibouguac and Fundy national parks as needed to prevent the onset of writer's block. Time and again, I have relied upon their advice and suggestions. Their encouragement and support have been unfailing at every stage of this project, as in everything else.

# GLOSSARY AND ABBREVIATIONS

| | |
|---|---|
| 1st ABTF | First Airborne Task Force |
| AFHQ | Allied Force Headquarters |
| AWOL | absent without official leave, US Army |
| AWL | absent without leave, Canadian Army |
| BAR | Browning automatic rifle |
| CCO | Chief of Combined Operations, UK |
| CCS | Combined Chiefs of Staff, US–UK |
| CGS | Chief of General Staff, Canadian Army |
| CIGS | Chief of the Imperial General Staff, UK |
| CMF | Central Mediterranean Force, Canadian Army |
| CMHQ | Canadian Military Headquarters, London |
| CO | Commanding Officer |
| COHQ | Combined Operations Headquarters, UK |
| EM | enlisted man, US Army |
| FGCM | Field General Court Martial |
| FSSF/1SSF | First Special Service Force |
| GHQ | General Headquarters |
| LMG | light machine gun |
| MG | machine gun |
| MP | military police |
| NCO | non-commissioned officer |
| NDHQ | National Defence Headquarters, Ottawa |
| NRC | National Research Council, Canada |
| NRMA | National Resources Mobilization Act |
| OC | Officer Commanding |
| OIC | Officer in Command |
| OR | Other Ranks, Canadian Army |
| OSRD | Office of Scientific Research and Development |
| RCAF | Royal Canadian Air Force |
| replacement | US Army term for reinforcement personnel |
| reinforcement | Canadian Army term for replacement personnel |
| SOE | Special Operations Executive |

"The eyes of Canada and the United States are upon us. Let them see that, as in the past, we move only forward."

— Brigadier-General Robert T. Frederick
Commander, First Special Service Force

# The First Special Service Force

The world has certainly been informed enough of the unguarded frontier, the long peace between our two nations. This is another step from the static to the active; from "We will not interfere with each other" to "We will do big things together." The Force is an intensely dramatic embodiment of our common effort in a cause that commands the faith of all of us.

*— Sholto Watt, War Correspondent*
*The Montreal Star* [1]

As this book [*The Canadian Army, 1939–1945*] is necessarily only an outline of events, we could not spare a great deal of space for any one topic; nevertheless, the Canadian component of the Special Service Force gets, I think, considerably more space to itself than any other unit of the Army. This is as it should be.

*— Colonel C.P. Stacey to Major-General Robert T. Frederick*
*10 December 1947* [2]

IN THE SUMMER OF 1942, six months after the American entry into the Second
World War, the Canadian Army authorized the movement of nearly seven hundred
soldiers to the United States for training as part of the First Special Service Force.
Formed at the request of the British Combined Operations Headquarters, the Force
was originally intended as a special operations unit capable of conducting raids and
long-range sabotage operations in the alpine regions of occupied Europe. Trained for
a parachute descent into enemy territory and the destruction of hydroelectric dams or
other vital installations, the Force was a unique experiment in US–Canadian military
collaboration that grew out of the desperate need of the Allied nations, in 1942, to find
some means of striking at Nazi Germany at a time when that enemy had yet to suffer
a serious reverse in battle against Allied forces.

Officers and men of the First Special Service Force were drawn from the armies of
both Canada and the United States, representing a unique development in the history of
both nations—a combined "North American" military formation in which soldiers from
the two armies served together without regard for nationality. Although the intended
sabotage mission never materialized, in late 1942 the Force underwent extensive
reorganization and received new training in preparation for a role in sustained combat. In
the autumn of 1942 and continuing throughout the winter, Force training emphasized
small unit tactics and weapons training, marking the transition from a highly specialized
sabotage unit to a versatile, light infantry and assault formation. Upon its commitment to
action in Italy in the winter of 1943, the First Special Service Force (FSSF) fought with
distinction during the difficult mountain fighting on the approaches to Cassino and
during the defence and breakout from the Anzio beachhead in the first half of 1944.

At the time, the Force came to symbolize the united purpose of the democratic
nations. "The men of the [Force] take a tremendous pride in their international
composition," wrote a Canadian war correspondent in 1944. "Americans serve under
Canadian officers and vice versa ... you couldn't tell whether you were talking to
Americans or Canadians in the Force, and indeed the Force gives the impression of
having formed something new, a synthesis of North America, but of North America at
its best."[3] At the time, the submergence of nationalist sentiment within the Force was
pointed out as an object lesson for a world that remained torn apart by such prejudices.
Today the Force is remembered in both Canada and the United States as a uniquely
shared and proud inheritance of the North American peoples.

The First Special Service Force was largely without parallel and stands today as an
anomaly in US–Canadian military cooperation. Prior to this, Canadian soldiers had
never served in such close association with the United States Army, and throughout and
after the long Cold War, continuing military cooperation between Canada and the
United States has resulted in no similar examples of such near-complete integration.

Throughout the 1920s and much of the 1930s, relations between the two North American nations had remained distant and strained. Referring to a ceremonial visit to Arlington National Cemetery by Canadian soldiers in 1927, historian J.L. Granatstein described these Canadians as the first "redcoats" to appear in the American capital since 1814, when the British arrived to burn it down.[4] While relations had obviously improved significantly during the intervening century, even by as late as 1939 the Canadian Army did not have service representation in Washington independent of Great Britain. Nevertheless, by the summer of 1942 Canadian and American soldiers were training together at Fort William Henry Harrison, an unused National Guard post outside Helena, Montana, named, ironically, for an American president who had been elected in part because of his leading role in the invasion of Upper Canada during the War of 1812. By the end of 1943, American and Canadian soldiers were serving in the line together, fighting under the command of officers and NCOs from both countries. That which made the First Special Service Force unique also makes it significant, especially given the continuance of a close, if not always uncomplicated, military relationship between Canada and the United States.

This book recounts the history of the First Special Service Force from a Canadian perspective, focusing in particular on the issues surrounding the 1st Canadian Special Service Battalion, the official designation given to the Canadian element of the FSSF. Throughout most of the history of the Force, this Canadian "battalion" existed only as an administrative entity, a convenience adopted for the sake of pay and discipline. Though paid as Canadian soldiers and remaining subject to Canadian military law, Canadian officers and men were dispersed throughout the Force without regard for nationality. Canadian and American soldiers wore the same uniforms, carried the same weapons and answered to the same superiors regardless of nationality. An American private could answer to a Canadian sergeant, who in turn took his orders from an American or a Canadian officer. The 1st Canadian Special Service Battalion, meanwhile, was a "paper unit" that existed as a separate formation of Canadian soldiers on only two occasions: the first being upon its arrival at Fort William Henry Harrison in 1942 and the second on 5 December 1944 when the First Special Service Force was disbanded and the Canadians returned to their own army.

Despite its somewhat ethereal nature, however, the 1st Canadian Special Service Battalion became the subject of a disproportionate amount of high-level consideration at National Defence Headquarters in Ottawa, Canadian Military Headquarters in London, the Canadian Army Joint Staff in Washington and Canadian Army field headquarters in Italy. Were it possible to gauge the success of a paper unit by the volume of letters, official reports and telegrams it generated, the 1st Canadian Special Service Battalion would have to be judged a resounding success. Unfortunately this mass of correspondence required the near-constant attention of Canadian authorities up to and including the Chief of General Staff and the Minister of National Defence, who were repeatedly called upon to make special provision for a formation of Canadian soldiers that never exceeded nine hundred in number.

Throughout the history of the First Special Service Force, issues of pay, discipline and national authority remained important concerns for the Canadian Army. From the beginning, Ottawa insisted on its right to approve or reject any proposed deployment of Canadian soldiers overseas, an insistence that the American authorities quite understandably viewed as a limit upon the free and unimpeded use of the First Special Service Force. Frustrations existed on the Canadian side as well, including repeated complaints to Ottawa that the Canadians of the Force received less pay for doing the same job as their American counterparts. Although the 1st Canadian Special Service Battalion was never brought in line with US Army pay scales, the pay issue came to be overshadowed by more pressing concerns upon the unit's entry into combat.

Within two months of the First Special Service Force arriving in Italy and joining the US Fifth Army in its advance up the Italian peninsula, the provision of Canadian reinforcement personnel to the Force appeared as the most serious difficulty encountered in connection with the 1st Canadian Special Service Battalion. While manpower remained a key concern to the Canadian Army throughout the Second World War and on two occasions assumed crisis proportions, it must be said that this was an unanticipated concern in regard to the First Special Service Force at the time of its creation. Given the nature of the mission first assigned to the Force—a parachute descent into occupied-Norway for the purpose of sabotaging German-controlled hydroelectric dams and power plants, followed by an escape by some undetermined means—reinforcement of the FSSF upon its commitment to combat was not expected to be an issue. During one of the initial planning sessions US War Department officials described the FSSF in two words as "sacrifice troops." When the intended mission in Norway was cancelled, however, Force training was reoriented to a role as elite light infantry. Unfortunately no corresponding arrangements were made for replacing casualties in the unit with Canadian and American soldiers trained to the standard of the original men, an oversight that from January 1944 onwards threatened the very existence of the First Special Service Force.

Given the severe losses incurred in the mountain fighting that followed the unit's arrival in Italy, casualty replacement became a serious difficulty for the Force as a whole and the Canadian element in particular. With the FSSF attached to the US Fifth Army in Italy, the Canadian element found itself separated from the rest of the Canadian Army with no means of replacing its losses. One month after entering combat, the 1st Canadian Special Service Battalion was reduced by casualties to half its combat strength, leading the acting senior Canadian officer of the FSSF, Lieutenant-Colonel Thomas P. Gilday, to recommend to his superiors that the Canadians be withdrawn from the Force. Though his request was turned down, over time the difficulties surrounding casualty replacement and the provision of Canadian reinforcements became the most serious threat to the unit's continued existence. By the autumn of 1944, as the Canadian Army and the Mackenzie King government grappled with shortages of infantry reinforcements and an emerging conscription crisis, these issues became even more pronounced.

Although nearly every historical account of the First Special Service Force has noted the international complications encountered in connection with the unit, there have been no in-depth studies of the Force based on research into both Canadian and American records. To date, the focus of historical literature has centred upon the operational history of the Force, beginning with *The First Special Service Force: A War History of the North Americans* (1947) by Robert D. Burhans. This detailed history of the Force in combat, written by the unit's former intelligence officer, remains unsurpassed as the authoritative operational history of the First Special Service Force.

In addition to popular historical accounts, most notably Robert H. Adleman and George Walton's *The Devil's Brigade* (1966), which became the basis of David L. Wolper's feature film of the same title, official histories in Canada and the United States have focused on the First Special Service Force. In the United States, operational accounts of the First Special Service Force appear in several volumes of the US Army in World War II series, which provide less detail than the work by Burhans but place the First Special Service Force within the context of US Army operations in the Aleutian Islands, Italy and Southern France. Training and organization of the Force, meanwhile, is detailed in Stanley W. Dziuban's *Military Relations Between the United States and Canada, 1939–1945* (1959), a volume of the US Army official series, which also considers the unit within the context of the US–Canadian military relationship.

In Canada volumes of The Official History of the Canadian Army series represent the only existing accounts dedicated to the Canadian element of the First Special Service Force. These are necessarily brief, given that the authors, Colonel C.P. Stacey and Lieutenant-Colonel G.W.L. Nicholson, were limited in the space that could be provided to a single battalion of the Canadian Army. Nevertheless, *Six Years of War: The Army in Canada, Britain and the Pacific* (1955) and *Arms, Men and Governments* (1970) by Stacey and *The Canadians in Italy, 1943–1945* (1956) by Nicholson provide brief overviews of the 1st Canadian Special Service Battalion.

Both the Canadian and American official histories point out that the international character of the Force led to difficulties, though these were far less apparent in Dziuban's account, which is based largely upon American sources. From his study of

United States records, Dziuban concluded, "The administrative complications were in the over-all so small and were handled so competently by the Canadian administrative personnel that they were hardly apparent to U.S. members of the force staff, and they had no practical impact on the force's fighting capabilities."[5] In comparison, Stacey's conclusions seem rather sobering. Surveying the difficulties involved in organizing the 1st Canadian Special Service Battalion and maintaining it in the theatre of war, including the inordinate amount of high-level consideration devoted to this battalion-sized formation, Stacey offered the following advice:

> The First Special Service Force was a fine fighting unit, and the relations of Canadians and Americans within it seem to have left very little to be desired. Nevertheless, the administrative and other difficulties that were encountered in connection with it—in matters of pay, decorations, and the tendency of the United States to regard Canadian members of this international unit as Canadians serving in the U.S. Army—suggest that any such enterprise should not be undertaken on another occasion without careful thought.[6]

Stacey's account was necessarily brief, given that his task was to write the official history of the Canadian Army in the Second World War. Nevertheless, Stacey's and Nicholson's work identifies several of the difficulties and complications arising from Canadian participation in the First Special Service Force.

From 1942 to 1944, some fifteen hundred Canadian soldiers served in the First Special Service Force and 155 were killed fighting in Italy and southern France.[7] Following upon its success on Monte la Difensa, the Force continued fighting its way through the half-frozen mud of the Apennine mountains, earning an enviable combat record in the process but suffering 1,400 casualties in the month of January 1944 alone—a loss of more than half the unit's combat strength. In February the Force arrived on the Anzio beachhead, where it spent the next four months holding the line along the Mussolini Canal on the right flank of the Allied perimeter. It was at this time that the Force commander, Brigadier-General Robert T. Frederick, expressed grave concern over the long-term viability of the Force. Having made no provision for replacing its losses with trained replacements—either Canadian or American—Frederick was of the opinion that the FSSF should be disbanded at the earliest opportunity. This, he felt, would be in the best interests of both nations. With the Force committed to holding the line at Anzio, however, and owing to the international complications involved, it was not until nine months had passed that his recommendations could be acted upon.

When it was finally decided to disband the First Special Service Force on 5 December 1944, the official report of the Canadian element recorded: "News of the break up of the Force was met with mixed feelings. It was a great surprise to all and it can only be estimated that 50% were glad and 50% sorry to leave."[8] While it is misleading to say that nearly half of the men were pleased by the decision (their reaction might better be described as resigned acceptance), this final report gives some indication of the serious difficulties plaguing the Force during the last months of its existence. While many Force veterans remember 5 December 1944 as perhaps the worst day of their life, the final report of the 1st Canadian Special Service Battalion indicates that many were willing to accept disbandment as the only reasonable decision at that point. For the surviving "originals" of the Force—the men who had been with the unit from its formation in Helena to disbandment in Southern France—it was simply not the same Force with which they had come overseas. Casualties among the original men, all of them selected soldiers who had spent more than a year in training together before their arrival in Italy, and the replacement of these casualties by eager but inadequately trained newcomers had led to a gradual but unmistakable erosion of the unit's elite character.

As Canadians today send their soldiers to serve alongside and, more recently, under the operational command of the United States Army, they would do well to consider the history of the First Special Service Force, one of the finest fighting units in the Second World War—but also a combined effort that began under happier circumstances than it ended.

While the First Special Service Force proved repeatedly in combat that Canadian and American soldiers could be moulded into an effective fighting unit—a "synthesis of North America at its best"—their achievements in the field were often set against a background of frustrating miscommunication and bureaucratic tangles in Ottawa, Washington and overseas. Although the front line achievements of the Force—hard-won victories against a determined enemy—figure prominently in existing accounts of the First Special Service Force, these need to be qualified by an understanding of how the bi-national composition of the unit led to unanticipated difficulties behind the scenes. Without detracting from what Canadian and American soldiers were able to achieve together, by viewing the Force from the perspective of higher headquarters it becomes possible to understand why the unit was disbanded and why, in spite of its achievements, there has been no attempt by Canada and the United States to repeat the experiment.

## CHAPTER 1

# The Talented Mr Pyke

The War Department was working on the assumption that
they were entirely responsible, at the request of the Chief of
Combined Operations, for the development of this project
in North America. Here, it should be noted that during our
conversations with Mr. Pyke, it appeared that he had got off
on the wrong foot in Washington and now wanted to move
the control of the project to Canada.

— *Major-General J.C. Murchie*
*Canadian Vice Chief of the General Staff*
*23 June 1942* [1]

ON THE MORNING OF 30 MAY 1942, Major-General Maurice Pope arrived at his
Washington office, ready to begin another day at his post as Canada's senior armed
services representative in the United States. As the official spokesman for both the
Canadian Chiefs of Staff and the Cabinet War Committee, Pope occupied a position
lying somewhere between soldier and politician. Among his many responsibilities in
Washington, the general was charged with maintaining continuous contact with his
British and American counterparts and keeping himself and his superiors in Ottawa
informed of recent developments in the Allied war effort. Should the need arise, Pope
also attended meetings of the Combined Chiefs of Staff (CCS) when matters of
concern to Canada were under discussion. [2] The CCS, however, being the supreme
Allied strategic directorate responsible for the direction of a global war, almost never

discussed matters concerning Canada. That morning Pope could look forward to another day of scheduled meetings and informal chats with his British and American colleagues. Among these visits, the arrival of Mr Geoffrey Pyke would have been regarded as only slightly unusual, and even then, due more to the odd appearance and personality of the visitor than to anything that was likely to be said during the meeting.

As Lord Louis Mountbatten's representative in the United States, Geoffrey Pyke had been appointed by the British Chief of Combined Operations to serve as the director of a secret Anglo–American project, code-named Operation Plough. Although not directly involved with this project, Pope was already vaguely familiar with the nature of Pyke's work, there having been some earlier correspondence passed between project planners and the Canadian National Research Council regarding the development of a snow vehicle.[3] During their conversation Pyke mentioned plans to visit Ottawa within the next two weeks and requested a meeting with Lieutenant-General Kenneth Stuart, the Canadian Chief of General Staff, in order to present certain proposals in connection with his work.[4] While there is no indication that Pope considered this visit to be unusual at the time, the development of a snow vehicle only went part way in explaining the motives behind Pyke's request. At the close of this meeting Pyke took his leave, and Pope ordered the necessary cable sent to Ottawa: "Mr. Geoffrey Pyke, head of mission and director of programmes, Combined Operations U.K., desires to visit Ottawa latter half of next week in order to lay certain proposals before Chief of the General Staff." It was the first in a series of events that would lead ultimately to the dispatch of Canadian soldiers to the United States and the formation of a Canadian element within the First Special Service Force.

The origins of Operation Plough as a joint British–American project lay in General George C. Marshall's visit to the United Kingdom in April 1942. The purpose of this visit by the US Army's Chief of Staff was to effect some initial coordination between the Western Allies in preparation for the invasion of occupied Europe. Having entered the war after the Japanese attack on Pearl Harbor and an ill-advised German declaration of war against the United States, the Americans were anxious to see some progress made in breaking Germany's hold on the European continent.

During Marshall's first meeting with the British Chiefs of Staff Committee on 9 April, much of the discussion centered around plans for the build-up of American forces in Britain under Operation Bolero and the cross-Channel invasion that Marshall hoped would follow in the spring of 1943, designated Operation Roundup. Having outlined this best-case scenario, Marshall also presented plans for an emergency landing on the Continent in late summer 1942, Operation Sledgehammer, to be conducted only if necessary to prevent the collapse of the Soviet Union. Intended to draw German forces away from the Eastern Front, the proposed Sledgehammer invasions would be conducted as a "sacrifice landing," a last-ditch effort to prevent German victory in the east. Understood to be a desperate gamble, the operation was planned as an emergency response to the worst-case scenario. Indeed, at this dark stage of the war, desperate gambles of this kind were becoming increasingly common.

At the conclusion of these discussions Marshall accepted invitations to three British headquarters but singled out Lord Louis Mountbatten's Combined Operations Headquarters (COHQ) at Richmond Terrace as the first he would like to see.[5] COHQ was the British headquarters responsible for effecting inter-arms coordination in preparation for an amphibious assault on the European mainland. For Mountbatten, a relatively young commander only recently appointed to the Chiefs of Staff Committee, Marshall's interest in the work of Combined Operations was greeted with great enthusiasm. During the American general's visit, Mountbatten impressed the American general with his ability to direct the efforts of soldiers, sailors and airmen. When asked by Marshall how this could be made to work so well, Mountbatten replied, "Well, after all, we all speak the same language. Come to think of it, so do you and we. Why don't you send me some American officers?"[6] Mountbatten was eager to build upon the foundations of Anglo–American cooperation that were being established in the spring of 1942. Perhaps equally important for Marshall, Mountbatten's commitment to offensive action and carrying the war to the shores of Europe seemed to stand out from that of the other British commanders he had met.

It was amid these friendly discussions that Mountbatten first introduced Marshall to Geoffrey Pyke, one of three "long-haired" civilian scientists who were working for the Director of Experiments at COHQ. Pyke has been described as an eccentric genius, although many who knew him described the British scientist in far less charitable terms. His personal habits were notably unpleasant, as Pyke only rarely shaved, bathed, changed his clothes or chose to wear socks. By all accounts, he was also an exceptionally difficult man to work with, one who had a very short fuse when it came to dealing with his military colleagues. "Pyke, who had little use for Service people—indeed, he had little use for anybody—used to bitterly quote G.K. Chesterton's Father Brown: 'It isn't that they cannot see the solution: they cannot see the problem.'"[7] Pyke was also in the habit of referring to the officers of Mountbatten's headquarters as "the numbskullery," which certainly did nothing to improve relations with his colleagues.[8] The feeling was often mutual, with military professionals barely concealing their disdain for Pyke's dishevelled appearance and irritating habits—such as calling meetings in his bed chamber when he imagined himself to be deathly ill or because he was simply "too busy to get dressed."[9]

On the day of Marshall's visit, however, Pyke was at the top of his game as he outlined his proposals for Operation Plough. Pyke's plan called for the creation of specialized commando detachments, trained in winter warfare and equipped with armoured snow vehicles. Capable of either parachute or glider landings in the snow-covered regions of occupied Europe, and with the mobility afforded by the proposed snow vehicle, these highly trained groups would be able to conduct long-range sabotage operations against key industrial targets. Using Norway as an example, Pyke argued that the detachments could land on glaciers or frozen lakes and from there proceed with attacks against hydroelectric dams, using their vehicles first to transport explosives to the target and then to effect an escape. "Escape to where?" remained an open question, but in Pyke's estimation these attacks would cause damage far in excess of the limited numbers of men involved and would compel the Germans to reinforce their garrisons, thereby deploying a disproportionately large number of troops in a continuing anti-sabotage role. "The Germans ... 'occupy' the Norwegian people but do not really occupy the 125,000 square miles of country," argued Pyke. "What we must try to do is either drive them out or compel them to this costly necessity ... Far from wanting to drive the Germans out of this area we want, under certain conditions, as many as possible of them to come in."[10]  By this means Pyke hoped to create a Norwegian quagmire for the Germans, a drain on their resources that he compared to the exploits of T.E. Lawrence in the Arabian peninsula during the First World War.[11]

Pyke's plan already enjoyed the support of Mountbatten, whose mandate for the development of new weapons and tactics almost required him to remain open to this sort of unconventional scheme.[12] Further, the responsibilities of Mountbatten's command—the only British headquarters responsible for conducting offensive operations at a time when the Axis nations stood at the height of their power—accorded well with a certain affinity for desperate undertakings. Winston Churchill was also behind the project, for reasons that are probably best attributed to the Prime Minister's enthusiastic support of commando forces and his predisposition toward operations in Norway. The Prime Minister, in fact, is said to have raised with such frequency the possibility of conducting raids in Norway that the subject became known as the "recurrent nightmare" of his staff. During his visit to COHQ, Marshall also became convinced of the plan's potential, and when Mountbatten offered the Plough project to the United States, he readily accepted responsibility for the development of both the snow vehicle and the raiding force.

While Marshall's acceptance of Operation Plough cannot be attributed to any single factor, all parties concerned would have recognized that there could be no further development of the project in the United Kingdom. British war industry was already stretched to the limit and simply did not have the capacity to turn out a working snow vehicle for the winter of 1942–1943. It also seems likely that, at least at this stage of the war, Marshall shared some of Churchill's enthusiasm for the establishment of commando forces, and this probably played a role in his support for the Plough project. During his visit to the UK, Marshall also approved the formation of Ranger battalions by the US Army, to be organized and trained along lines similar to the British Commandos. The formation of such units, Marshall reasoned, would provide select volunteers with an early entry into combat. The intention was that these units would then be disbanded prior to the invasion of Europe, thereby providing the US Army with a pool of veteran officers and NCOs to lead the assault forces.[13]

Another factor contributing to Marshall's acceptance of the Plough project was his desire to foster good relations within the alliance. A few days after his return to the United States, nine American officers received orders to proceed to the UK—Marshall placed a high premium on cooperation with the British, and he had accepted Mountbatten's request for American officers to join the staff at Richmond Terrace. It is not unreasonable to conclude that Marshall expected Operation Plough to achieve similar ends by drawing the Western Allies into closer cooperation with each other. Finally, a successful diversionary operation in Norway during the winter of 1943 accorded perfectly with Marshall's proposed timetable for Operation Roundup and his hopes of opening a second front in northwest Europe that spring.

On 21 April 1942, General Marshall called a meeting of his staff at the War Department for the purpose of introducing them to the Plough project. In a memorandum circulated prior to this briefing, Marshall summarized the intent of the operation as follows:

> If a snow vehicle, armored, carrying adequate guns and a small crew can be developed, it is possible that it may be used to considerable effect against critical points. They have in mind establishing a glacier base from the air in Norway, from which they could operate against the hydroelectric plants on which Germany depends to get out valuable ores. They have in mind the use of these vehicles in sudden raids so as to force German troop concentrations in a wasteful manner in the rear of coastal garrisons.[14]

In this presentation, Marshall made it clear that Plough enjoyed both his and Mountbatten's personal support. He also took the opportunity to note Geoffrey Pyke's impending arrival in the United States, it having been decided that the British scientist should follow his project across the Atlantic. "The civilian concerned," Marshall warned, "is a very odd-looking individual, but talks well and may have an important contribution to make."[15] He requested that Pyke be given an opportunity to explain his ideas regarding the proposed operation. Once the project was underway, the British scientist would stay on in Washington, assuming an advisory role as Mountbatten's representative and assisting with the development of the snow vehicle. Ideally, said Marshall, Pyke could be "taken in charge" by American officers, his creativity "channeled to Army specifications."[16]

Pyke had little use for army specifications. Before he left Britain, someone suggested that he might be better received in the United States if he accepted a commission and arrived in uniform—"a polite way of suggesting that he really should do something about the way he dressed."[17] To this Pyke replied, "I am quite willing to be clothed as a general—in the Salvation Army."[18] In truth, the officers at COHQ were happy to be rid of the scientist, and they fully expected the Americans to cut him down a notch—or several—upon his arrival in the United States. They would soon be proven correct in this assumption.

In his first meeting with representatives of the War Department, Pyke presented his ideas to a committee that included the Deputy Chief of Staff, Lieutenant-General Joseph T. McNarney; the Chief of Supply (G-4), Brigadier-General Raymond Moses; and Dr. Vannevar Bush of the Office of Scientific Research and Development (OSRD).[19] During his detailed presentation Pyke continued at length explaining his theories regarding snow as a "fourth element" in warfare, and concluded his talk with a request for further research into the physical nature of snow before the use of actual vehicles in any tests. Although it is uncertain whether he made any more comparisons to Lawrence of Arabia, the American officials were not particularly impressed by his lecture. When the OSRD representatives objected to Operation Plough on the grounds that a working snow vehicle could not be designed and built from scratch within a time-frame of nine months, Pyke became impatient and spoke angrily. Meanwhile, his British Army assistants, Brigadier Nigel Duncan and Major E.A.M. Wedderburn, said nothing to help ease the tension because Pyke had warned them prior to the meeting that they were not to interfere in the discussion. Having made a decidedly poor first impression upon the American committee, Pyke concluded that the meeting had accomplished nothing and that Plough was off to a difficult start in the United States. Nevertheless, the OSRD had its orders from Marshall and accepted the project on the condition that development of the snow vehicle receive first priority from the War Department in the allocation of resources.[20]

Following shortly upon the conclusion of this meeting, Operation Plough came to be divided into two separate paths of development. The first, taken by the OSRD, was responsible for bringing the snow vehicle into production, while the second, taken by the Operations Division of the War Department, handled the organization of the Plough force and drew up plans for its employment.

It was in the field of developing the snow vehicle that Canada first became involved with Operation Plough. Towards the end of April the National Research Council of

Canada received numerous requests for information on existing snowmobiles. Further, the Canadian Army was asked to nominate an officer from the Winter Warfare School for short-term duty as an advisor in the United States.[21] In May a representative of the Council's Mechanical Engineering Division joined the OSRD research committee headed by Dr. Bush. In this advisory capacity Canada was able to share the results of considerable research conducted on track-driven snow vehicles prior to the war.[22] It is important to note, however, that Canadian involvement at this stage was limited to assisting American engineers with the technical problems of developing the snow vehicle. There were no plans in May 1942 for the establishment of a Canadian element in the Plough force.

The initial period of vehicle testing and trials witnessed a flurry of activity as OSRD researchers sought to push development ahead as quickly as possible before the snow disappeared from the southern Rockies. Moving in stride with the hurried pace of research and development during the first two weeks of May, Geoffrey Pyke's relationship with the Americans underwent a rapid deterioration. Prior to the first vehicle tests, Pyke took the position that an Archimedean screw design—using two long, threaded cylinders for traction—offered the best form of propulsion for the snow vehicle. He remained committed to this theory even after field testing in the Sierra Nevada demonstrated it to be impracticable.[23] To Pyke's way of thinking, if the Archimedean screw design did not work well, this simply meant the engineers were not trying hard enough—a view he readily discussed with anyone who would listen, regardless of security concerns.[24] It was not long before US Army and OSRD officials began to ignore him, choosing instead to communicate directly with his assistants, Duncan and Wedderburn. Throughout the month, these two British officers attended numerous tests of experimental snow vehicles, tests from which Pyke was very deliberately excluded.

The result was a series of irate cables to Mountbatten in which Pyke bitterly accused the Americans of selling the Plough project short.[25] At first, Mountbatten seems to have dismissed these complaints as nothing more than Pyke's usual antics being played out on the other side of the ocean. His reply urged Pyke not to allow personal grievances to interfere with the greater effort of winning the war. That done, the CCO probably considered the matter closed—until he was forced to reconsider upon receipt of an angry, 3,000-word telegram in which Pyke elaborated on the nature of his difficulties and tendered his resignation from the project.[26] The situation was obviously more serious than Mountbatten had first imagined, but for the moment there was little that he could do, being fully engaged at the time with planning a cross-Channel raid on the French port of Dieppe. Promising to look further into the situation during his upcoming visit to the United States, Mountbatten refused to accept Pyke's resignation and asked that he carry on with his work, at least for the time being. Although it was unclear whether Pyke had any work to carry on with, given his exclusion from the project, he agreed to stay on until Mountbatten had had a chance to visit.

Considering that vehicle development was already throwing Pyke into tantrums, he would likely have found the progress of operational planning equally discouraging. While the OSRD handled the details of bringing the snow vehicle into production, the task of evaluating Plough from a military standpoint fell to Major-General Dwight D. Eisenhower's Operations Division of the War Department. On 22 May, Eisenhower called on Lieutenant-Colonel Robert T. Frederick, one of more than a hundred staff officers working in the Operations Division, to produce a detailed strategic assessment of Operation Plough. Here again Pyke was excluded, as operational planning was rightfully considered to be a military function requiring the strictest measures of security. Nevertheless, in the absence of any useful task to perform, the British scientist appears to have begun plotting.

This was the context of Geoffrey Pyke's meeting with Canadian Major-General Maurice Pope in Washington on 30 May. Finding himself isolated and without a role to play in what he considered to be his own project, Pyke had become increasingly frustrated with the development of Plough in the United States. Arriving in Pope's office to request an audience with Canadian officials in Ottawa, clearly, Pyke hoped that some form of increased Canadian involvement in the project would provide him with a means of bolstering his dwindling influence. Bringing in a new partner—one that he had not yet completely alienated—would provide Pyke with a second chance, a channel through which he could again hope to exert some influence over Operation Plough. While this may have been an unrealistic expectation on Pyke's part, his exclusion from any kind of active role in vehicle testing seemed to have left him with plenty of spare time in which to develop such schemes. To his credit, Pyke carefully kept these plans to himself, demonstrating that he could, in fact, keep a secret when he wanted to.

Lord Louis Mountbatten arrived in Washington on 3 June for the purpose of continuing his earlier discussions regarding Operation Roundup and the invasion of Europe. In this regard, the British CCO's task in Washington was to convince the American chiefs of staff that there could be no invasion of Europe in 1943.[27] Mountbatten had also committed, however, to look further into the Plough situation during his visit, and he took the opportunity to discuss these matters in person with Pyke. In the course of their discussion he came to agree with his representative that the project was not receiving due consideration in the United States, and he decided to raise these issues the next day during a meeting with Major-General Eisenhower at the War Department.[28]

Mountbatten and Eisenhower had first met only a few days earlier, during Eisenhower's visit to the UK to discuss invasion planning. Like Marshall, Eisenhower had established an immediate rapport with Mountbatten and had come away impressed by the British commander's willingness to engage the Germans.[29] Their meeting in Washington was conducted on equally friendly terms, with Eisenhower offering his assurance that Pyke would henceforth be kept fully informed of developments.

Having addressed Mountbatten's concerns over Pyke's status in the United States, the meeting turned to a discussion of Lieutenant-Colonel Frederick's assessment of Operation Plough. The report was scathing, with Frederick pointing out that while Norway offered promising terrain for such an operation, no available aircraft was capable of carrying the snow vehicle and dropping it by parachute. Gliders, meanwhile, were not feasible because their use would require every second man in the assault force to be trained as a pilot. Further, there existed no workable plan for evacuating the raiding force once its mission was accomplished. Every soldier landed in Norway would ultimately be killed or taken prisoner. As an alternative, Frederick suggested that subversive acts by native Norwegians could effect equal or greater damage to the German war effort at far less cost than could an American combat force. In closing, Frederick noted that Operation Plough threatened to interfere with more important tasks, and he recommended that "the plan proposed by Mr. Geoffrey Pyke for United States operations in Norway … not be undertaken as proposed."[30]

Mountbatten did not doubt the soundness of these objections; Frederick's report had been well reasoned, meticulous, and presented valid concerns that needed to be addressed. In Mountbatten's view, Eisenhower had offered his assurance that the project would receive due consideration and he judged Ike to be an honest and capable man.[31] Nevertheless, the meeting seemed to confirm some of Pyke's earlier assertions that Operation Plough had met with significant resistance in the United States. While the opposition was not overwhelming, it was enough to convince Mountbatten that before his return to the UK, it would be necessary to establish the project on more stable footing if its survival was to be assured.

There is no documentary evidence recording the precise moment of Mountbatten's decision to approach the Canadians requesting their participation in the Plough force. Pyke, however, almost certainly had a hand in this decision, either directly by suggesting the idea during his initial meeting with Mountbatten or indirectly through his innumerable difficulties in the United States. The inclusion of Canadians in the assault force would also have held certain attractions for Mountbatten, who as CCO had just spent the past few months planning a large-scale raid on Dieppe. Throughout this period, the Canadian government had been pressing to have its soldiers assigned to combat. In April and May, pressure from the Canadian government, along with

Winston Churchill's support of those demands, had been a key consideration in the selection of the 2nd Canadian Infantry Division for the Dieppe raid. In June, these same demands influenced Mountbatten's decision to suggest Canadian participation in the Plough force, and he very likely discussed this possibility with Churchill prior to departing for Washington. In any case, Pyke's upcoming visit to Ottawa presented an ideal opportunity for raising the subject.

For the moment, however, Mountbatten returned to the wider war, attending meetings with the American chiefs of staff and presenting British views on invasion planning and the operations proposed earlier by Marshall during his visit to the UK. During these visits, Mountbatten also took the opportunity to remind President Roosevelt that Prime Minister Churchill had taken a rather strong interest in the project. In a subsequent meeting with the President's advisor, Harry L. Hopkins, he was able to secure further assurances that Pyke would not be obstructed from a role in Operation Plough. "If, in the future, the military attempted to close doors to Pyke, the resourceful 'assistant President' would forcefully reopen them."[32] On the evening of 10 June, with business in Washington concluded, Mountbatten and Pyke boarded a train bound for Ottawa via Montreal, travelling in company with the newly appointed commander of the Plough force, Robert T. Frederick.

There have been a number of explanations for Frederick's appointment to command the Plough force, all of them noting the unusual nature of the decision. A Coast Artillery officer by training, Frederick later attributed the decision to other more qualified officers turning down the job.[33] Indeed, Frederick's initial reaction to Eisenhower's offer was to protest that he was completely unqualified for the position, noting in particular his complete lack of infantry training and his unfamiliarity with parachuting, mountain operations and winter warfare.[34] Others have detected what may have been Mountbatten's influence on the decision, that the CCO noted Frederick's objections to the plan and shrewdly calculated that these would disappear if he were placed in command of the operation.[35] Appointing Frederick to command Operation Plough would perhaps offer a means of silencing one of the project's harshest critics. Regarding Major-General Eisenhower's role in the decision, it is worth noting that on 8 June General Marshall told Ike that he was being considered for the job of commanding general, US European Theater of Operations.[36] At this stage of his career Eisenhower would probably have considered it counterproductive to overrule the British Chief of Combined Operations on an admittedly minor point of detail. In any case, on 9 June, Frederick was called into Eisenhower's office and told: "Frederick, take this plough project. You've been over the whole thing. You're in charge now. Let me know what you need."[37] One day later the modest and unassuming Lieutenant-Colonel Frederick was sitting with Mountbatten and Pyke on a train destined for Canada.

Arriving in Montreal the next day, Mountbatten had approximately one hour in which to discuss matters with the Canadians before boarding a return flight to the UK.[38] On hand to meet him was Lieutenant-General Kenneth Stuart, Chief of the Canadian General Staff. Although their discussion was necessarily brief, Mountbatten was able to outline the project and request all possible assistance from the Canadians before handing the proceedings over to Pyke and Frederick. With that, he departed, leaving Pyke as his personal representative in North America, able to speak with the full authority of the British Chief of Combined Operations.

Pyke was determined to make full use of this authority during his stay in Canada. On the day following their arrival, he and Frederick moved to Ottawa for a preliminary meeting at National Defence Headquarters (NDHQ). By the time of this meeting, which was held in the evening of 12 June, Pyke had already requested a series of interviews with personnel ranging from Captain T.P. Gilday of the Canadian Army's Winter Training School to the Deputy Minister of Transport.[39] The meeting at NDHQ was a general discussion of the Plough scheme, with Pyke outlining the concept of the operation and Frederick commenting on its development in the United States.[40] Lieutenant-General Stuart, in turn, "expressed his desire to cooperate and find the right men for planning, testing, etc. He suggested that the planning and intelligence organization might be placed in Washington D.C., whereas the testing of the machines might be done in conjunction with the Canadian Winter School."[41]

Absent from the minutes of this discussion, however, is any mention of Canadian soldiers serving in the combat element of the First Special Service Force. The discussion ranged from vehicle development and testing to intelligence and demolition studies but did not include specific strategic questions nor a single mention of Canadians serving in the raiding force. It was not until the following day that Frederick appears to have raised the subject. Colonel W.A.B. Anderson, a staff officer at NDHQ, provided the following account of a conversation that took place that day:

> Lt.-Col. Frederick is of the opinion that the U.S. authorities will wish to obtain the services of a number of Canadians who have had experience living outdoors in winter conditions. Lt.-Col. Frederick pictures the force consisting of a mixture of Americans, Canadians and Norwegians. He anticipated therefore that officers as well as other ranks would eventually be desired from Canada.[42]

Anderson's account conflicts with Frederick's own recollections of the visit. Referring to the reasons for Canadian participation in a 1946 letter to Robert D. Burhans, Frederick wrote: "The reasons expressed at the time were vague, but I believe the real reason was that Pyke considered the Canadians experienced cold-weather people. Neither the White House nor General Marshall knew anything about the planned Canadian proposal until after I returned from Ottawa."[43] According to Frederick, "The United States did not propose Canadian participation. It was proposed by Mountbatten and Pyke."[44]

While the source of this misunderstanding is unclear, Anderson's account indicates that Frederick himself first raised the possibility of Canadian participation in the Plough Force on 13 June. Had Mountbatten raised the issue with Lieutenant-General Stuart during his layover in Montreal, there would almost certainly have been some discussion of this during the preliminary meeting at NDHQ on 12 June. Perhaps during the train ride from Washington to Montreal Mountbatten and Pyke persuaded Frederick to raise the topic with the Canadians. It is not difficult to envision a newly appointed lieutenant-colonel being swayed to accept a certain line of thinking during an eighteen-hour train ride with the charismatic British Chief of Combined Operations. While Anderson's memorandum identifies Frederick as making the initial request, Frederick later denied any responsibility, pointing instead to Mountbatten and Pyke. It is possible that the suggestion of Canadian participation was simply an off-handed remark, which was later forgotten by Frederick—especially if his superiors later came to look unfavourably upon the creation of a combined US–Canadian outfit. Whatever the cause of this misunderstanding, the subsequent actions of Geoffrey Pyke would have only added to the confusion surrounding the issue.

After the meetings in Ottawa, Frederick returned to Washington to begin establishing a headquarters for the project. Pyke stayed on in Ottawa to continue discussions with the Canadians and on 15 June he met with Colonel Anderson at NDHQ to suggest a new direction for Operation Plough. "At 1130 hours Mr. Pyke visited my office and intimated that it might be desirable for the planning headquarters for this project to be located at or near Ottawa."[45] Of course, this went against Anderson's understanding that the project was under American direction, and he replied that nothing concerning such a move had been suggested by US authorities. When Pyke pressed the issue, asking how Canada might respond to such a request, Anderson declined to comment and wrote the following in his memorandum of the conversation:

> Due to the somewhat indefinite nature of Mr. Pyke's remarks, and of the action which he proposed to take, I took steps at the end of the meeting to make it perfectly clear to him that nothing which had been said or discussed was to be construed as indicating N.D.H.Q.'s possible reaction to a formal request for the organization of the planning Headquarters for this project in Canada.[46]

Here once again, Pyke was attempting to undermine American control of Plough. During a telephone conversation that evening, when Frederick asked Pyke if there had been any new developments, the latter replied, "Nothing special. Colonel Anderson, whom you remember, is coming to Washington the day after tomorrow."[47] Pyke may have presumed Anderson's visit was the result of his suggestion to move the project to Canada. He was correct, to some extent, but not for the reasons he expected. Anderson was not going to Washington to make a case for moving the project headquarters to Ottawa; his task was to settle a number of questions regarding Pyke's status in North America. Specifically, Anderson intended to confirm that Mountbatten had, in fact, placed the project under American control, and he also hoped to obtain some idea of the part the Canadian Army might be expected to play.[48] To this point there had been a number of indefinite suggestions, but Anderson's superiors now considered it time these were settled. Having noted Pyke's difficult relationship with the US authorities, however, the Canadians thought it best to deal with the War Department directly. Before Anderson proceeded to Washington, the CGS informed him to make it clear that Canada preferred responsibility for Operation Plough to remain with the United States. Mr Pyke's activities, it seems, were winning no more friends in Canada than they had in the United States.

Colonel Anderson's meeting with General McNarney on 18 June represents a turning point both for Pyke and Canadian involvement in Operation Plough. At the War Department Anderson began by noting that Pyke had requested the project be moved to Canada and then he stated his understanding that Mountbatten had delegated the project to the US War Department. To this McNarney replied that the War Department had, in fact, been working under the assumption that they were solely responsible for the development of Plough in North America. Agreeing that this seemed to conflict with Pyke's views on his own status, McNarney explained that Mr. Pyke had gotten off on the wrong foot in Washington, and his latest antics were evidence that he now desired to move control of the project to Canada.[49] While McNarney may have been surprised to learn the extent of Pyke's scheming, he was not overly concerned by it. Now fully aware that the British scientist was playing a double game, Anderson and McNarney arrived at one of the first jointly made decisions regarding Operation Plough when they resolved that in the future Mr. Pyke would make his representations solely to the US War Department rather than the Canadian authorities.

If Anderson and McNarney's meeting effectively sidelined Pyke, the reverse is true for the Canadian Army: from this conversation came a more definite suggestion that Canadian personnel might be required for the combat force. McNarney anticipated that the force might ultimately consist of 1,000 all ranks, but stated that "when this matter had crystallized further it would be possible to determine the extent to which the participation of Canadian personnel was required."[50] Two days prior, Marshall had signed orders establishing the Plough force, which was authorized to include United States, Norwegian and Canadian soldiers as necessary for the accomplishment of the mission. These orders, interestingly enough, were written by Frederick himself, indicating that while he may have been reluctant to take credit for first suggesting Canadian participation, he was not adverse to the idea itself.

Although the Norwegian government-in-exile, perhaps not surprisingly, declined to participate in a project that envisioned the destruction of their nation's hydroelectric dams, the Canadians eagerly seized upon the idea of a combined US–Canadian military formation. As mentioned earlier, it was a rare day in Washington when the Canadians we re consulted on matters pertaining to the conduct of the war. Participation in a joint effort under the direction of the War Department in the United States and Combined Operations in Great Britain offered a means of exerting some small influence in matters of great strategic importance. Canadian personnel would compose roughly half of the raiding force, with a Canadian officer appointed as Frederick's second-in-command.

On 23 June, Major-General J.C. Murchie, the Canadian Vice Chief of General Staff, informed the Minister of National Defence of these developments, detailing Anderson's visit to the United States and McNarney's request for an undetermined number of Canadian soldiers. Three days later Prime Minister Mackenzie King approved Canadian Army participation to a maximum of 500 all ranks, although final orders to this effect were held in abeyance pending an official request from the War Department; the number was soon raised to nearly 700 officers and men.[51] When the request arrived on 12 July, preparations were already underway to recruit the Canadian personnel from units across Canada and from among formations of the Canadian Army overseas.

By the very nature of its origins and formation, the First Special Service Force was an unlikely and unexpected development, primarily because it seems that until approximately three days before the actual request was made the US War Department did not intend to request Canadian participation in the Force. In hindsight, the records of Canada and the United States indicate that the development may have been the result of confusion and misunderstanding, assisted in no small measure by the actions of Lord Louis Mountbatten and his eccentric assistant.

The confusion engendered by Pyke's activities has, in turn, been reflected in the literature by the many and varied explanations of how the Canadian Army first became involved in the First Special Service Force. The official history of the Canadian Army, for example, simply avoids the issue by opening the discussion of Canadian participation in the Force with Prime Minister King's approval of the decision on 26 June 1942.[52] Adleman and Walton's *The Devil's Brigade*, on the other hand, suggests that credit for the idea belongs to Winston Churchill,[53] while Robert D. Burhans accepts Frederick's account, tracing Canadian participation in the Force to a suggestion by Lord Mountbatten to the Canadian CGS during their conversation in Montreal on 11 June.[54] Closest to the mark, Stanley W. Dziuban, the American official historian, points to McNarney's discussion with Anderson on 18 June, though the reasons behind Anderson's visit to Washington manage to avoid comment.[55] Still others maintain that the origins of Canadian participation in the First Special Service Force are simply not apparent.[56] Given the shady nature of Pyke's activities in Ottawa, which become glaringly evident upon an examination of Canadian archival sources, the perennial confusion on this issue seems entirely understandable.

Upon his arrival in the United States, Pyke, quite naturally, attempted to remain involved in all aspects of the project, though he faced significant opposition as US officials grew increasingly annoyed by the British scientist's meddling. To the Americans, Pyke became an unwelcome distraction, to be tolerated when necessary and ignored whenever possible. In the face of such opposition, with the Americans attempting to sideline both him and his project, Pyke enlisted the considerable support of Mountbatten to prevent this from happening. The result was a series of meetings and messages, angry telegrams and so on, leading ultimately to Pyke, Mountbatten and Frederick's visit to Ottawa and the creation of the First Special Service Force as a combined North American military formation. In the spring of 1942, few could have foreseen this as the probable, or even possible, outcome of Pyke's proposals for the development of an armoured snow vehicle. It was, for the most part, an unplanned and completely unlikely development, and here the subsequent and largely unanticipated difficulties encountered in administering the Force might best be regarded as a reflection of the confused and somewhat accidental nature of its origins.

CHAPTER TWO

# Being Special in Helena, Montana

We speak the same language, think much the same, have many
similar customs, and are probably closer than the people of any
other two nations. It is simply that in our military services there
are many differences in training, terminology, customs and
practices that we must adjust if the personnel of both armies
are to be united and trained in a single Force.

*Colonel Robert T. Frederick*
*Commander, First Special Service Force*
*22 October 1942[1]*

IN THE SUMMER OF 1942 the Washington headquarters of Operation Plough
attended to wide-ranging matters of planning and organization. With the decision to
activate the First Special Service Force, it became necessary first to locate suitable
training facilities and then to secure the required personnel. In June, Frederick's staff
considered several possible training areas before finally settling upon a vacant National
Guard post outside Helena, Montana. Situated on a grassy plain overlooked by the
Sawtooth Range of the Rocky Mountains, Fort William Henry Harrison offered both
level ground for parachute operations and more rugged terrain for mountain and ski

instruction. In July, this sleepy, half-abandoned post became transformed into a hive of activity as construction crews set about expanding the existing facilities with new mess halls, tent platforms, and classrooms, along with jump training facilities such as parachute-drying towers, C-47 mock-ups and a parachute-packing shed.[2]

Construction of the Force itself, meanwhile, became the responsibility of Major Kenneth G. Wickham, the Force Adjutant (S-1). After arriving for service in Washington on 21 June, Wickham spent his first week at headquarters determining the numbers of officers and enlisted men required for the proposed operation. By the beginning of July, Wickham had established the tables of organization that became the organizational framework of the Force. On 11 July, they also became the basis of an American request for 47 officers and 650 other ranks from the Canadian Army, to be made available by 1 August.[3] Wickham then turned to hammering out the details of Canadian participation in the Force, and on 12 July met with a representative of the Canadian Army, Major D.D. Williamson.

While requesting Canadian soldiers for service in a combined unit had proven relatively simple, arriving at a workable agreement of service that was acceptable to both countries proved rather more difficult. With nothing in the way of example or precedent upon which to base this agreement, Wickham and Williamson spent the next three days negotiating difficult matters of organization.

From the outset, it became apparent that Canadian and American authorities viewed their joint undertaking from fundamentally different perspectives. The first indication of this came when Frederick suggested that Canadian soldiers take the oath of service and obedience to the United States.[4] Noting that this would necessarily require the discharge of these soldiers from the Canadian Army, Frederick's first priority at this point was to place Canadians and Americans on an equal footing in terms of pay, records and discipline.[5] Frederick considered the pay issue particularly important; since US Army base pay scales and parachute pay were higher than Canadian allowances, this would present a source of cleavage between Canadian and American soldiers.

While Frederick's suggestion that the Canadians be released from their own army and transferred to the United States may have presented the most practical solution, Williamson advised him that there were significant political objections to it.[6] First among the objectors, the Canadian Chief of General Staff, Lieutenant-General Stuart, advised that he saw no reason for the discharge of Canadian soldiers or their being required to swear allegiance to the United States. Although Stuart also recognized the pay issue as a potentially thorny one, he was not willing to see soldiers dismissed from the Canadian Army in order to serve in what he considered a joint US–Canadian unit. After the three days of discussion, the two officers arrived at a tentative agreement that, although never formally ratified by either government, became the foundation of the

US–Canadian partnership in the Force. The problem of an oath of allegiance was circumvented by having the soldiers swear obedience to their officers, regardless of nationality, in lieu of an oath of allegiance to the United States itself. Legal authority remained unresolved, however, with the Wickham–Williamson agreement stating that discipline for all members of the Force would be in accordance with US Army regulations, although this contradicted Ottawa's insistence that its soldiers remain subject toCanadian military law and the King's Orders and Regulations.[7] Both parties agreed that for administrative purposes Canadian personnel would receive their pay and pensions from within the Canadian system, while their rations, equipment and quarters would be provided by the United States.[8] To handle Canadian pay and administration, the Force would receive a paymaster, pay sergeant and records sergeant from the Canadian Army.[9] Overall, although the Wickham–Williamson agreement left a few issues unresolved, it became the basis of a lasting allocation of responsibilities within the Force.

While these discussions were taking place, preparations continued at Fort William Henry Harrison, and a call for volunteers went out across the United States and Canada. In the United States, recruits were required to be between the ages of eighteen and thirty-five years, physically rugged and able to withstand severe physical hardship. Willingness to undertake parachute training was a must, as was some degree of experience in an outdoor occupation, such as that of a forest ranger or a lumberman, or a background in hunting, trapping or prospecting.[10]  In the interest of speed, the Adjutant General's office formed committees of army examiners and civilian psychologists to make a circuit of bases throughout the United States. According to Kenneth Wickham, however, "in the various Western camps to which they went, instead of doing the interviewing themselves, they set up committees of post officers to make the selections. These post officers, in turn, seized upon the opportunity to get rid of undesirable men, literally emptying their stockades."[11] While the post-war characterization of American Forcemen as criminals and misfits has been greatly exaggerated in movies and in print, these men did present some degree of contrast to the volunteers arriving from Canada for service in the United States.[12]

In Canada, volunteers were selected from every possible source, including units already serving overseas. Upon selection by a committee of medical and army examiners, volunteers faced a second cull by Canadian officers who were themselves marked for service with the Force. Unlike the members of committees formed in the western United States, these officers had a vested interest in ensuring the quality of the soldiers selected. The Canadian mobilization orders stated that only fully trained soldiers were eligible to volunteer, with preference given to those with previous winter training or deemed "suitable for service under winter conditions." Further, as it was initially anticipated that the lowest rank in the Force would be sergeant, selections were made with an eye to ensuring that the Canadian volunteers were either NCOs already or "privates who are considered as good N.C.O. material."[13] In the American system, the wide range of skills demanded of Force soldiers qualified even the lowest ranking men as Technician 4th Grade, a technical rating equal to sergeant.[14] With no similar technical ratings in the Canadian Army, volunteers selected on the basis of being considered "good NCO material" were judged according to their experience as soldiers and their potential for leadership. As for the senior Canadian officers, experience was considered a valuable asset. While many of the Canadian junior officers selected for the Force were recent graduates of officer training schools, fully fifty percent of the selected senior officers were drawn from the ranks of the Canadian Army Overseas, many of whom had answered the call in 1939 and had been training ever since.[15] As these soldiers were considered representatives of the Canadian Army as a whole, only the best were allowed past concentration points in Ottawa and Calgary and allowed to board trains bound for Helena at the beginning of August.

Proceeding to the United States as the "2nd Canadian Parachute Battalion," a designation adopted for reasons of secrecy, the first contingent of Canadian soldiers arrived at Fort William Henry Harrison at noon on 6 August. Force veterans liken the early days at Helena to joining a North American Foreign Legion, with kilted Canadians forming-up alongside US Cavalrymen in campaign hats, making their introductions in "a thousand and one different accents."[16] Assigned to a four-man tent in a group of two Americans and two Canadians, one former Canadian police officer recalls finding himself sharing quarters with a Canadian trapper, a Montana sheep herder and a former illicit whisky distiller from Kentucky.[17] "The camp has only been under construction two weeks but progressing rapidly ... Met Col. Frederick, O.C. Joint Forces, who outlined briefly the plans for training" and a few other details regarding the organization of the unit.[18]

With an eye toward completing the training as quickly as possible, the Force adopted a unique Table of Organization, or War Establishment, that separated the brigade-sized formation into discrete combat and service echelons. While the Service Battalion, composed entirely of American personnel, handled matters of maintenance and administration, the Combat Force was left to devote its entire energy toward training. In August 1942, Canadians comprised almost half of the Combat Force, where the four-man tent groups became the basis of crews for the snow vehicle, which was now designated the T-15 Weasel. With Americans and Canadians fully integrated throughout, the Combat Force was subdivided into three light regiments of 600 men each. Within each regiment there were two battalions, each consisting of three 100-man companies.

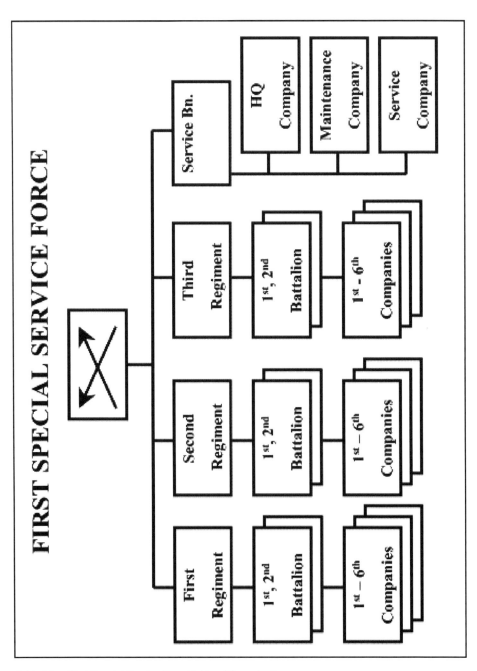

Table 2.1    First Special Service Force Table of Organization

Canadian officers were appointed to command one of the three regiments, three of six battalions and ten of the eighteen companies within the Force.[19] At the platoon level, where many of the junior officers were American, a large percentage of their more experienced senior sergeants were Canadian. Each platoon was composed of two sections, which represented a departure from the standard US infantry platoon of three squads. Throughout the Force, it was understood that officer appointments were temporary; holding them was contingent upon ability, and further promotions would be made without regard for nationality.[20] "It was a solid intermixture where no one country dominated, where no national cliques formed, and where a man could rise according to his comparative ability."[21]

In practice, Canadian soldiers were integral to the Force and did not form a separate contingent of their own. On paper, however, they remained grouped within the 2nd Canadian Parachute Battalion for administrative purposes. While this distinction made little difference to the men on the ground, in Ottawa the administration continued to treat the battalion as a serving unit of the Canadian Army. On 4 August, the CGS appointed Lieutenant-Colonel J.G. McQueen, formerly of the Calgary Highlanders, as the Officer Commanding, 2nd Canadian Parachute Battalion. Recalled from the UK only a few days prior, McQueen, as the senior Canadian officer at Helena, assumed responsibility for all matters pertaining to Canadian personnel and their participation in the First Special Service Force, in addition to his regular duties within the Force chain of command. His orders offer a statement of how the Canadian authorities viewed their newly formed partnership with the United States Army:

> You have been appointed Officer Commanding the 2nd Canadian Parachute Battalion. This Battalion will form part of a composite force to be known as the First Special Service Force, which is being organized by the United States in co-operation with the Canadian Government ...
>
> The operational employment of personnel of the 2nd Canadian Parachute Battalion and/or the dispatch of such personnel from this continent will be matters for the determination of the Canadian Government in consultation with the Government of the United States ... You will not commit any of the said personnel to any operational employment or to such dispatch until you have referred the matter to the Department of National Defence ...
>
> You may in your discretion permit any or all of the [Canadian] personnel ... to be allocated by [Colonel Frederick] ... to sub-units within the Force, in such manner as you consider advisable ...
>
> So allocated, you will order them to place themselves under the command of and to obey all lawful orders of the respective sub-units to which they are posted, whether these officers be Canadian or American unless and until you

otherwise order. You will, however, always retain and exercise the powers of a Commanding Officer with respect to … the administration of discipline and the punishment of offences, [which] shall be dealt with under Canadian Military Law and the King's Regulations.

You will be responsible for bringing and will bring to the attention of the Department of National Defence … any matters affecting the training, welfare, administration, and discipline of Canadian personnel in the First Special Service Force.[22]

Having given its approval to Canadian participation in the Force, Ottawa retained the right to decide upon any proposed deployment of Canadian personnel overseas. Discipline and authority remained vested in the senior Canadian commander of the Force, although soldiers of both nations were required to obey the lawful orders of their officers regardless of nationality. Finally, while Canadians were to be distributed throughout the Force, McQueen's orders made very clear that he answered to Ottawa, not to Frederick or Washington.

In Helena, training began immediately in accordance with a three-phase schedule aimed at preparing the Force for operations that winter. While the details of the proposed operation in Norway were kept a closely guarded secret, it was essential that training proceed as rapidly as possible, starting with an abbreviated course in parachute jumping. Leaving the finer details of parachute packing to the Service Battalion, some US personnel made their first jumps within two days of arrival in Helena, though "crash courses" of this kind were the exception rather than the rule. Of the Canadians, most were considered ready to jump by the fifth day, but after consultation with Frederick, it was decided that instructors would check each man individually and await the delivery of special parachute jumping boots to help prevent unnecessary injuries. This delay meant that it was seven days from the Canadians' arrival before Lieutenant-Colonel McQueen made the first jump on 13 August.[23] "On Thursday I jumped by myself," wrote McQueen, "in order that I might assess the training and feel convinced that the men were ready." McQueen suffered a fractured ankle in the attempt, but considered this the result of high winds on the afternoon of his jump. He deemed the training sufficient, and Canadians began making their qualification jumps the following day.

"It must be realized," wrote McQueen after his injury, "that in this type of training casualties are bound to occur and while every effort is made to cut these to a minimum the fact must be realized and accepted."[24] On 13 August, McQueen became one of the first casualties, though he was certainly not the last. Throughout August, injuries sustained during parachute training ensured a steady stream of personnel to the infirmary at Fort Harrison. In the case of minor sprains and abrasions, the men were treated and released without any significant interruption to their training. More serious injuries, however, including those suffered by Lieutenant-Colonel McQueen, were another issue entirely.

From the earliest stages of training at Fort Harrison, it was understood that anyone who proved incapable of keeping pace with the group would be reassigned immediately. Anyone falling behind due to injury, refusal to jump or falling-out during physical training could expect a prompt return to his former unit. Even before the first soldiers had arrived at Fort Harrison, Frederick expected that "the speed with which the force will be assembled, the special background required of each member ... and the rigorous training to be undertaken will result in a certain percentage ... becoming unfit for the mission to be performed."[25] Recognizing that these losses were bound to occur, Frederick had ordered, "In the interests of the morale of the entire group, the individual should leave the force on the day that the decision is made."[26]

The same policy applied to every member of the Force, including Lieutenant-Colonel McQueen. On 17 August, Frederick wrote to NDHQ in Ottawa, requesting McQueen's reassignment to the Washington planning headquarters and the appointment of another officer to command the Canadian element of the Force. "Although Col. McQueen will be able to get around with a cast on his leg after a short time," wrote Frederick, "it will not be possible for him to undergo training ... Due to the intensive training which must be accomplished by all members of this Force during the next three months, anyone who is prevented from undergoing training for an appreciable period will be thrown too far behind to enable him to continue."[27]

McQueen, for his part, was bitterly disappointed that he would not be allowed to return to the Force. When asked to recommend a replacement, he suggested either Major D.D. Williamson or Major R.A. Keane, though he expressed a decided preference for Keane due to his "greater level-headedness."[28] Unfortunately Major Keane had to be ruled out when he also broke his leg during parachute training. By default, that left Williamson, and despite McQueen's reservations about this officer being a well-meaning loudmouth, Frederick almost insisted that McQueen's replacement be promoted from within the Force.[29] "It appears undesirable at this time to send an officer who is not yet familiar with the project or problems of training, and would have to devote a considerable amount of time to getting on the ground and familiarizing himself with the conditions."[30] As a result, on 5 September, Major Williamson was promoted to the rank of lieutenant-colonel and appointed senior Canadian officer at Helena. He did not, however, assume McQueen's former position as the Force Executive Officer. Instead, Frederick appointed an American officer, Colonel Paul D. Adams, as the unit's second-in-command. Frederick was a fine judge of talent, and Adams was an excellent officer—as evidenced by his post-war rise to the rank of four-star general. It was with some disappointment, however, that the Canadians accepted their loss of influence in the unit.

If McQueen's injury and subsequent transfer from the Force necessitated some hasty rearrangements, the same may be said of the almost constant flow of officers and men admitted to the hospital or returned to Canada "at their own request"—meaning that they failed to meet the training standards. On one particularly bad day, 25 August, thirty-seven men were admitted to the hospital, and there were an unusually large number who balked at the doors of the aircraft and refused to jump.[31] In August and September 1942, nine officers and 250 men returned to Calgary, approximately 180 at their own request, 60 for medical reasons and less than a dozen in disciplinary cases.[32] Those remaining, now qualified as parachutists, continued their training, concentrating on the use of American small arms, demolitions, unarmed combat and rigorous physical training.[33]

The men proceeded to the firing ranges for training in the American automatic carbine, followed by lectures and demonstrations on the use of explosives. Each soldier received demolitions training so that he would be capable of carrying out such a task by himself if the need arose. "There is an abundance of training in explosives and the instructors are most competent." Force candidates also received advanced training in unarmed combat, Frederick having secured the services of Captain Dermot Michael ["Pat"] O'Neill, formerly of the Shanghai police, the British embassy at Tokyo, and the Office of Strategic Services. O'Neill first trained a cadre of instructors, who were then rotated between the regiments. "This training is very popular with the troops and a great keenness and interest is shown." By the end of September, forced marches and calisthenics were "built up to such a pitch that an ordinary person would drop from exhaustion in [the] early stages … In connection with running, each officer and man must be able to run a mile in less than ten minutes, and it is worth mentioning that the majority can do it in around seven."[34]

For the most part, discipline and morale in this early period at Helena were described as quite good, with a noticeable improvement individually when the men qualified as parachutists. "Rations and quarters are extremely good and receive favorable comment from all ranks. The relationship between Canadian and American personnel is most satisfactory." By the end of September, while relations between Canadian personnel and American officers and men continued to be of the highest order, Lieutenant-Colonel Williamson was beginning to notice considerable grumbling among the Canadians in regard to pay. "It is obviously difficult with men completely mixed as they are," he wrote, "to have the lad in front of him jump out of the plane (which is nerve wracking business at the best) and you know that he is getting $50.00 per month extra for doing it, while you are not getting anything." According to

Williamson, "morale hinges on the pay question, and I can't recommend too strongly that equivalent rates of pay be adopted and at the earliest possible moment."[35]

By this time, 259 officers and men had been returned to Canada for various reasons, and while Canadian and American authorities recognized that casualties and other losses were bound to occur during training, the initial planning had established no coordinated means of providing Canadian replacements to the First Special Service Force. From the outset, the American element received authorization from the War Department to carry a thirty percent overstrength in personnel until it was dispatched overseas.[36] This was deemed sufficient to account for any losses incurred during training, as these were simply deducted from the existing surplus of personnel. With no corresponding surplus of Canadian personnel, however, by the end of August it had been necessary to request 150 reinforcements from Canada.[37] Although the decision to recruit entirely new personnel from Canada conflicted with Frederick's earlier policy of releasing anyone who fell behind due to injury, making the original policy appear rather wasteful, it is clear that both Frederick and the Canadian authorities expected this to be the only occasion when reinforcements would be required. On 31 August, Williamson justified the request by stating that the "150 Canadian personnel expected to arrive today and tomorrow will bring strength to a figure which, on completion of parachute training, will allow for normal wastage and ensure 50% of the Force being Canadian."[38]

Beyond such stop-gap measures, no one at this early stage could have foreseen the need to provide the First Special Service Force with reinforcements on a continuing basis. During the planning stages of Operation Plough, one representative of the Operations Division had commented on the impossibility of maintaining the unit upon its commitment to combat. Describing the Force as "sacrifice troops," the official had added, "I'd put them down as lost troops and be willing to pay for it—if they accomplished [their mission]."[39] Operation Plough was intended to deliver a series of crippling blows to the German occupation of Norway. Barring any unexpected changes to the plan, there would be no need to maintain the First Special Service Force beyond its first operational tasking. Nevertheless, when the plan changed (as plans are apt to do in time of war), the difficulties inherent in a combined US–Canadian formation of this kind came to assume greater importance on both sides of the border.

In late September, during a visit to the UK to discuss developments with Mountbatten, Frederick came to realize that there had been a complete lack of coordination within the British High Command. For example, the British Chief of Air Staff expressed serious reservations regarding Operation Plough, adding that he was reluctant to divert the bombers necessary to parachute the Force and its vehicles into Norway without proof that the Plough force could do more damage to the enemy than could be done by bombing Germany directly.[40] In London, Brigadier Colin Gubbins of the Special Operations Executive informed Frederick that his organization already had a plan for destroying Norwegian hydroelectric stations using Norwegian saboteurs. Further, the Norwegian government-in-exile had voiced strong opposition to the Plough project, expecting the destruction of hydroelectric facilities to cause greater hardship for the Norwegian people than for the German occupiers. In light of these developments, on 26 September, Frederick cabled the following message to Washington:

> Suspend effort on present line … New plan may be radically different and not concerned with hydroelectric or other industrial installations … Inform Adams at Helena to cease training on hydroelectric installations and to stress general tactical training to include attack of fortifications, pill boxes, barracks and troop concentrations. Change in weapons may be necessary to provide greater firepower, so suspend further small arms training pending a decision.[41]

Returning to the United States in October, Frederick reported the results of his visit to Lieutenant-General McNarney, who ordered all planning stopped and took the matter to General Marshall for a decision. One can only guess the Chief of Staff's reaction to the news, given that he had originally adopted the Plough project at the suggestion of Churchill and Mountbatten. Exasperated, Marshall and McNarney spent the next week considering whether to retain the Force for another role or to order it disbanded. Given the considerable investment already made in training and equipping the Force, not to mention development of the snow vehicle, Marshall decided to retain the First Special Service Force for possible employment in other theatres. Nevertheless, the cancellation of Operation Plough made it necessary to consult the Canadian authorities regarding their continued participation in the Force.

On 16 October, Frederick delivered a letter to Lieutenant-Colonel McQueen, now stationed at the planning headquarters in Washington, communicating the War Department's formal request of a decision regarding the Canadian element of the First Special Service Force. Noting Ottawa's earlier instructions to the senior Canadian officer of the Force that Canadian personnel would not be committed to any combat operation or moved from the North American continent without prior approval from the Canadian Department of National Defence, Frederick voiced his concern that limitations on the movement of the Canadian element impeded the Force as a whole. "In the event that the Canadian personnel would not be permitted to engage in an operation to which the Force is assigned," he wrote, "the strength of the combat echelon would be so greatly reduced as to make it inadequate for any probable employment."[42] With the United States now spending large amounts on the clothing, housing, equipment, medical attention, and training of Canadian personnel, Frederick requested that "in fairness to the United States, the Canadian Government should at this time specifically state any limitations upon the combat employment of the Canadian personnel of the Force."[43] What Frederick and the US War Department wanted, given the cancellation of Operation Plough, was a written statement by the Canadian Department of National Defence "of the theaters of operation in which Canadian personnel of the Force may be employed," together with advance notice of any other restrictions which the Canadian Government might wish to place on the Canadian element of the Force.

As in May when Geoffrey Pyke had arrived in his office regarding a visit to Ottawa, Major-General Pope of the Canadian Joint Staff Mission once again found himself at the centre of developments. After a long talk with McQueen, Pope referred the matter of Frederick's letter to the acting Chief of General Staff, Major-General J.C. Murchie, who agreed with Pope that Canada should retain the right to approve participation in any projected operation. At the same time, however, Pope agreed with Murchie that once this approval had been given, "the Canadian Government should not further reserve the right to withdraw the Canadian element from participation."[44] This would reserve the right of the Canadian Government to veto any particular project in principle, while simultaneously acknowledging that once approval was given, operational planning would be left to the United States.

The Canadians made these recommendations after a close examination of the Canadian position in other theatres of the war. Comparing the FSSF to other examples in which Canadian soldiers found themselves serving alongside Allied forces, Pope and Murchie decided that the circumstances of the Force were entirely different from those affecting other commands:

> In the event that a Canadian force, acting in combination with the forces of our allies, did not propose to proceed with a given operation, this would not affect the independent action of the forces of the other allies involved.... Should, however, the Canadian element of the First Special Service Force be similarly withdrawn, it would mean, in effect, the disappearance of the Force as such, and the cancellation of the project to which it had been assigned.
>
> This essential difference between the First Special Service Force and other Canadian forces acting in combination with allied troops seems to be of sufficient importance to warrant the relinquishment of the rights of the Canadian Government to withdraw from any operation once its approval of the general project had been given.[45]

Recognizing these unique characteristics of the First Special Service Force, Canadian authorities must have been aware of the great leverage provided by this partnership with the United States. Frederick was correct that in the event of the Canadian personnel being withdrawn from the Force, the entire unit would be required to undergo a lengthy reorganization. The Canadians, nonetheless, were unwilling to state specific limitations in advance, as this would, in effect, allow the United States to send the Force anywhere not specifically ruled out, without notification. In recognition of the difficult situation this created for the United States, however, the Canadians decided that once approval was given for a proposed employment of the Force, "we can safely leave the operational planning to the United States authorities. They are not given to rash military undertakings."[46]

In Ottawa, a meeting of the Cabinet War Committee on 28 October accepted these suggestions as the basis of continued Canadian participation in the First Special Service Force. The minutes from this meeting make clear, however, that maintaining good relations with the United States had an important influence on the decision: "Though the future of employment of this unit is doubtful, beyond its existence as a 'stand-by' force, acceptance … is recommended as a token of intimate cooperation between the two countries."[47] It remained to be seen, however, whether the United States would agree to the condition that Canada should continue to exercise right of approval prior to any deployment of the FSSF.

On 30 October, Major-General Pope proceeded to the War Department "to ask the US Army some pretty direct questions" regarding Canada's role in the First Special Service Force.[48] Specifically, Pope was instructed by the CGS to ask: "Does the U.S. Army really want us to continue our association with this Special Service Force? Will the U.S. Army agree to our conditions of continued association, namely that any operational projects contemplated be subject to approval by this headquarters?"[49] Meeting first with Frederick, Pope was unable to get any answers and was referred to General McNarney, who on behalf of the War Department accepted the Canadian conditions. The continued participation of the Canadian element of the Force was thereby assured, at least for the time being.

The decision to retain the Force for another role necessitated significant changes both in Helena and Washington. At the planning headquarters Frederick's staff began to consider a number of possible alternate uses for the Force, along with a fair number of impossible ones. In October a recommendation of using the FSSF in the Soviet Caucasus was seriously considered before being rejected because the terrain and tactical situation were not believed suitable.[50] By November, attention had shifted to the

Mediterranean theatre, where "developments in the military situation indicate a very profitable use of the 1st Special Service Force as a Ranger unit for operations in the Mediterranean against Sardinia, Italy, or Sicily. Some modification in specialized equipment will be necessary, and amphibious training will be required."[51]

In Helena these "modifications" included the adoption of heavier armament, reflecting the change from a sabotage to a combat role. While the Thompson sub-machine-gun was retained, carbines were exchanged for heavier M-1 rifles along with an assortment of heavier weapons including the Browning light machine-gun (LMG), the Johnson LMG, 60mm light mortars, flame throwers and the new "bazooka" anti-tank gun.[52] Sections were increased from eight to twelve men, and although the Force still lacked heavy mortars and machine-guns, "the light machine-guns and light mortars in the Force's 108 sections exceeded in number those weapons in an infantry division."[53] Meanwhile, the intensive training program continued, now entering its second and third phases of tactical problems and battle drill, followed by instruction in skiing, mountain climbing, living in cold climates and use of the snow vehicle.[54]

Late in October, Colonel Frederick had assembled his officers for a meeting in which he voiced his opinion on some of the unique challenges presented by the bi-national composition of the Force. "We have an unusual problem in this Force … We do not have the common background in military training and experience that would normally be the case of an officer in either of our armies. I do not mean that this presents insurmountable problems," noted Frederick, adding that in his consideration the difference between a Canadian and an American was not readily appreciable. "We speak the same language, think much the same, have many similar customs, and are probably closer than the people of any two nations. It is simply that in our military services there are many differences in training, terminology, customs and practices that we must adjust if the personnel of both armies are to be united and trained in a single Force."

To that point, Frederick had believed that this integration had proven largely successful, though he noted that in most cases the Canadians had been required to go further to reach this common ground, given the use of American weapons and equipment by the Force. "The response of Canadian officers and men to these new conditions, many of which may seem strange, unnecessary, or unreasonable, has not only been gratifying to me, but is an indication of the sincerity of purpose with which they view the task before us." In closing, Frederick stated his views on competitive training, referring specifically to the three regiments of the Force but with obvious implications for his philosophy on US–Canadian relations within the unit:

> I have particularly avoided formal competition between units of this Force. Competition is a two-edged sword; it can cut both ways. The elation of a unit

that wins a competition does not offset the sense of depression in the units that lose. If this … is to be a single Force we must have unity throughout, and not a group of mutually snarling units, suspicious of the others and mutually hostile … Once competition becomes serious, then it becomes a disintegrating factor. [55]

In these first months of arduous training, officers and men of the First Special Service Force laid the foundation of a working partnership between Canadian and American soldiers. So successful were Frederick's training policies and his insistence on complete integration that throughout much of the unit's history, observers frequently noted that within the Force it was often impossible to distinguish between Canadian and American soldiers. Invaluable as the common language and customs of these soldiers, who were "probably closer than the people of any two nations," may have been, Frederick and his officers of both nationalities certainly deserve a share of the credit for this achievement.

At the same time, difficulties regarding pay had arisen on the Canadian side, and the continuing need to replace training casualties made it clear in Ottawa that the original estimate of Canadian participation in the order of five hundred all ranks had undergone substantial revision. From the perspective of the US War Department, Canadian participation generated only minor headaches, with the exception of a persistent concern that a Canadian withdrawal from the First Special Service Force would mean the disappearance of the Force and the cancellation of the project to which it had been assigned. In effect, given the cancellation of Operation Plough, the Canadians now wielded the right to veto any proposed employment of the First Special Service Force, despite the fact that the United States was responsible for an overwhelming share of the resources being devoted to the maintenance and training of this unit. Certainly, it was a less than ideal state of affairs for all concerned, but one that was likely to persist until a mission could be found for this highly trained and specialized force.

A double retreat ceremony is performed at First Special Service Force headquarters at Fort William Henry Harrison, as US and Canadian soldiers lower their respective flags at sundown. The FSSF activated on 20 July 1942 and was at first equally composed of American and Canadian volunteers. The men trained and were sent into combat in mixed units. Helena, Montana, 1943. *(NA-CP SC 187844-S)*

Force training emphasized physical and mental endurance. The soldiers seen here are on a particularly grueling route march that covered a remarkable 76 kilometres in one day. Marysville, Montana, 1942. *(CWM 19900261-012)*

Forcemen pick their way down a ravine during a September 1942 route march near Helena, Montana. The walking sticks are being used as substitute ski-poles in preparation for ski training during the winter months. *(CWM 19900261-013)*

Parachute training in the Helena Valley, summer 1942. Parachute qualification was one of the first orders of business for volunteers arriving at Fort William Henry Harrison, a process Colonel Frederick hoped might help "separate the sheep from the goats." *(CWM 19900261-017)*

A soldier struggles with his deployed parachute in a stiff breeze during parachute training at Helena. While Canadian soldiers were officially grouped within the 2nd Canadian Parachute Battalion for administrative purposes, in practice they were integral to the Force and did not form a separate contingent. *(CWM 19900261-018)*

Parachute beginners of the First Special Service Force are familiarized with the feel of the 'chute in a special harness rigging. The sergeant instructor is showing the suspended beginner the proper way to hold his feet on landing. Fort William Henry Harrison, Montana, 1943. *(NA-CP SC 187833-S)*

Preliminary to their actual jump from a transport plane, these doctors of the First Special Service Force are thoroughly oriented to the feel of a parachute by wearing the practice harness shown here, 1943. *(NA-CP SC 187742-S)*

Doctors of the First Special Service Force practice the jump exit from a grounded transport plane. Captain George F. Evashwick (Turtle Creek, Pennsylvania; HQ det. 2nd Regt) a paratroop field surgeon, is jumping while other doctors wait their turn. Fort William Henry Harrison paratroop training centre, 1943. *(NA-CP SC 187744-S)*

The day before their first jump, men of the First Special Service Force receive final instructions on the adjustment of their parachutes, 1943. *(NA-CP SC 187834-S)*

Members of the First Special Service Force hooked up and ready to make their first jump from a C-47 aircraft over Fort William Henry Harrison, in 1943. Six C-47s were assigned to the Force for parachute training. *(NA-CP SC 187746-S)*

With the jump master kneeling at the extreme lower right, these paratroop field surgeons await the call to make their first jump. Colonel Robert T. Frederick, Force commander, made his initial jump after fifteen minutes of briefing. *(NA-CP SC 187747-S)*

The coveted "Buzzard Claws" are pinned on paratroop field surgeon, Capt. Carl A. Brakel (Seattle, Washington; HQ det. 3rd Regt) after he completed his training at Fort William Henry Harrison. *(NA-CP SC 187749-S)*

This mixed group of US and Canadian soldiers of the First Special Service Force is at bayonet practice.
A Canadian officer, not in the photo, is drilling the men. *(NA-CP SC 187832-S)*

In the barracks – this line of footwear suggests the range of training for Force soldiers: from the left, low-quarter dress shoes,
regulation army boots, mountain-climbing boots, ski boots, parachute jump boots and Arctic overshoes. *(NA-CP SC 187837-S)*

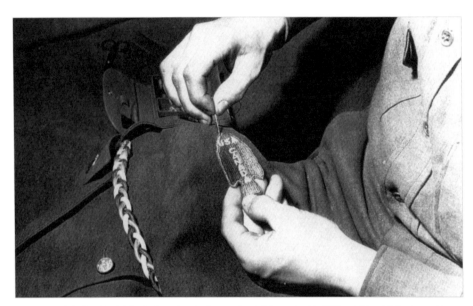

The insignia of the First Special Service Force is an Indian spearhead of deep red, with "USA" and "Canada" forming a white "T" against the background. The patch is worn on the left shoulder. A soldier is shown here sewing the coveted emblem to his shirt. The braided cord of red, white and blue also signifies the wearer as a member of the Force. *(NA-CP SC 187847-S)*

The complete integration of US and Canadian soldiers in the joint First Special Service Force is shown in this photo of a soldier from each nation playing checkers in their barracks. Only at their disbandment in Southern France on 5 December 1944 did Canadian and American soldiers of the Force again form separate ranks. Fort William Henry Harrison, 1943. *(NA-CP SC 187845-S)*

A more or less common sight in Helena, Montana, is this one showing a Canadian and a US soldier enjoying the company of their girlfriends in 1943. *(NA-CP SC 187846-S)*

## CHAPTER THREE

# Finding a Mission in 1943

As this Force is designed for a special mission, there are no reinforcement implications. Brigadier Weeks informs me that Colonel Frederick told him that when the Force leaves the United States it will not be reinforced.

*Lieutenant-General Kenneth Stuart*
*Canadian Chief of the General Staff*
*20 April 1943*[1]

FORCE TRAINING AT HELENA CONTINUED beyond the cancellation of Operation Plough, maintaining its emphasis on skiing, mountain climbing, and living in cold climates, albeit with increasing amounts of time spent on battle drill and weapons use. Just as the War Department hesitated to throw away the investment made in training the Force, preferring instead to retain the unit for an undetermined role, the continued training for winter combat attests to the desire of Force officers to avoid throwing away weeks of training. At the same time, the volume of rifle, light machine-gun, 60mm mortar, and anti-tank rounds fired on the ranges emphasized the unit's expected transition to an assault infantry role.

Firing bazookas, in particular, became a favourite among the men, as did demolitions training and Pat O'Neill's classes in unarmed combat. During an inspection of the training at Fort William Henry Harrison between 2 and 4 December, a team from US Army Ground Forces Headquarters provided a mixed review of the training received by the First Special Service Force:

> In general, the training was energetic and determined. Physical condition of the Force was excellent. All ranks seemed demolition conscious and were exceptionally well versed in that phase of training. On the other hand, the training program is too broad and instruction is too general. Not enough attention is devoted to the perfection of details … Enthusiasm and morale of officers and men were excellent.[2]

In his letter to Colonel Frederick, Lieutenant-General Lesley J. McNair also commented on the relative inexperience of the unit's junior officers, but noted that in those subjects relating to the original mission intended for the Force—especially demolitions—soldiers of all ranks demonstrated considerable skill.

In Canada, the cancellation of Operation Plough sparked additional consideration of the unique problems presented by the First Special Service Force. On 26 November, a discussion at National Defence Headquarters concluded that continued Canadian participation in the Force required immediate decisions regarding the questions of pay and reinforcements. Throughout the fall there had been growing discontent among the Canadian element of the Force owing to the fact that Canadians received far less pay than their American counterparts. As Lieutenant-Colonel Williamson repeatedly complained in his reports, Canadians received "less than half their American friends' parachute pay. We now have Canadian Staff Sergeants drawing less money than the American privates under them."[3]

In November, attempts to authorize US Army pay scales for Canadian officers and men serving in the Force were blocked when the Royal Canadian Air Force representative pointed out that Canadian airmen stationed in Alaska were similarly situated, drawing far less pay than American personnel.[4] Special concessions to one group would undoubtedly lead to requests from others, something the Canadian paymaster-general was unwilling to contemplate at the present time.

While the pay situation remained unresolved, Canadian authorities considered far more pressing the need to establish a system of providing reinforcements to the FSSF. Lieutenant-Colonel McQueen received instructions to obtain the views of the American authorities in Washington as to the best method of maintaining the Canadian element of the Force during the training phase and after the unit moved overseas.[5] Also in November, the Canadians met a request from Colonel Frederick for one hundred additional personnel by ordering the transfer of trained paratroops from the 1st Canadian Parachute Battalion.[6] Currently undergoing parachute training at Fort Benning, Georgia, these reinforcements from the 1st Parachute Battalion provided a convenient, albeit temporary, solution to training attrition within the Force.

At the end of November, Captain R.W. Becket departed Helena for Fort Benning, where he was to select the one hundred Canadian paratroop reinforcements and arrange for their transfer to the First Special Service Force.[7] At the same time, the CGS wrote to McQueen informing him of developments in Ottawa:

> Consideration is now being given in Canada to the setting up of a permanent training establishment which can undertake the training of paratroop reinforcements for the Special Service Force and the 1st Parachute Battalion.
>
> Our present plans are that the Special Service Force will be provided with reinforcements from the 1st Parachute Battalion; reinforcements for the latter, in turn, being trained at Shilo. I would, therefore, be glad to have your advice as … a guide to us in determining the rate at which reinforcements must be trained for the Special Service Force.[8]

In order to maintain the Canadian element of the Force, Canadian authorities were prepared to establish a quota of reinforcements from the new training centre in Shilo, Manitoba. At this important juncture, however, Frederick made a decision that, in hindsight, seems inexplicable and inexcusable.

While Colonel Frederick certainly appreciated the decision to provide qualified paratroops as reinforcements, in the long term something more permanent would undoubtedly be required to maintain the Canadian element of the Force. Nevertheless, he refused the Canadian offer, "recommend[ing] that no further Canadian personnel be provided between now and the date of departure of this Force to a theatre of war, and that no system be established for the reinforcing of the Force in the theatre of war."[9] Probably basing his decision on the belief that the Force would soon move overseas, Frederick may have still hoped that the Force was to be used in a single, devastating attack on some vital point of the German war machine. Further, as always, he remained adamant that replacements from other units were to be avoided whenever possible, as outsiders could not be expected to meet the demanding requirements or possess the specialized skills of the original men. Noting recent preparations toward a role as assault infantry, the Canadians found Frederick's decision rather odd, but they acceded nonetheless:

With the nature of operations envisaged, there would appear to be a distinct possibility that the Force would be used more than once, in which case, I think it highly probable that further reinforcements will be required. However, the Americans do not appear to be making provision in this direction.[10]

On 18 December, having decided to make no special provisions for supplying Canadian reinforcements to the Force, NDHQ directed that special training facilities at Shilo would be provided only for the 1st Canadian Parachute Battalion.[11]

Returning from Fort Benning on 10 December, Captain Becket arrived at Fort Harrison with ninety-seven reinforcements from the 1st Parachute Battalion. "A good looking group of boys, and really looked smart marching through camp," recorded the War Diary. "All but one are qualified parachutists, some qualified in both England and U.S.A."[12] A special training regiment was soon established in order to bring the recruits in line with a few of the more specialized areas of Force training and to allow those who had received their parachute training in Britain to requalify according to American standards. Overall, the new arrivals were integrated into the Force with little difficulty, although some were understandably upset when they were denied a Christmas furlough and held back for additional training. While most of the newcomers took this in stride, in January a group of seventeen recruits took matters into their own hands and went AWOL. When these men were apprehended, all were found carrying return bus tickets to Lethbridge, Alberta.[13] Taken into custody and returned to Helena, the men were demoted and confined to base.

After the Christmas furlough, ski training continued into January and February 1943, usually beginning before daybreak and continuing until dark. Under the supervision of Captain Kiil of the Royal Norwegian Army and his assistants, even those who had never skied before made good progress—comments regarding "Skiwegians," "torture boards," and "misery sticks" notwithstanding.

In February, Force officers began to note a decline in morale "owing to the fact that these men, all selected volunteers, are impatient for action and consequently are exhibiting considerable restlessness."[14] Months after the cancellation of Plough, the unit was still in training and no new mission had materialized. Soon it would be spring, and with the snow already disappearing in Europe, the Force would be stuck in training for another year. Constantly led to expect assignment to combat at any time, but seeing no possible use for the FSSF in the winter of 1943, on 3 February Frederick wrote the following to Lieutenant-General McNarney:[15]

**MEMORANDUM FOR THE DEPUTY CHIEF OF STAFF**

**Subject: First Special Service Force**

The time has been reached when it is necessary to decide the future of the First Special Service Force. The First Special Service Force was created specifically for the accomplishment of the Plough Project at the request of British authorities, but in October, 1942, the Project was dropped due to the impracticability of executing it during the winter of 1942–1943. Reasons for abandoning the project were that planning information furnished by the British mission assigned to the project was faulty and erroneous, airplanes to drop the Force into the combat area are not available, and the Norwegian Government did not favour the project or its objective.

At the time that the Plough Project was dropped, a new mission for the First Special Service Force was sought. After consideration of several possible missions, it was directed that the Force complete its winter training with a view to its employment in Sicily, Sardinia or Italy early in 1943. In accordance with the last directive, the Force has continued its winter training and an attempt has been made to prepare the Force for any operation in which it may be employed.

At the present time, there appears to be no possible employment for the Force in a winter operation during this winter. To hold the Force in training without its engaging in combat before the winter of 1943–44 would bring about difficult problems.

The personnel of this Force, both United States and Canadian, volunteered for hazardous duty and have subjected themselves to a course of training more demanding and rigorous than has ever been attempted elsewhere, in order that they might be in top condition for combat … Both officers and men are beginning to get restless and have frequently stated that they volunteered for this Force in order to get into combat early. The problems of morale and discipline that might arise if the Force is continued in training for a prolonged period might become serious…

The expense incident to maintaining this Force is great and is not justified unless employment of the Force in an operation utilizing its special equipment and training is definitely foreseen. The United States is providing highly specialized and valuable training not only for United States Army personnel, but also for about seven hundred Canadian officers and enlisted men…

The combat personnel of the Force are now in excellent physical condition, and as a result of the training are able to withstand severe and difficult conditions. While a prolonged period of training would bring about greater proficiency in tactics, use of weapons and the performance of specialists, the detrimental effect on physical condition and spirit of the personnel would offset the gain.

The employment of the Force is limited by the necessity of securing from the Canadian authorities an agreement for the participation of Canadian personnel in the Force. More than a third of the officers and enlisted men of the Combat Echelon are Canadians, and to employ the Force without the Canadian personnel would seriously reduce the combat strength.

The commitment of the War Department to British authorities for the continuation and training of this force are understood, but it is believed that unless definite employment … in the near future is foreseen, the unit should be discontinued and the personnel reassigned…

Considering the capabilities of this Force and the limitations upon its use, one of the following missions offers the most profitable use and should be decided upon at this time:

a. Participation in an operation in the Aleutian Islands, if one is to be undertaken during the spring of 1943. The Force could participate in a strong attack to drive the enemy from Kiska or could be used independently in an operation against the enemy on Attu. In view of the interest the Canadian Government must feel in the Aleutian Islands, it is believed that agreement to the employment of Canadian personnel in this area would be readily obtained…

b. Transfer of the Force to the United Kingdom for employment on the Continent of Europe as a raiding force. Canadian authorities should not object to participation of the Canadian personnel. This employment offers little or no use for the special snow vehicles and would not require the winter training troops have received…

c. Assignment of the Force to North Africa and employment as a raiding force either in Africa or in the Mediterranean area. The Canadian Government should not object to this employment of Canadian personnel … The specialized training, other than winter training, received by personnel of the Force should particularly fit them for this type of operation. The presence of the Force in this area would ensure its being available where its employment is most likely.

[signed] Robert T. Frederick
Colonel, First Special Service Force
Commanding

Frederick's report of February 1943 highlights the difficulty involved in finding a mission that was suited to the highly specialized training and capabilities of the First Special Service Force. Having volunteered for an early entry into combat, the officers and men now found themselves in Helena at a time when, in some cases, their former units were already fighting in North Africa. Significantly, Frederick made repeated reference to the need for Canadian approval of any proposed employment, the limitations this placed on the Force as a whole, and the expense incurred by the United States in training these men.

On 3 February, the day of Frederick's suggestion that "the time has been reached when it is necessary to decide the future of the First Special Service Force," the US War Department ordered all winter training suspended, pending a decision on the date of the unit's departure from the United States and the theatre to which it would be assigned. A decision was forthcoming within less than a week when General Eisenhower reported that he could use the Force in the Mediterranean but "that the unit should be amphibiously trained and should maintain its parachute proficiency until such time as he [Eisenhower] could determine its exact method of employment."[16] In other words, while there was still no definite use for the Force, the unit would require amphibious training before it could be used at all. From this came a decision: in April the Force would proceed to the Naval Operations Base at Norfolk, Virginia, for amphibious training.

Prior to the Force's departure for Norfolk, Frederick reversed his earlier decision and requested additional reinforcements from the Canadian Army. "As matters now stand, there will be an opportunity to train additional personnel for the 1st Special Service Force, prior to its employment abroad."[17] Recognizing that the Canadian element was not quite up to its authorized strength, but that an opportunity to train new men had presented itself, on 24 February NDHQ was sympathetic and authorized a second draft of reinforcements drawn from the 1st Canadian Parachute Battalion.[18] The newly-promoted Major Becket once again made his way to Fort Benning to recruit six officers and a hundred and twenty-five other ranks.[19]

The results were far from encouraging. On 1 March, Becket telephoned Fort Harrison to report that certain complications had arisen. Specifically, very few men in the 1st Battalion were willing to volunteer for the Force. Becket attributed this to a number of factors, including the development over the past four months of a strong esprit de corps in the 1st Canadian Parachute Battalion. Second, immediately prior to Becket's arrival, the officer commanding the battalion had authorized two weeks' leave in Canada beginning on 22 March, a vacation the troops would have to forego upon transferring to the Force. This leave had been granted in recognition that the 1st

Battalion would soon depart for overseas, which introduced an additional difficulty for Becket as the First Special Service Force no longer seemed to offer the possibility of an early entry into combat. Finally, some of the men recruited earlier from the 1st Battalion had written disparagingly of the Force. According to Becket, "Most of these men would appear to be those who suffered punishment or demotion for AWOL. It appeared to me that these letters were used actively by the officers for adverse propaganda."[20] During his visit Becket was able to recruit only twelve men. One officer also volunteered provisionally but later withdrew his statement.[21]

Upon learning the results of Becket's visit, NDHQ was unwilling to issue orders compelling the transfer of personnel from the 1st Canadian Parachute Battalion, but suggested that it might be possible to secure the required reinforcements after the men had returned from their two weeks' leave in Canada.[22] When McQueen suggested this to Colonel Frederick, however, the Force Commander could not accept further delay as it would not allow sufficient time to train the reinforcements. Though the evidence suggests the Canadians found it bewildering that Frederick could not accept a few weeks' delay, there was nothing to do besides accepting his decision. On 23 March, Lieutenant-General Stuart noted, once again, that the Force would receive no further Canadian personnel. "This is based upon recommendations from the Commander, First Special Service Force, who has definitely indicated that, as the Force is a task force of highly trained specialist troops, it would not be practicable to reinforce … from training sources available here."[23] Noting that only the recent decision to provide the Force with amphibious training had allowed it the time to take on additional reinforcements, Stuart did not anticipate "that we will continually call upon the 1st [Parachute] Battalion to reinforce the 2nd Battalion … as the role and employment of the two units is quite different."[24]

To confirm these arrangements, however, Stuart arranged a visit to Helena in early April by the Deputy Chief of General Staff, Brigadier E.G. Weeks. Arriving on 5 April, Weeks met with Colonel Frederick, Lieutenant-Colonel Williamson and the officers of the Force. Overall, the Deputy CGS was very impressed with the state of training in the Force. "Considerable stress has been laid on physical fitness and toughness, and the personnel, both officers and Other Ranks are in excellent condition, being the result of very strenuous winter training."[25] Describing the relationship between Canadians and Americans as "very cordial and satisfactory," Weeks reported "an excellent esprit de corps, and as far as I could notice, the integration is complete."[26]

During this same visit, Frederick, somewhat inexplicably, again raised the question of reinforcements:

The Commanding Officer stated that during the next few months it might be possible to make special arrangements to complete parachute training in the case of Canadian reinforcements who were not trained in this subject. If it is decided not to send further Canadian reinforcements, the Commanding Officer would like to be so advised and in this event would fill up his Force with U.S.A. troops.[27]

It is possible that Frederick's earlier refusal of reinforcements, as recorded in Canadian correspondence of March 1943, was the result of a misunderstanding. Given Frederick's unwillingness to accept the two weeks' delay in providing trained parachutists, his willingness in April to accept Canadians trained only as infantrymen indicates the level of confusion at Force headquarters as to when the unit would proceed overseas. It is also possible that Frederick simply failed to realize that the arrangements for providing additional personnel could not be made on short notice and then cancelled, repeatedly, without frustrating some highly placed officials at NDHQ. While Weeks appeared to have taken the Force Commander's latest reversal in stride, others were less graceful. In Ottawa, Stuart's patience was wearing thin, and on 20 April the CGS made a tersely worded recommendation to the Minister of National Defence:

> I recommend that no further reinforcements be sent to the First Special Service Force and we accept the fact that the Canadian component will be slightly less than 50% of the total strength of the Force. To date we have despatched to the First Special Service Force a total of 54 officers and 955 O.Rs.
>
> It follows that we have produced our fair share of personnel for this Force and, if you concur, I will have Colonel Frederick informed immediately that it is not proposed to send any further Canadians as reinforcements.[28]

Meanwhile, on 11 April, the Force had departed Helena by train bound for Norfolk, Virginia, there to begin amphibious landing exercises on Chesapeake Bay. Training consisted mostly of carrying weapons, including mortars, machine-guns and flame-throwers, down the cargo nets or otherwise lowering them by line and coal bags into the landing craft. The loading time of boat teams usually averaged about sixty seconds during their second attempt at debarkation, a performance that earned high praise from the instructors at Norfolk. At the completion of this training, Colonel James Howe, the executive officer of the training centre, offered the following assessment of the First Special Service Force:

> This was the best example of debarkation into landing craft that I have observed … The Special Service Force, because of its organization, the superior type of personnel, their varied training, and their extreme mobility, are ideally suited for assignment to the assault waves of a ship to shore operation. They

could well be employed as the first wave of a Division Task Force ... By reason of their physical stamina and high morale they could overcome beach defenses and push inland ... They should then be relieved by standardized infantry, withdrawn to transports, and used in subsequent operations.[29]

Considering the Force ideally suited to an assault role at the spearhead of an amphibious landing, he noted that "with the inclusion of short periods of training [between] phases of offensive combat, these troops would become the most versatile and most effective combat troops in any army."[30]

Transferred to Fort Ethan Allen, Vermont, at the end of April, the Force was held in readiness, marking time and pending final orders for dispatch overseas.

In May 1943 a decision had still not been reached regarding the employment of the First Special Service Force, although the matter was now being discussed at the highest levels of command. On 25 May the Combined Chiefs of Staff held their sixth meeting of the Trident Conference at the White House. Among those present, Winston Churchill and George C. Marshall took the greatest interest in the future of the First Special Service Force, although Sir Alan Brooke, General McNarney and President Roosevelt all took some part in the discussion. To begin, General Marshall reported on the specialized training received by the Force, as well as on the high state of readiness among its officers and men. In the opinion of all United States and British officers concerned, the Force should be given battle experience as soon as possible. "It could be reassembled for its proper role before the winter," noted Marshall, who also pointed out a number of areas for immediate employment including the Aleutian Islands and Italy. At this point Churchill stepped in, saying that because the Force had been designed for use in a particular type of warfare, it would be a shame to see it wasted—especially if there were a chance of the Force being used in its proper role. With planners going so far as to suggest Burma as a possible destination, the British Prime Minister voiced his influential opinion that the Force had been designed for winter warfare and that it would be a pity to dissipate it in the steaming jungles of Southeast Asia.[31] "Nevertheless," he added, "it would be quite easy to create an opportunity for its employment if it were sent to the United Kingdom."[32] At Churchill's suggestion, the Force was ordered to proceed to the UK in the summer of 1943.

On 28 May, Frederick addressed a gathering of his officers, explaining how the near-constant changes of the past months had been the result of ongoing uncertainty as to

the mission for the Force. "[Frederick] said that one day in Washington within 14 hours the Force had been assigned to 6 different missions. At present the Force was not assigned to any mission but it was sufficiently trained that it must expect to be alerted at any time and leave with little or no notice."[33] That being the case, it is not difficult to attribute Frederick's repeatedly cancelled requests for additional Canadian personnel to the confusion surrounding when the Force would proceed overseas. In early June, when the recent decision of the Combined Chiefs of Staff seemed to confirm that the Force would not be departing from the United States for at least several weeks, Frederick used the time to make his way to Ottawa in order to explain the earlier confusion and make a final request for Canadian reinforcements.

Visiting Ottawa in person, Frederick sorted out any misunderstandings and allayed some of the frustration at NDHQ. As a result of his visit, the Canadians agreed in principle to the provision of an additional six officers and a hundred and fifty other ranks, to be made available at the earliest opportunity. With the Force scheduled to depart for the United Kingdom on 25 July, "Frederick observed that this reinforcement, if made, should be done within the next two weeks as the unit would be required to reach a state of readiness as from the 1st of July."[34]

Within a week Ottawa had confirmed these arrangements, stating that the reinforcements would be dispatched on 24 June.[35] True to form, however, Frederick responded that, once again, the plan had changed—24 June would be too late. Frederick's latest orders proved to be the real thing. After a long string of false alarms, on 9 June the War Department advanced the unit's date of departure for overseas to 11 July, bound not for the UK, but for the Aleutian Islands, where the First Special Se rvice Force was slated to spearhead the assault on the Japanese-held island of Kiska.

Occupied in the summer of 1942, the Alaskan islands of Kiska and Attu represented the only North American territory to fall under Japanese control during the Second World War. The islands of the Aleutian archipelago, forming a natural bridge between Asia and North America, consist mostly of barren tundra and mountains, alternately swept by cold winds or enshrouded in fog. Garrisoned by Japanese soldiers and operated as a base for submarine and flying boat patrols, Attu and Kiska in 1943 offered little of value to the conquerors aside from their prestige value. "A strong case could have been made for leaving the Japs to freeze … on Kiska and Attu, where they were at most a nuisance to American operations in the Pacific. However, their presence naturally worried the inhabitants of Alaska, British Columbia and the Pacific Coast states, and there was thus a 'political' motive for ejecting them."[36] In August 1943 the First Special

Service Force would become part of the combined US–Canadian effort to dislodge the Japanese from their only foothold in North America.

Earlier, in May, an American invasion force had landed on Attu, initiating a bloody campaign that ended in the utter destruction of the enemy garrison. Of the nearly 2,500 Japanese on the island, only 24 allowed themselves to be taken prisoner.[37] In the summer of 1943, landing on Kiska promised more of the same, though on a much larger scale. With the Japanese garrison of the island numbering almost 6,000, and including both civilians and soldiers, American planners expected the forthcoming invasion of Kiska to prove costly for both sides.[38]

While the invasion of Attu was still in progress, Major-General Maurice Pope of the Canadian Joint Staff Mission in Washington had heard a suggestion that it might be appropriate for Canada to lend its support to the Aleutian campaign. When he approached General Marshall with the idea, the Chief of Staff agreed with him and on 24 May informed him that the United States would welcome Canadian support in future operations.[39] At the end of the month, the Cabinet War Committee approved the dispatch of a Canadian brigade group to the Alaskan theatre to take part in the invasion of Kiska.

Selecting the 13th Canadian Infantry Brigade to join an American task force, the Canadian government had high hopes that the employment of a Home Defence brigade, consisting of personnel conscripted under the National Resources Mobilization Act (NRMA), would help lessen public hostility toward these soldiers who had been unwilling to volunteer for overseas service in Europe.[40] Eager to see the NRMA troops committed to an operation that was in keeping with their intended role—the defence of North America—the Canadian government informed the United States of its decision to send the 13th Infantry Brigade to Alaska. At this time, Canada expressed no opinion regarding the use of the First Special Service Force because that unit was believed to be on its way to the United Kingdom.

On 12 June, Major-General Pope received a letter from the US War Department in which General McNarney informed him that there had been a change of plans and the Force was now being ordered to the Aleutians. Having interpreted the Canadian government's approval to use the 13th Brigade in Alaska as a green light to send the First Special Service Force as well, the United States inadvertently committed a breach of earlier agreements that any proposed operational employment of the Force be subject to Canadian approval. Upset by what could easily be construed as a unilateral decision to send the Force to Alaska, Pope recorded in his diary:

> This was hardly giving us a chance because: (a) we had approved the use of certain named Canadian troops for the Aleutians, in which the Special Service Force was not included, and (b) we had approved the despatch of the Special

Service Force to the United Kingdom. I therefore called him [McNarney] up and went out to the Pentagon to ask him if he would not give the Canadian Government a chance to express its approval, telling him at the same time that the C.G.S. had intimated to me yesterday that the prior use of this Unit in the Aleutians would also be approved. McNarney saw the point and together we redrafted the letter.[41]

After all the discussion and the guarantee that Canada would retain the right to approve the movement of its soldiers overseas, in practice this was how the decision-making process worked. On 14 June, Ottawa gave its rubber stamp to the decision.

The First Special Service Force departed from Fort Ethan Allen by train at the end of June and arrived in San Francisco on 3 July, where it was housed in isolation on Angel Island for reasons of security. Although the final destination remained unannounced, the arrival of winter stores and cold-weather equipment provided strong indications that the Force was being sent to the Aleutians. Within the week, the men had begun loading onto two Liberty ships, the SS *Nathaniel Wyeth* and *John B. Floyd*. On 11 July, the two ships passed under the Golden Gate Bridge, bound in convoy for Amchitka Island, the Force staging area for operations against Kiska.[42] *(See map, Figure 3.1.)*

In the forthcoming invasion, the Force would lead the assault, landing in darkness some five hours ahead of the main invasion. Tasked with securing the beachhead, clearing obstacles and marking the routes inland, FSSF casualties were expected to be heavy. For the Canadian element, recently redesignated the 1st Canadian Special Service Battalion, these anticipated casualties posed an especially difficult problem as the Force was proceeding into combat with no means of replacing Canadian losses. "Whereas the U.S. element is approximately 20% overstrength, which in all probability will take care of their casualties from the forthcoming operations, this Battalion is now 6 officers and 150 O/Rs short of its authorized strength. Some system, it is hoped, will be set up now to make up the above shortage plus anticipated casualties."[43] Estimating that casualties might run as high as forty percent, Lieutenant-Colonel Williamson suggested, "If our continuance as an integral part of this Force is intended, a total of 22 officers and 375 O/Rs will be required on our return to the U.S.A."[44]

The operational history of the First Special Service Force began in the early morning hours of 15 August 1943. Approaching in rubber boats across still waters on a cloudless, moonlit night, the First Regiment under Lieutenant-Colonel Marshall touched down

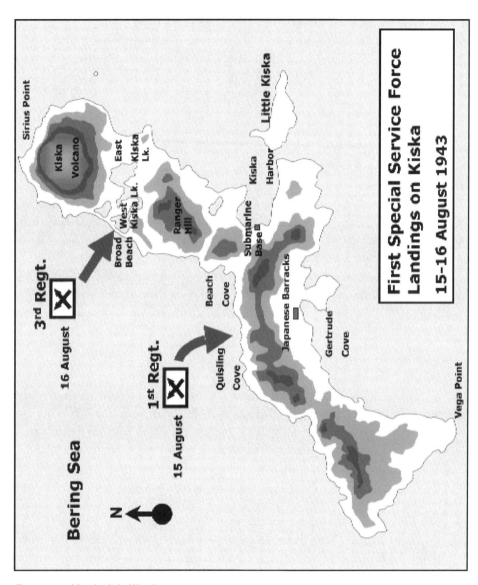

Figure 3.1   Map by Lyle Wood

unopposed at points along Kiska's north shore near Beach Cove. Securing the landing zones and moving inland, Force patrols scoured the island but found nothing. The following evening, Frederick, who had also gone ashore with elements of Force Headquarters, reported by radio; "Reached objective without meeting a single enemy or exchanging a shot. Hills terrific. Fog dense … Hoping for better hunting."[45]

The search continued into the next day, but it soon became obvious that the Japanese had managed to evacuate Kiska undetected. "Speculation is rampant as to whether any Japs other than a handful are still on the island. If there are not, the navy, who have claimed to have had such a tight ring about Kiska, will have some explaining to do."[46] The Japanese were not on the island, and the navy did have some explaining to do. It soon became apparent that the Japanese had evacuated the island several days earlier. Patrols searched several caves and huts, finding abandoned weapons, equipment and provisions. Searches uncovered quantities of cooked rice in pots and mess kits on tables, indicating that the evacuation had taken place in the middle of a meal.

Toward midnight on 16 August, a second landing, by Lieutenant-Colonel Walker's Third Regiment at the north end of the island near West Kiska Lake, met with similar results and confirmed that the island was abandoned: "Jap equipment and supplies found. Kiska extensively patrolled. No enemy contacted."[47]

On 18 August a slightly embarrassed meeting of the Combined Chiefs of Staff discussed the landings on Kiska. It decided that the FSSF should be made available in other theatres as soon as possible. To this end, the Combined Chiefs ordered the unit returned to the United States and began considering other opportunities for its employment. Dispatch to the United Kingdom remained a possibility, offering the potential for diversionary operations into Norway, possibly in support of Operation Overlord. The Mediterranean was another option, as the Force would be a valuable asset in the tough mountain fighting up the Italian peninsula or along the Dalmation coast in support of Yugoslavian partisans.[48] "The Force is at present gaining experience in the Kiska operations … There is still time therefore for the possibilities of its further employment to be fully explored."[49] While the final decision would have to await consultation with the commanders in the Mediterranean and the United Kingdom, on Adak Island the Force boarded ships and, on 24 August, began its long return journey to Fort Ethan Allen via San Francisco.

Upon the Force's arrival back in the United States, there ensued a last-minute round of administrative changes, including a final, almost desperate, attempt by Lieutenant-

Colonel Williamson to resolve the Canadian reinforcements situation before proceeding overseas. On 12 September, he boarded a flight to Ottawa, the object being to secure the personnel needed to bring the Canadian element up to its authorized strength. Though he was able to secure sixty-five replacements during this trip, the additions still left the 1st Canadian Special Service Battalion understrength and without a system of replacing its losses once it was committed to combat.[50] At the same time, the Combined Chiefs reached a decision: after consultation with General Eisenhower in the Mediterranean, the FSSF was being sent to Italy. Departing on 28 October, Williamson commented on what might be considered the most significant failure of the planning stages for the First Special Service Force as a bi-national military formation:

> The Battalion is proceeding overseas 10 officers and 131 other ranks short of its authorized strength. This is greatly deplored by the writer, particularly so because the necessary authorization to build to strength on a number of occasions was received but the time allowed on each occasion for their procurement, selection, necessary training and assimilation was always practically impossible to meet.[51]

In hindsight, the failure to establish an ongoing system of providing US and Canadian replacement personnel to the First Special Service Force stands as perhaps the most significant oversight of this period of organization and training. More than one historian of the Force has attributed this problem, at least on the Canadian side, to Lieutenant-General Kenneth Stuart's recommendation of 20 April 1943 that no further Canadian reinforcements be provided to the First Special Service Force.[52] Had Stuart lived to read these historical accounts, he may have pointed out that his recommendation had been based upon Frederick's refusal, in December 1942, of a Canadian offer to supply parachute-trained reinforcements, as well as the Force commander's repeated reversals on the issue until the unit proceeded overseas. Interestingly, archival sources in the United States, including Frederick's personal papers, contain no mention of the Force commander having ever refused an offer of Canadian reinforcements. Similar to Geoffrey Pyke's activities in Ottawa in June 1942, the full story only becomes apparent upon an examination of both Canadian and American accounts.

In fairness to both Frederick and Stuart, the failure to establish a permanent system of replacing casualties in the First Special Service Force might best be attributed to the nature of the proposed mission for which the Force had been created. Operation Plough was intended as a single raid into enemy territory. In effect, the Force was considered a single-use weapon, and there were, consequently, no reinforcement implications for the original mission.

Given the Force's orientation towards a role in sustained combat after October 1942, however, it seems highly unfortunate that Frederick did not accept the Canadian offer to provide reinforcements to the unit on an ongoing basis, or that Adams, who was responsible for the day-to-day management of the unit, did not recommend doing so. Why these officers missed an opportunity to secure further Canadian replacements remains uncertain, although Frederick was, in all likelihood, hesitant to take on new men when the unit could, seemingly at any moment, find itself en route to an operational theatre. Further, Frederick considered the training that his men received within the First Special Service Force to be far better than could be received elsewhere, an opinion which he appeared to share with several outside observers who came into contact with the unit. For this reason, and given that he was constantly led to expect assignment to combat on short notice, Frederick's decision becomes understandable. The continuation of this policy of non-acceptance after the cancellation of Operation Plough, however, was one of the regrettable results of the near-constant changes and conflicting orders that characterized the unit's search for a mission in the opening months of 1943.

Lieutenant Albert "Link" Washburn was a technical adviser attached to the First Special Service Force in 1942-43 as an army Specialist Corps training officer in rock climbing and cold-climate survival techniques. Here he demonstrates the packing of the soldier's winter rucksack. All the items on the table go into the sack. (NA-CP SC 187835-S)

Here, soldiers are seen jumping from a wall during training at Fort William Henry Harrison. Force personnel received extensive preparation in demolitions, jump training, endurance, mountain and winter warfare. In addition, courses in hand-to-hand combat were emphasized, along with night patrolling tactics. Captain Pat O'Neill gave unarmed combat training, and boxing was very popular. *(G. Ronald collection, CWM 19820091-001 M-5)*

The rugged terrain of the Montana hills provides ideal training conditions as the Force prepares for a parachute descent into occupied Europe for the purpose of destroying German-held hydroelectric dams and other targets. Unfortunately, Operation Plough was cancelled before the Force had a chance to put many of its unique capabilities to use. *(G. Ronald collection, CWM)*

Ascending the steep precipices of the Rockies by means of belaying ropes, these soldiers are mountain climbing near Fort William Henry Harrison in 1943. The jackets and hoods worn by the men are reversible, being white on the other side to provide camouflage when set against a snowy background.  *(NA-CP SC 187838-S)*

A para-ski trooper of the Force, dug in for sniper practice. The effectiveness of the camouflage afforded by the white winter outfits is well illustrated by this photo. *(NA-CP SC 187840-S)*

Two white-camouflaged men of the Force prove that they can live and work under all kinds of winter conditions by operating their radio during training at Fort William Henry Harrison, 1943. *(NA-CP SC 187842-S)*

In winter the soldiers are taught complete living skills. This soldier is taking advantage of an improvised dugout to cook himself a warm meal. *(NA-CP SC 187843-S)*

The climate and terrain of Fort William Henry Harrison affords excellent ski practice for the First Special Service Force, 1943. *(NA-CP SC 187841-S)*

Captain Carl A. Brakel, Paratroop Field Surgeon (Seattle, Washington; HQ det. 3rd Regt) takes off his parachute after making his first jump, 1943. *(NA-CP SC 187748-S)*

This para-ski trooper, just landed by parachute, immediately adjusts his bindings. Training at F o r t William Henry Harrison continued through 13 April 1943. Amphibious training followed at Camp Bradford in Norfolk, Virginia and continued with advanced infantry, scout and raider tactics at Fort Ethan Allen in Burlington, Vermont, until June 1943. *(NA-CP SC 187839-S)*

Alligator detachment in support of combined Canadian-American advance across Kiska, 15/16 August, 1943. Assigned to General Corlett's 34,000-strong task force (ATF9) charged with assaulting Japanese-occupied Kiska in the Aleutians, 1st and 3rd Regiments of FSSF paddled ashore at 0130 hours to land at Beaches 9, 10, and 14 (Gertrude Cove, Lilly Beach, and Witchcraft Point, Broad Beach). *(NA-CP SC 245211)*

A Canadian 25-pounder emplacement with a dugout for troops directly behind the gun, on Monument Hill, Kiska Island, 1943. On D+1, the 3rd Regiment FSSF, 13th Canadian Brigade Group and US 184th Infantry were to advance from the Northern Sector to join the Southern Sector, where they would join the 1st Regiment in an advance toward the main Japanese naval base and army installations. On 15 August, 2nd Regiment was on an Amchitka airstrip waiting for a call to parachute onto Kiska, but the drop was cancelled upon discovering that the Japanese had evacuated the island 18 days earlier. *(NA-CP SC 245238)*

An American soldier takes a close look at Japanese guns atop South Head on Kiska, 1943. As part of the Southern Sector landing, the plan was for 1st Regiment FSSF to attack this area surrounding the main Japanese naval base. *(G. Myers photo, NA-CP SC 325836)*

The "Stars & Stripes" again flies over Kiska after fourteen months of Japanese occupation, 1943. *(G. Myers photo, NA-CP SC 325837)*

## CHAPTER 4

# A "Special" Reinforcements Crisis

Have now received representation from Gilday, Acting OC. He states strength is now reduced to between 250 and 300 after heavy fighting and that without reinforcements the battalion will eventually waste to virtually nothing. He feels the battalion has created an excellent impression on the Americans but that the situation is becoming increasingly difficult due to increasing numerical disparity and the time has come when this commitment should be terminated.

*Brigadier-General A.W. Beament*
*OIC, Canadian Section, GHQ, 1st Echelon*
*15 January 1944*[1]

The First Special Se rvice Force arrived in Italy on 17 November 1943, during a stalemate in the US Fifth Army's drive towards Rome. After landing at Salerno in September, Fifth Army had driven the German Army up the peninsula toward Naples, then inland up the Volturno River valley and into the mountainous country of the interior. In October the weather turned foul, and the onset of the rainy season made it difficult to sustain the momentum of the advance. Streams became flooded, washing out bridges and roads and leaving the weary troops and their vehicles mired deep in the mud of the Italian countryside. By mid-November, the US Fifth Army advance had ground to a halt before the Mignano Gap, a bottleneck leading to the Liri valley and the road to Rome. Here the Germans occupied a series of hilltop strongholds from which they were able to dominate the lowlands with mortar and artillery fire.

This belt of fortifications was the Winter Line, and at Mignano the German defence was anchored on Monte Sammucro to the north and the Monte Camino–La Difensa–Maggiore hill mass to the south. In November, two attempts by British and American soldiers to seize the latter peaks had met with failure, the attackers being driven off Monte la Difensa with heavy losses. From positions overlooking all accessible approaches to the summit, German snipers, machine-gunners and mortars had been able to dominate the narrow gorges leading up the mountain, frustrating all attempts to seize this key point in the German defences. Difensa, meaning "defence" in Italian, was a fortress. On 23 November the FSSF was assigned to the US II Corps under Major-General Geoffrey Keyes, and the next day Frederick received orders for an assault on Monte la Difensa.[2] After months of false alarms and cancelled missions, there was no longer any question that the Force would see combat.

Incessant rain marked the last week of November 1943 in central Italy as Frederick and his staff made their reconnaissance of Monte la Difensa. Occupying a line halfway up the mountain was the US 36th Division, whose troops had inherited the position from the American 7th Infantry Regiment after it was kicked off the upper reaches of the mountain by the Germans on 12 November.[3] Beyond 36th Division's lines, Force patrols discovered that German snipers and machine-gunners overlooked all accessible approaches to the summit and were able to dominate the narrow gorges leading up the mountain, just as they had done during the 7th Infantry's week-long effort to take Difensa. When these patrols confirmed that all accessible approaches to the summit remained blocked, the only solution became to consider the "inaccessible" ones.

With German machine-guns commanding the more gradual slopes of Difensa, Force patrols began scouting the north face of the mountain, which was largely undefended likely because the Germans considered the near-vertical cliffs in this area to be impassable. It was here in the last week of November that Force reconnaissance patrols located a narrow rift that could be negotiated with some difficulty by an assault battalion, provided that the men were able to use ropes and were not too heavily loaded with arms and ammunition.[4]

Fifth Army's plan for the upcoming offensive called for a simultaneous attack by two army corps against the Camino–Difensa complex. On the far left, the British 46th Division would open the attack, launching a diversionary assault against Hill 360 that was intended to draw enemy forces away from the Camino hill mass. This would be followed by a 56th (City of London) Division attack against Monte Camino and a First Special Service Force ascent of Monte la Difensa. Simultaneous capture of both peaks was considered essential as German defenders holding out on Camino would be able to overlook the approaches to the Difensa summit, and vice versa. Supporting the initial phases of the Camino–Difensa assault would be a series of bombing and strafing runs by Allied aircraft, combined with the largest artillery barrage of the Italian campaign.[5] As the Force made its way up Monte la Difensa, 925 guns of the US II Corps and British X Corps would cover its approach, including 820 guns firing directly against the Camino–Difensa hills.[6] This massive artillery support plan for Operation Raincoat was intended to produce one of the "most powerful and intense concentrations ever produced in battle on a small area."[7] *(See map, Figure 4.1.)*

Assigning Lieutenant-Colonel Williamson's Second Regiment to lead the attack, with Third Regiment's 1st Battalion in reserve, the assault force carried out a ten-mile march to the base of Difensa on the night of 1/2 December. "We went up the mountain, remaining under the cover of brush and tree cover until the whole Regiment was concealed as daylight broke," recalls Bill Story. "It stopped raining overnight and the sun came out in the morning." Remaining hidden throughout the day, the Force began its ascent to the Difensa summit on the evening of 2 December.

Throughout the night one of the largest artillery concentrations since El Alamein rained high explosives onto enemy positions above. According to Fifth Army operational records, "925 pieces of all calibers poured ton after ton of high explosive, white phosphorous, and smoke shells into the enemy's positions. The rumble and roar of the guns echoed from mountain to mountain, and the noise of exploding shells reverberated until the ground trembled."[8] Although the Germans had blasted their positions out of the solid rock and were not likely to be killed in the bombardment, it was hoped that the barrage would at least serve to keep their heads down until the Force could reach the summit.

As the shells and bombs crashed into the Camino–Difensa hill mass, the reinforced 3rd Battalion of the 104th Panzergrenadier Regiment withdrew to their pillboxes and caves at the Difensa summit to wait out the attack.[9] Monte La Difensa was an ancient volcano, crumbled away on one side and almost vertical on the other. At the summit lay the bowl of the crater, a shallow depression where bunkers and caves formed the centre of the German position. Far below, Second Regiment emerged from the cover of a ravine to begin a six-hour ascent of the rocky slopes towards an assembly area at the base of the cliffs. Prior to last light, noise of their movement was drowned out by the constant waves of Allied aircraft overhead, followed after dark by an intensified artillery barrage, which resulted in a "murderous seething and crackling [that] thundered along the Camino–Difensa ridge."[10]

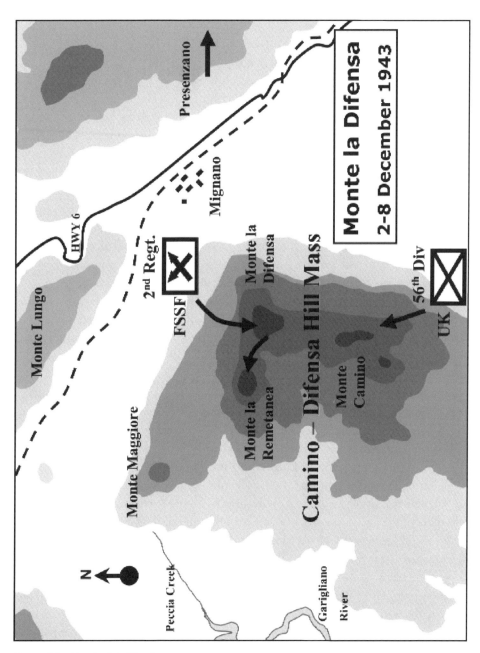

Figure 4.1    Map by Lyle Wood

By 2230 hours, Second Regiment had arrived at the base of the summit crown, and from there 1st Battalion under Lieutenant-Colonel T.C. MacWilliam of Moncton, New Brunswick, started up the cliffs, freehand at first and then using ropes. It took nearly three hours for the heavily loaded assault battalion to reach the top of the cliffs, bringing them to within 350 metres of the summit. Then 1st Company deployed on the left, 2nd Company in the centre and 3rd Company following behind and to the right as they made their way toward the summit crest, the noise of their ascent covered by the ear-splitting roar of artillery. It was not until after the barrage had moved on to more distant targets at 0430 hours that the sound of a battalion advancing over rock-strewn ground alerted the defenders. In the darkness a German voice challenged two of the Force scouts, Sergeant Howard Van Ausdale and Sergeant T.E. Fenton. A burst of gunfire, and then a storm of tracers, mortar rounds and illumination flares followed. The shooting started before dawn; surprise had been achieved, and the assault battalion was able to take advantage of the darkness and confusion to launch a downhill assault against the German defences that were facing in the other direction.

Daylight broke and darkness was replaced by fog on the mountain as advance elements of MacWilliam's battalion fought it out with Panzergrenadiers in limestone caves and pillboxes that had been blasted out of the solid rock. These positions had remained largely untouched by the preceding artillery barrage and now formed the main line of enemy defence around the shallow depression at the summit. As the strongpoints were cleared by gunfire and grenades, enemy soldiers began to emerge from the fog with their hands in the air. One of these Germans was seen waving a white flag, but when Captain W.T. Rothlin went out to accept the surrender, he was immediately cut down by a machine-gun in the rear. In response, the nearest section of Rothlin's 1st Company opened fire, killing the decoy and several others.[11]

Clearing the enemy positions with small arms fire and grenades, by 0700 hours the 1st Battalion was firmly established on the peak of Monte la Difensa. Behind them, the remainder of the Second Regiment was scrambling up the cliffs to reinforce the attack. At this point, Lieutenant-Colonel MacWilliam gave his last order, directing the battalion to reorganize and prepare to pursue the enemy as they withdrew across the fog-shrouded ridge connecting Monte la Difensa to Monte la Remetanea. Meanwhile, the reserve battalion from Third Regiment was working feverishly to bring up ammunition and evacuate the wounded. Unfortunately, with a crossfire of mortar rounds flying between Difensa and Remetanea, MacWilliam had just given the order for 1st Company to advance when he was killed by a shell that exploded near his command post. With German artillery and mortar explosions bursting across the summit, and 1st Battalion now deprived of its commander, Colonel Frederick signalled Second Regiment to hold their positions until more ammunition arrived.

In the first two hours of fighting, the First Special Service Force had mounted a successful surprise attack and captured a height of land where the Germans had been holding out since the first week of November. For the Force, however, holding Difensa would ultimately prove more difficult than taking it. On the Allied face of the mountain, pack trains from Third Regiment and the Service Battalion worked beyond the limits of exhaustion to carry water, ammunition, rations and blankets to the summit, while the German-held Peccia valley to the west flashed with gunfire and echoed with unnatural screaming as artillery and German Nebelwerfer rocket-mortars pounded the heights of Difensa.

Soldiers of Second Regiment at the summit were not the only ones to suffer under this bombardment. On the night of 3 December, First Regiment, in reserve at the base of the mountain, received orders to send a battalion to strengthen Force defences at the summit. As the men of First Regiment's 1st Battalion began climbing the trail, however, a burst of tracer fire from an enemy machine-pistol pointed them out to German forward observers, who immediately called down fire from German artillery on Monte Maggiore. Caught in the open, 1st Battalion suffered heavy casualties and was unable to move out according to plan.[12] Pack trains from Third Regiment were also targeted by the Germans and suffered numerous casualties as they struggled under extreme difficulties to carry cans of water, ammunition, mortar shells and other necessities up the mountain.

In the days to follow, fighting in the Force's sector became a war of patrols as both sides attempted to control the saddle ridge between Difensa and Remetanea. At noon on 4 December, one of the Force patrols reported a heavy concentration of mortars and machine-guns on the opposing ridge. Later in the day, the interrogation of two prisoners revealed that the Germans were preparing an attack for that night.[13] This intelligence was later confirmed when a large formation of Germans came under observation southwest of Remetanea and was subsequently targeted by II Corps artillery. Whether or not this action broke up the German counterattack is uncertain, but the threatened attack never materialized. The next morning, a break in the otherwise miserable weather allowed Second Regiment to begin preparing for a move across the saddle to secure Monte la Remetanea.

On the afternoon of 5 December, two FSSF battalions attacked down the ridge from Difensa toward Remetanea, where they encountered determined resistance from Panzergrenadiers who had decided to fight it out. With elements of the 129th Panzergrenadier Regiment, who remained entrenched on Monte Camino in the British sector, able to pour harassing fire on the assaulting Force battalions, it was not until the following day that Second Regiment's 1st Battalion was able to make the crossing and secure Remetanea. Finding the crest of the mountain abandoned, Frederick dispatched a situation report to the 36th Division command:

Our attack … has progressed beyond the crest of 907 [Remetanea]. We are receiving much machine-gun and mortar fire from several directions, principally from the draw running S[outh] W[est] from LA DIFENSA, from the Western foothills of MAGGIORE, and from the Northern slopes of CAMINO. We are endeavoring to place arty support fire on the troublesome areas, but it is difficult due to very low visibility….

German snipers are giving us hell and it is extremely difficult to catch them. They are hidden all through the area and shoot bursts at any target….

German reinforcements approach up the draw southwest of Camino, but I am unable to tell whether they are reinforcing or attempting to organize a counterattack.

In my opinion, unless the British take Camino before dark today it should be promptly attacked by us from the north. The locations we hold are going to be uncomfortable as long as the enemy holds the north slopes of Camino.[14]

Frederick also warned that the combination of falling temperatures and cold rain was beginning to produce casualties from hypothermia and exhaustion among the lightly equipped Second Regiment. The suffering caused by exposure was especially severe for the wounded until they could be evacuated to the regimental aid station, which lay halfway down the mountain. "Men are getting in bad shape from fatigue, exposure and cold … They are willing and eager, but are becoming exhausted."[15]

At this point the more serious difficulty on Monte la Difensa, however, was the adjacent peak of Monte Camino remaining in enemy hands. Facing each other across a saddle connecting the two crests, German positions on Camino traded mortar and machine-gun fire with the Force on Difensa throughout the week until, on 6 December, the British 56th (City of London) Division managed to take and hold the Camino hilltop. With this last stronghold in Allied hands, the Force set about clearing enemy troops from the surrounding area. On 8 December the last pockets of organized German resistance were eliminated.[16] That same day, the US 142nd Regimental Command Team relieved the First Special Service Force and took responsibility for defending the newly won ground in the Difensa–Remetanea sector.

After making their way down the mountain, the First Special Service Force withdrew from the line on 9 December 1943 for a week of rest and recovery at Santa Maria. With the capture of Monte la Difensa, the unit's contribution to Fifth Army's Raincoat offensive had been a decisive one: the Camino–Difensa hill mass, the southern anchor of the German Winter Line, was now firmly in Allied hands, leaving the heights of Monte

Sammucro to the north as the only remnants of the German defences overlooking the Mignano Gap and guarding the entrance to the Liri Valley. For their contribution to the success of the recent operation, the Force received the following commendation from Lieutenant-General Mark Clark, Fifth Army's commanding general:

> The Special Service Force was given the task of capturing LA DIFENSA, an extremely difficult piece of high ground in the MT. MAGGIORE hill mass, the possession of which was vital to our further advance in that sector. The mission was carried out at night in spite of adverse weather conditions and heavy enemy rifle, machine-gun, mortar and artillery fire on the precipitous slopes over which it was necessary to attack. Furthermore, the position was maintained despite counterattacks and difficulties of communication and supply. The fact that you have acquitted yourself well in your first action under enemy fire is a tribute to fine leadership and a splendid reward for time spent in arduous training.
>
> You are now out of the line for a rest and an opportunity to prepare yourselves for further operations. You must take this opportunity to prepare your troops in every way to carry out your future assignments in such manner as to add to your already creditable record.[17]

In the six-day fight for Monte la Difensa, the First Special Service Force suffered 511 casualties, roughly a quarter of its total combat strength: 73 dead, 9 missing, 313 wounded and 116 hospitalized for exhaustion.[18] Of these, Canadian losses amounted to 27 killed, 86 wounded and 41 suffering from fatigue.[19] Although some of the exhaustion cases were already beginning to recover and many of the wounded could be expected back eventually, it became painfully obvious that without reinforcements the Force would not survive many similar missions.

Two days later, Lieutenant-Colonel Williamson made a trip to Avellino in order to bring this situation to the attention of Brigadier-General A.W. Beament, the officer responsible for Canadian reinforcements in the Mediterranean theatre. In view of earlier decisions not to provide reinforcements to the Canadian element of the Force, however, there was nothing that Beament could do. A second visit to the Canadian headquarters made no more progress. "Brigadier Beament ... would have no part of the reinforcement angle in view of the C.G.S. decision not to reinforce." Returning to Santa Maria empty handed, Williamson noted, "It now becomes a matter ... for N.D.H.Q. to decide whether we are to be reinforced or continue to be a wasting asset and withdraw from the Force when the Battalion peters out."[20]

Meanwhile, efforts to secure American replacements for the FSSF encountered no serious difficulties, the greatest concern being to ensure that US Army replacement depots provided qualified personnel. On 9 December, the Force Adjutant requested replacements from US II Corps, his letter stressing the importance of physical and mental ruggedness among the volunteers and adding that these men should be hand-picked by Force officers.[21] With the Force having proven itself on Monte la Difensa, the request received the full support of the commanding general of the US Fifth Army, as Clark had now taken a personal interest in retaining the unit for future operations.[22] Over the next two weeks, training consisted mostly of trying to get the men back into fighting condition. "The severity of the last show has burnt them out and there are still a number of cases of trench feet and dysentery. A number of the wounded have returned, but the Force will go into the next show considerably understrength."[23]

On 21 December the Force departed Santa Maria and began moving toward the front, slated to join in the offensive against the northern shoulder of the Mignano Gap. Like gates overlooking the entrance to the Liri Valley, the Mignano Gap had its lock forced to the south by the fall of Monte la Difensa, but the task still remained to bust the door off its northern hinges. Assigned to guard the right flank of the II Corps advance, over the next two weeks the Force's First and Third Regiments would mount two distinct and separate operations against Winter Line positions in this sector. *(See map, Figure 4.2.)*

The western spur of Monte Sammucro, or Hill 720, overlooked the San Vittore start-line and the valley through which tanks of the US would advance during the next phase of the II Corps offensive. Although the hilltop had already been taken by the US 36th Division, several miles of the lower slopes to the west remained solidly in German hands. On 22 December the First Special Service Force, supported by the 141st Infantry and the 504th Parachute Infantry, received orders to clear the western slopes of Sammucro. With an armoured field artillery group and three airborne artillery battalions laying down a preliminary barrage, Frederick's plan was for First Regiment to conduct a downhill assault at night against prepared German defences on the western slopes. Owing to delays and poor trail conditions, however, the attack could not be brought off on schedule, and First Regiment spent the rain-soaked night of 23/24 December under whatever shelter they could find among the rocks of the treeless hillside.

It was not until Christmas Eve that First Regiment could move up to its start-line. Although the intent was that a one-hour artillery barrage would begin at 2300 hours, more delays postponed the barrage by three hours. At 0300, German artillery returned fire. This barrage threw First Regiment's attack into disorder when a mortar round landed near the 2nd Battalion command post, severely wounding the battalion commander, Lieutenant-Colonel Jack Akehurst, and killing his adjutant, Lieutenant M.A. Cotton, and one of the NCOs, C.H. Dawson. Although Colonel Marshall moved

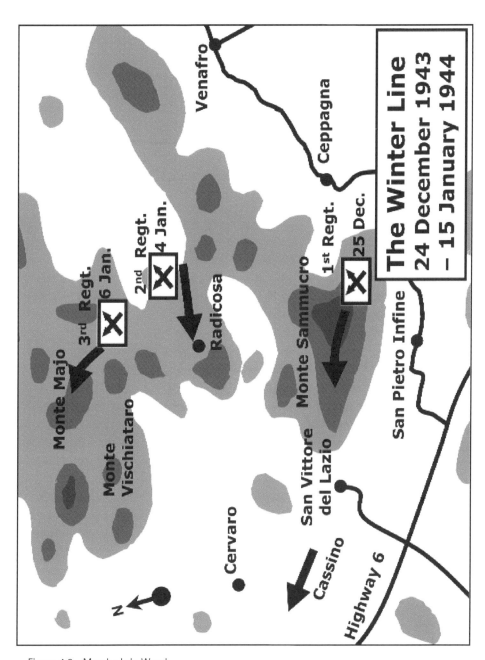

Figure 4.2   Map by Lyle Wood

up to take charge of 2nd Battalion, the attack could not get started until shortly before dawn.

Stepping off on a bitterly cold Christmas morning from the heights of Monte Sammucro, First Regiment conducted a frontal assault against the prepared defences of the 3rd Battalion, 71st Panzergrenadier Regiment. "Strong enemy opposition was encountered and the regiment was caught under very heavy shell fire, which inflicted heavy casualties."[24] Though the attack was successful, subsequent shelling and losses from trench foot and exposure reduced several companies of the First Regiment to between twenty and thirty percent strength.[25] On Christmas Day, First Regiment was relieved by elements of the 36th Division.

After a short rest, on New Year's Day the First Special Service Force received orders for the next phase of the advance: again to act as flank protection on the right of II Corps as it pushed down the valley toward the Rapido River and Monte Cassino. This next phase of the attack was designed to force the Germans to fall back along Highway 6 toward the Gustav Line—the next belt of defences beyond the now-crumbling Winter Line positions. On the north shoulder of the advance, overlooking the recently won slopes of Monte Sammucro, lay the dominating mass of Monte Majo. Advancing from the vicinity of Sammucro on 4 January, First and Second Regiments captured three of the Majo foothills, clearing the way for Colonel Walker's Third Regiment to lead the assault against the main objective.

In ascending the snow-covered hills below the heights of Monte Majo, Third Regiment secured scores of nameless peaks and struggled to keep lines of communication open, with mule trains and pack boards offering the only means of delivering ammunition and provisions to the front. High winds and below-freezing temperatures took a heavy toll, as did intermittent shelling by German artillery. Trench foot, exhaustion and hypothermia became a daily experience for all three regiments, as much of the high country was covered in several inches of snow and temperatures hovered below freezing. With all three regiments below strength, on 6 January Major-General Keyes, the corps commander, attached two battalions of infantry and an engineer company to the First Special Service Force, forming Task Force B under Frederick's command. For artillery, Keyes placed the US 36th Division's artillery in direct support of the Force. Since the heights of Monte Majo overlooked the approaches to Monte Cassino, its capture was essential to the success of the II Corps advance.

On the night of 6/7 January the augmented Third Regiment was ready for a fight, and Walker selected 1st Battalion under Canadian Lieutenant-Colonel Thomas P. Gilday to lead the assault on the crest of Monte Majo. Setting out shortly after dark, the battalion was moving steadily toward the summit by 2200 hours when enemy machine-gun fire opened up from various points, including a few positions in the rear that had been bypassed by the 1st Battalion advance. Scattered machine-gun fire quickly developed into a full-scale firefight as Gilday's company commanders led their troops in a flanking movement against the enemy's main defences along the summit crest. By midnight, a battalion of Austrians and Poles from the German 44th Infantry Division was driven from its positions on the heights. The following morning a patrol from Gilday's 2nd Company reached Colonel Walker to report that the crest of Monte Majo had fallen—but with great difficulty.[26] Atop the mountain the "entire regimental position was subjected to heavy artillery and mortar fire" in addition to a series of counterattacks over the next two days, which were stopped cold by Third Regiment using captured German machine-guns and large quantities of ammunition seized during the attack.[27]

For another week all three regiments of the Force were involved in countless skirmishes and unending toil as they made their way through the trackless hills. Bitter cold, difficult terrain and a fiercely determined German resistance exacted a heavy toll from all three regiments. Entries in the War Diary of the 1st Canadian Special Service Battalion provide some insight into the nature of Force operations during this period:

> January 8: Today's casualty return ... lists 100 names, half of them frostbite and exposure, the rest battle casualties. The weather in the hills is very cold, with high wind and snow. German resistance is quite severe, artillery and mortar fire is taking its toll.
>
> January 9: Today's Force casualty return has 122 names, again nearly half are frostbite and exposure. There soon won't be much left of the Force if casualties keep up at this rate.
>
> January 10: News from the front is bad ... The Force is being thrown into one action after another with only a handful of able-bodied men left and no sign of their being relieved. Seventy-three names on today's casualty report, 40 frostbitten feet. Those returning to camp on light duty say it is really rugged and they are all played out. Three weeks tomorrow since they left here.[28]

Fought across the freezing, snow-covered slopes, Force operations in January 1944 came to assume the character of a slugging match as the combat echelon secured one hilltop after another and was bled white in the process. For those who survived, the mountain fighting of January faded into a blur, as recalled by Force veteran John R. Dawson:

> All through these actions, our regiment was terribly understrength, and a major factor in our lives was toting all our weapons and the ammunition for

them with skeleton crews. Somehow we did, but the greatest memory I have of this period is utter weariness, and generally of firing not at people, but squares on the map, wisps of smoke, muzzle blasts in the darkness.[29]

In the wake of these operations the high ground secured by the First Special Service Force became a pivot upon which the Fifth Army swung toward the Gustav Line and Monte Cassino, the dominating height of land that both sides understood would be the next major obstacle blocking the Allied drive on Rome. On 15 January the Force withdrew from the front in order to begin reorganizing for the coming offensive. As remnants of the combat echelon filtered into the base camp at Santa Maria, the losses suffered over the past month became painfully clear. The combat echelon had been devastated, with losses running approximately fifty percent in all three of the combat regiments.

| | ASSIGNED STRENGTH | | EFFECTIVE STRENGTH | |
|---|---|---|---|---|
| | Officers | Enlisted Men | Officers | Enlisted Men |
| 1st Regiment | 29 | 480 | 14 | 217 |
| 2nd Regiment | 35 | 491 | 26 | 276 |
| 3rd Regiment | 36 | 527 | 23 | 277 |
| TOTAL | 100 | 1498 | 63 | 770 |

Table 4.1: First Special Service Force Assigned and Effective Strengths, 20 January 1944.[30]

Among those returning from the mountains was the commanding officer of the 1st Battalion, Third Regiment, Lieutenant-Colonel Gilday. When he arrived at Santa Maria in the second week of January, Gilday learned that the recent loss of two officers had left him as the senior Canadian officer of the Force.

On 1 January, Frederick had relieved Lieutenant-Colonel D.D. Williamson of his command, ordering him to pack his bags and leave the Force immediately. Second Regiment officers reported that Williamson had lost his nerve and behaved erratically during the attack on Monte la Difensa.

> Williamson came in from the front … he had been called into the Force Commander's C.P. in the morning [and] shown statements signed by some of his regimental officers declaring lack of confidence in him as a result of the La Difensa operation four weeks ago. Not one officer said a word to him about it and he was given no intimation that they lacked confidence in his leadership until he was handed the declarations four weeks after. He felt that

he might have been told. He was asked how quickly he could be packed and leave as he had been relieved from command. He had no opportunity to defend himself—a most unfair way to handle the case and especially to treat the man who had helped create the Force and who has been at the helm through its many turbulent and trying times.[31]

Although the initial entry in the Canadian War Diary records resentment at Williamson's summary dismissal, subsequent entries may point to the necessity of Frederick's decision, noting that Williamson was subsequently treated for battle exhaustion at the 14th Canadian General Hospital in Caserta before being transferred to the United Kingdom at the end of the month.[32]

While Lieutenant-Colonel Robert S. Moore succeeded Williamson as commander of the Second Regiment, the position of senior Canadian officer and commander of the 1st Canadian Special Service Battalion passed formally to Lieutenant-Colonel Jack Akehurst, who was still in the hospital recovering from wounds suffered on Monte Sammucro.[33] With Williamson gone and Akehurst in the hospital, on 12 January Lieutenant-Colonel Thomas Gilday assumed temporary command of the 1st Cananadian Special Service Battalion. His promotion came just in time to deal with a breaking crisis over the issue of Canadian reinforcements.

While American replacements had been filtering into Santa Maria since late December, with 250 arriving between 24 January and the end of the month, Canadian numbers continued to fall owing to the decision not to provide reinforcements to the unit. By 14 January, with nearly half of the Canadian element either dead or wounded, Gilday decided that it was time to force a decision on the matter. Travelling to Naples the next day, he explained the situation to Brigadier-General Beament, outlining the full extent of the problem.

Less than half of the Canadians in the Force were still on their feet. Under normal circumstances approximately fifty percent of the wounded could be expected to recover, but given the large number of frozen feet and cases of trench foot, Gilday predicted that no more than twenty-five percent would actually return to the Force owing to "the strenuous type of work our troops are required to perform." In the past month, these Canadians had performed exceptionally well in battle, "acting in a straight infantry role as shock troops for the Fifth Army."[34] To replace the considerable losses suffered by the combat regiments during this period, said Gilday, the Americans were now bringing in replacements. If the Canadians did not do the same, they would soon comprise less than a third of the combat element.

Gilday recommended three possible courses of action: (1) reinforce the Canadian element to full strength, (2) withdraw from the Force and return the men to the Canadian Army, or (3) simply allow the remnant of the 1st Canadian Special Service Battalion to waste away. Noting the difficulties involved in training Canadian reinforcements to use American weapons while the Force was in a theatre of war, but also considering the morale implications if the remaining Canadians were abandoned to their fate, Gilday suggested that there was only one solution:

> We have acquitted ourselves well in battle. There is a good feeling and many strong friendships between the Canadians and Americans of the Force. As new American reinforcements come in and Canadians become fewer in number, it will be increasingly difficult to keep the friendly spirit and good relations that now exist. The Canadian element is liable to become a source of embarrassment to the Americans. It will also become increasingly difficult to keep the existing high morale when it becomes known that the Canadians are going to be allowed to slowly waste away.
>
> I strongly recommend that the Canadian element be withdrawn from the First Special Service Force while there is enough of it left to be of assistance to the Canadian Army. This withdrawal should take place immediately before the force is committed again in another phase of operations and while the force is undergoing re-organization.[35]

Although recognizing the matter as one of higher government policy, Beament was convinced that Gilday's recommendations were sound and represented the majority of Canadian opinion in the Force. Reinforcements, in any case, would be very difficult to obtain from Canadian Army sources as the officers and men selected would have to be volunteers and would inevitably take longer to train than American replacements. Incoming Canadians would be required to learn the use of American weapons and become familiar with US Army customs which would require weeks of training.

While unable to take action himself, Beament passed Gilday's suggestions along to Canadian Military Headquarters (CMHQ) in London that same day, adding, "I am personally impressed by the soundness of these views and am convinced that Col. Gilday's feeling is generally shared by the personnel of this Unit. Personnel of this Unit apparently feel rather keenly that they are losing touch with the Canadian Army … If 1st Canadian Special Se rviceBattalion were removed from the American Force this, of course, becomes rather simple."[36] If Gilday hoped his recommendations would produce a strong reaction from higher Canadian headquarters, he was probably not disappointed.

As it happened, the newly appointed Chief of Staff at CMHQ London, Lieutenant-General Kenneth Stuart, was personally familiar with the difficulties surrounding Canadian participation in the Force. During his tenure as CGS in Ottawa, there had been numerous occasions where these issues had required Stuart's personal attention, particularly in regard to the provision of Canadian reinforcements during the organization and training of the Force. On each of these occasions, US authorities had confirmed that since the Force was intended for a special mission, it would not be provided with replacements upon being committed to combat. That being the case, there is some evidence that General Mark Clark's recent reversal of this decision, committing the Force to a sustained combat role and providing the unit with American replacements, struck a nerve with Stuart and his staff at CMHQ.

On 17 January, Stuart's deputy at CMHQ, Brigadier E.G. Weeks, who had also had earlier connections with the Force regarding the reinforcements issue, commented on the developing situation: "In May 1943 Col. Frederick, commanding the Force, visited Ottawa, when it was decided, because of the time factor, that no further efforts would be made to despatch Canadian reinforcements. At this point it might be convenient to point out that, because of the special nature of the Force, the object was to employ it on some special operation, and once committed to battle, there was no intention to reinforce either with USA or Canadian personnel."[37] As for the situation within the Force, the Canadian reinforcements issue was becoming more difficult: "United States personnel are being reinforced. Battle casualties have noticeably decreased Canadian personnel in the Force. Both men and Officers notice the decrease in strength and it is beginning to have a noticeable effect on Canadian morale ... The Force is rapidly losing its character as the Canadian element decreases and morale is bound to be affected accordingly."[38]

If Beament was concerned and Weeks slightly annoyed, Stuart was rightly exasperated by the latest reversal in US policy regarding the First Special Service Force. On 18 January, Stuart recommended the withdrawal of the 1st Canadian Special Service Battalion to the United Kingdom, noting that this should be done immediately while the Force was reorganizing at Santa Maria and before it was again committed to active operations.[39] In the past, reinforcement of the Canadian element of the Force had only been accomplished at the expense of the 1st Canadian Parachute Battalion; Stuart's recommendation now was that the Canadians of the Force be returned to the UK and absorbed into the Canadian parachute battalion.

Realizing the necessity of consulting both Ottawa and Washington on this matter, Stuart noted that Canadian withdrawal from the Force would be difficult under any circumstances, but to do so while the unit was in combat would be impossible and would contradict earlier agreements with the Americans. That being the case, CMHQ urged the authorities in Ottawa to consult with Washington, approve the withdrawal of the Canadian element of the Force, and send instructions to that effect at the earliest opportunity.[40]

While awaiting the necessary approval from NDHQ, the staff at CMHQ considered what should be done with the 1st Canadian Special Service Battalion upon its return to the UK. In discussing the matter with Lieutenant-Colonel G.F.P. Bradbrooke, the officer commanding the 1st Canadian Parachute Battalion, and Brigadier James Hill of the British 6th Airborne Division, Weeks found that both officers were eager to accept the returning Canadians as reinforcements. The only difficulty, they noted, was that there were not sufficient vacancies in the 1st Canadian Parachute Battalion for the large number of Canadian NCOs in the Force. "From the point of view of morale in the 1st Canadian Parachute Battalion, it would be most unwise to freeze all promotions within the battalion for the purpose of absorbing the personnel in question."[41] Instead, Bradbrooke and Hill suggested the creation of a supernumerary company attached to the 1st Canadian Parachute Battalion, available both for active operations and as a reinforcement unit:

> Brigadier Hill suggested that personnel of this unit might be placed in a special company and put at the disposal of the British authorities for purposes similar to that for which the 1st Canadian Special Service Battalion was originally formed, i.e., to undertake one single operation, such as a landing deep in enemy territory.
>
> The original idea in regard to the 1st Canadian Special Service Battalion was that it was to be dropped somewhere in Norway for the purpose of sabotage. It was anticipated that it would do this single job and nothing more, and for this reason no arrangements were made to provide reinforcements. The present suggestion of Brigadier Hill has the same kind of task in view.[42]

This proposal was attractive to CMHQ for a number of reasons. After spending an entire year in training, the Force was, arguably, being squandered by the US Fifth Army—employed as "glorified infantry" with "all the special training going by the boards, except possibly mountain climbing."[43] Gilday's comments regarding General Clark's use of the First Special Service Force in a "straight infantry role" as Fifth Army shock troops had stung the authorities at CMHQ, who undoubtedly remembered that volunteers for service in the Force had been selected from among the best soldiers in the Canadian Army. Even private soldiers chosen for the unit had been singled out as potential NCO material. If they were not being used in the special role for which they had originally been selected, why were they now serving as line infantry in the United States Army? In addition to being in accordance with the original purpose for which the unit was formed, Hill's idea of a supernumerary company with the 1st Canadian Parachute Battalion would maintain the special identity of the unit and allow the soldiers to retain their present ranks.[44] Further, Brigadier Weeks added, this proposal "would have the advantage of being more or less acceptable from the Canadian public's point of view, in the event of criticism developing regarding the withdrawal of Canadians from a mixed USA/Canadian Force."[45]

On 26 January, CMHQ sent a long telegram to Ottawa, repeating Stuart's earlier suggestion: calling for the immediate withdrawal of the Canadian element from the Force and asking that the necessary arrangements be made in Washington.[46] The idea was to sell these suggestions to NDHQ, but the Chief of General Staff was not buying. Gilday's and then Stuart's recommendations for withdrawal were predicated on the Force not being engaged in active operations. From the perspective of NDHQ in Ottawa, however, "overseas" and "active operations" were essentially the same thing. Further, the Canadian Army Staff in Washington had warned Ottawa: "Any proposal to break up this combined unit, which is not only in a theatre of operations but is actually engaged against the enemy, would prove embarrassing to a degree and might be construed as hardly playing the game. It would certainly be difficult to put across and certainly would not enhance US regard for us."[47]

The result was a furious exchange of telegrams across the Atlantic, with CMHQ in London pressing for immediate withdrawal of the Canadian element while NDHQ in Ottawa considered other options. On 29 January, the Chief of General Staff in Ottawa, Lieutenant-General J.C. Murchie, cabled CMHQ asking Stuart to reconsider his recommendation to withdraw the Canadians:

> We are informed US is drawing reinforcements from general infantry pool. As there appears to be no dearth of volunteers for paratroops, we would like to be assured that you have fully explored possibility of reinforcing unit from normal reinforcement stream before approaching Washington.
>
> Owing to integration of Cdn and US personnel, you will appreciate that withdrawal would involve complete reorganization of First Special Service Force, which is not only in theatre of operations but actually engaged against the enemy. In these circumstances consider it desirable that full appreciation of all factors necessitating withdrawal be available for discussion in Washington.[48]

In response, Stuart argued that since the Force was being used as regular infantry, rather than the special purpose for which it had been originally intended, it would be better for the Canadians to fight as part of a Canadian infantry formation.[49] Noting that Gilday had called Beament in Naples on 29 January to re-emphasize the need to act quickly, but had since then been out of contact, along with the rest of the First Special Service Force, Stuart repeated earlier suggestions on Gilday's behalf, adding that he was in complete agreement that the Canadian element should be withdrawn immediately.[50]

The issue had reached a deadlock and time was running out. On 2 February, NDHQ relented, asking Stuart if there were "other reasons not disclosed in your telegram arising from present employment relationship with the Americans on which your strong recommendation for withdrawal is based?"[51] To this, Stuart might have responded that for the past year and a half the United States had repeatedly reversed its policies regarding the provision of reinforcements to the First Special Service Force and had shown little regard for the difficulties these constant changes caused the Canadian Army. Instead, knowing that the Force being out of contact could only mean one thing—a return to the front—Stuart resigned from the argument, leaving the matter for NDHQ to take up with the Minister of National Defence in Ottawa.

On 2 February, Murchie presented CMHQ's recommendations to the Minister, outlining both sides of the argument but now leaning more towards accepting the recommendations for withdrawal presented by CMHQ. In his memorandum to the Minister, Murchie gave the arguments both for and against the withdrawal of the 1st Canadian Special Service Battalion and its return to the Canadian Army:[52]

**2 FEB 44**
**The Minister**
**Employment of 1st Special Service Battalion**

A recommendation has now been received from the Army Commander [Stuart] that the Canadian portion of the First Special Service Force be withdrawn to the United Kingdom and utilized with the 6th Airborne Division, of which the 1st Canadian Parachute Battalion forms part.

It is reported that the Canadian element of the Force has been reduced by battle casualties to approximately 50% of its establishment and as the Force is again in action it is probable that a further decrease in strength will have taken place.

The arguments for withdrawing the remainder of the Canadian element and not reinforcing it with ordinary infantry reinforcements are summarized in Canmilitary telegram A.705 hereunder.

Against those the following factors must be considered:

a) The First Special Service Force was formed as a joint Canadian–United States enterprise, the personnel are completely integrated, and withdrawal of the Canadian element will necessitate a complete reorganization of the Force, which is actually engaged in operations against the enemy.

b) The United States have made a substantial contribution in equipping, training, quartering and transporting this Force to its present theatre of operations and there may be criticism if Canada withdraws from participation shortly after the Force has been committed to action, particularly if the Canadian personnel are returned to the United Kingdom.

On the other hand, the Force was formed and trained to undertake a particular type of operation which has not materialized. It is, in fact, being used in a straight infantry role with the United States Army. If, therefore, the special type of training which the Canadian personnel have received can be used to better advantage for the common cause in prospective operations being planned for the forces in the United Kingdom, there should be little objection to their being used for that purpose. I consider that the strong recommendations of the Officer Commanding the Canadian element of the Force [Gilday] and of the Army Commander must be given great weight.

     It is recommended, therefore, that before a final decision is made, further information be obtained through the Commander, Canadian Army Staff, Washington, as to the United States plans for the reinforcement and future employment of the Force and that he be authorized to inform the military authorities in Washington of the recommendations received from Canadian Military Headquarters Overseas and the consideration that is being given to them here.

     A telegram in that sense has been prepared for despatch if you approve.

[signed] P.E.
Brigadier,
for C.G.S. [Murchie]

In summary, although the Chief of General Staff had agreed with the recommendations of Canadian commanders overseas, it would be necessary for the Canadian Army Staff in Washington to discuss the matter with US authorities and arrive at an agreement that was acceptable to both countries.

Ironically, the decision to approach the US authorities and suggest the withdrawal of the 1st Canadian Special Service Battalion came only a few days after the entire argument became irrelevant. Gilday's, Beament's, and finally Stuart's recommendations had been predicated on the Force not being engaged in active operations. When Gilday first made this suggestion on 15 January, the Force had just emerged from a month of hard-fought, successful operations in the mountains of Italy. While the Force was undergoing a period of rest and reorganization at Santa Maria, the withdrawal of the Canadians could have taken place with a minimum of inconvenience. Instead, more than two weeks of argument and foot-dragging by Canadian authorities in London and Ottawa passed before an agreement was reached. Even then, the only decision made was that the issue should be discussed further in Washington. As it happened, when Stuart reported on 1 February that the Force was out of contact and that it was not known when it would again be possible to communicate with Gilday or Frederick, this signalled that the window of opportunity had closed.

Throughout the last week of January 1944 the plan had been that the Force would return to combat in February and conduct an assault-crossing of the Rapido River in support of US II Corps' operations against the German Gustav Line defences.[53] On the morning of 30 January, however, a Fifth Army courier arrived at Force headquarters carrying orders for an emergency change of plans. Within three hours the Force had left Santa Maria by truck convoy and moved to a staging area outside the port town of Pozzuoli, near Naples. Boarding a small fleet of landing craft the next day, by evening the First Special Service Force was bound in convoy for the Anzio beachhead, where nine days earlier an Anglo–American corps had conducted an amphibious landing in an attempt to outflank the Germans and break the stalemate at Monte Cassino. On 2 February, as the CGS discussed the fate of the 1st Canadian Special Service Battalion with the Minister in Ottawa, the Force was moving by convoy from the port of Anzio to a position north of Nettuno and digging in. Three miles further ahead lay the front lines, and that evening the combat echelon moved forward to take up defensive positions along the banks of the Mussolini Canal.[54]

Private Leonard (Fort Worth, Texas; 1 Co., 1st Regt) adjusts medic Private Wilson's (Vancouver, British Columbia; 3 Co., 1st Regt) first aid packboard of blankets and plasma at the 1st Regiment aid station. The FSSF was assigned to Italy and the Winter Line campaign in late 1943. During the assault on Monte la Difensa, FSSF positions at the summit were kept supplied up a narrow footpath by means of packboards such as the one seen here. *(NA-CP SC 187868)*

First Special Service Force pack mules ascend a hillside in the rocky Italian countryside. During the mountain fighting of January 1944, these mules provided one of the best means of moving food and ammunition to the front. *(G. Ronald collection, CWM)*

A wounded soldier is being lowered down the side of an Italian mountain by means of an equipment line. The patient is held in a rigid position, the rope being secured to the wounded man between the shoulder blades. Suspended from the rope by the snap links, he is carefully let down to a lower elevation. Piedimonte, Ceppagna area, 22 December 1943. *(NA-CP SC 191267)*

Three members of the First Special Service Force file cautiously along a mountain trail in the Venafro area of Italy, passing through a cluster of peasant houses. After the assaults on Monte la Difensa and Remetanea (Hills 960 and 907), the Majo hill mass was the objective, the north end of which overlooked Monte Cassino. By this time, the FSSF had already fought with distinction in its first action at Monte la Difensa, incurring over 500 casualties. Early January, 1944.
*(F.G. Whitcombe photo, LAC 128979)*

Although suffering with frozen feet and a shrapnel wound to his hand, Private N.L. Shaver (Battle Creek, Michigan; 6 Company, 3rd Regt) brings in a German prisoner near Venafro, Italy, January 1944.
*(F.G. Whitcombe photo, LAC 128980)*

Another prisoner arrives under escort of Warrant Officer Samuel Wolsborn (Seattle, Washington; HQ Co.) near Venafro, January 1944. *(F.G. Whitcombe photo, LAC 128983)*

Lt. W.H. Langdon (Timmins, Ontario; 3 Co. 2nd Regt) carrying full kit is about to go forward to join his unit of the First Special Service Force, north of Venafro, January 1944.
*(F.G. Whitcombe photo, LAC 128981)*

Germans, Canadians, and Americans milling about together in front of the Force clearing station at Le Noci, near Venafro. Six weeks of action in the mountains exacted a heavy toll on the FSSF; frostbite and exposure caused almost as many casualties as enemy fire. January 1944. *(F.G. Whitcombe photo, LAC 128982)*

T/4 Harlan Morgan (LeRoy, Montana; 3 Co. 2nd Regt) leading men up the mountain, passing a mule relay point and French medical aid station. Cervaro area, 14 January 1944. *(Gallagher photo, NA-CP SC 218510-I)*

Men of 5 Company, 3rd Regiment FSSF, take a break while moving up to the front. Left to right: Sergeant John P. Grantz, Cleveland, Ohio; Private N.E. Brown, Oshawa, Ontario; and Private Alva Thompson, Waverly, Iowa. 14 January 1944. *(Gallagher photo, NA-CP SC 228363)*

Five men of the machine-gun squad from 1 Company, 1st Regiment FSSF, prepare their "ten-in-one" ration supper in the extreme cold of the Appenine Mountains. Left to right: T/4 Michael Flannery, Amenia, New York; Private John Johnston, Montreal; T/4 Clifford E. Joiner, San Francisco; Sergeant Bill Leonard, Fort Worth, Texas; and Sergeant John R. Thompson, Danville, Illinois. Radicosa, 15 January, 1944. *(Gallagher photo, NA-CP SC 228336)*

Private John Johnston of Montreal, Quebec, is seen here in the Radicosa area during the Winter Line campaign of January 1944. He is carrying a Johnson .30 cal. automatic rifle – one of the special weapons carried by the Force and an unusual sight in the European Theatre. *(US Signal Corps, G. Ronald Collection, CWM)*

Colonel Edwin A. Walker, who assumed command of the First Special Service Force after Frederick's departure, is seen here observing enemy positions in the Radicosa area from his Command Post on Hill 1090. With him from HQ detachment are from left, Major Robert B. Holt of Yakima, Washington; Major J.M. Secter of Winnipeg, Manitoba; and Captain Frank W. Erickson, of New Jersey. 16 January 1944. *(Gallagher photo, NA-CP SC 228763)*

Artillery fire at Cassino observed by US soldiers. The First Special Service Force had been fighting in the area since Christmas as part of II Corps alongside the US 1st Armored and 34th Infantry Divisions. During this third and final phase of the Winter Line Campaign, the FSSF also fought alongside US 133rd and 141st Infantry and 504th Parachute Infantry Regiments, as well as the 36th and 45th Divisions. German units opposing them were the 5th Mountain Division and 44th Austrian Division, including the 132nd Grenadier Regiment and two battalions of the 71st Panzergrenadier Regiment. It would be another two weeks before they would move on to the Anzio beachhead. Cervaro, 15 January 1944. *(Gallagher photo, NA-CP SC 191265)*

A communications muleskinner points to Monte Cassino, where the Force was initially slated to take part in the assault on a German-held monastery. Instead, the unit was sent to Anzio, attached to Fifth Army's VI Corps, at the beginning of February 1944. *(G. Ronald collection, CWM)*

## CHAPTER FIVE

# Punch-Drunk:
# The Anzio Beachhead

The entire existence of the Force … was countenanced by the
War Department only because of its international character
and because of the interest of British officials, which no longer
exists … For the sake of United States and Canadian relations,
it may be best to let this unit pass out of existence while it is
still in its prime, rather than to sustain it through a period
when it will be remembered only for its faults and defects.

*Brigadier-General Robert T. Frederick*
*Commanding General, First Special Service Force*
*19 February 1944*[1]

In January 1944, four months of steadily grinding combat, interspersed with short,
deliberate moves forward, had seen the US Fifth Army advance only seventy miles
beyond the Salerno bridgehead. Conditions at the front were absolutely miserable, with
the advance pressing forward slowly and painfully, one mountain range at a time,
facing one belt of German defences after another. Operation Shingle, the code-name
for an amphibious landing at the seaside town of Anzio, was intended to circumvent

the German defences of the Gustav Line, thereby opening the way to Rome. The plan called for the US VI Corps under Major-General John P. Lucas to secure a beachhead at Anzio–Nettuno and move from there against the Alban Hills, which lay astride the two major highways leading to Rome, some fifteen miles southeast of the city. Meanwhile the remainder of Clark's Fifth Army would mount a major offensive across the Garigliano and Rapido rivers, hoping that a breakthrough from the south combined with the threat of an amphibious landing in the rear would force the Germans to abandon the Gustav Line and withdraw their forces north of Rome.

While Lucas himself expressed serious misgivings about the plan, his superiors, including Clark, Alexander and especially Churchill, were desperate for some means of breaking the deadlock in Italy. On 22 January, Operation Shingle went ahead as scheduled. Meeting no serious opposition at the waterline, the British 1st and US 3rd Infantry Division began moving inland and soon confirmed that the landings had caught the Germans completely off guard. By the end of the day, VI Corps had landed some 36,000 soldiers and 3,200 vehicles at Anzio, along with an enormous quantity of ammunition and supplies.[2] Although the landings had been an unqualified success, Lucas hesitated to press too far inland as this would threaten his lifeline to the coast and leave his corps vulnerable to a German counterattack. Instead, he ordered the landing force to consolidate its coastal foothold, dig in and wait for the hammer to fall.

As expected, German reaction to the landing at Anzio was swift and violent. By the evening there were some 20,000 German troops concentrating in the area, the first of eight divisions that would arrive in the first week to contain the Allied bridgehead. In the days following, both sides began a massive concentration of forces. The VI Corps sought to hold and expand the bridgehead while the Germans built-up in preparation for driving the Americans and British back into the sea. While the Allied intent had been to force the enemy to abandon the Gustav Line, the Germans reacted instead with a determined effort to eliminate this threat to their lines of communication. At the same time, Fifth Army's offensive against the lower Gustav Line stalled. An attempt to force a crossing of the Rapido River was repulsed with heavy casualties. In the British sector, the Germans were able to contain a small bridgehead on the north bank of the Garigliano. There would be no breakthrough in the Fifth Army sector, and VI Corps at Anzio was on its own—at least for the foreseeable future. Barricaded in a coastal enclave, with the entire length and width of the Allied position exposed to German artillery fire from the surrounding hills, VI Corps struggled to hold the line against a growing concentration of enemy forces. Far from breaking the stalemate in Italy and opening the road to Rome, by the end of January the Anzio landing was itself in danger of being overrun and annihilated.

On the morning of 30 January a Fifth Army messenger tore into the First Special Service Force's headquarters at Santa Maria: at Anzio the situation was taking a turn for the worse, and VI Corps desperately needed reinforcements. That same morning, as the FSSF began preparing for a move to the beachhead, the 1st and 3rd Battalions of Colonel William O. Darby's Ranger Force were being shot to pieces in the Pantano ditch, an irrigation canal leading toward the German-held town of Cisterna, which lay on the outskirts of the Anzio perimeter. Assigned to spearhead the 3rd US Division attack on Cisterna, the Rangers had attempted to infiltrate up the canal during the night, and at daybreak they had been caught in a German ambush. Of the 767 Rangers who set out for Cisterna, only six returned.[3] The situation on the beachhead was desperate, and on the morning of 1 February, the First Special Service Force disembarked at the port of Anzio. The three combat regiments proceeded to an assembly area overlooking the front lines and then moved forward on the evening of 2 February to take up positions on the Mussolini Canal. *(See map, Figure 5.1.)*

Beyond the raised banks of the canal lay the Pontine Marshes, a former malarial swamp that was now a thirteen-mile stretch of reclaimed farmland—treeless plains dotted by stone farmhouses and crossed at intervals by irrigation ditches. Constructed at enormous cost by the Fascist government of Italy, the Mussolini Canal now served as a massive anti-tank ditch on the southern boundary of the Allied perimeter, a barrier to forward movement offering full advantage to the defenders on both sides.

Upon relieving the 39th Combat Engineer Regiment on this 12,000-yard stretch of the canal (a length of ground representing roughly one quarter of the beachhead perimeter), the Force found that the area had been already partially wired and mined by the engineers. While British and American forces in the centre and left sectors of the Anzio perimeter were exposed to attack by German infantry and armour, the line of the Mussolini Canal was better suited to defensive actions on both sides; to this point it had remained the quietest sector of the Allied bridgehead.

Moving forward with Third Regiment on the left and First Regiment on the right, Frederick ordered the Second held in reserve, to be used as a counterattacking force in the event of an enemy breakthrough. Behind the front, the unit received attachments from the 160th Artillery Battalion, the 465th Parachute Field Artillery Battalion and a company of tank destroyers to provide fire support. Digging in along the line of the canal, the Force spent the next five days improving the existing defences and conducting nightly harassing patrols on the far side of the canal.[4] "The countryside is dotted with many farmhouses which offer opportunities for observation and for ambush. Aside from the fringes of trees along the roadside there is virtually no cover and in clear weather all movement may be observed easily."[5]

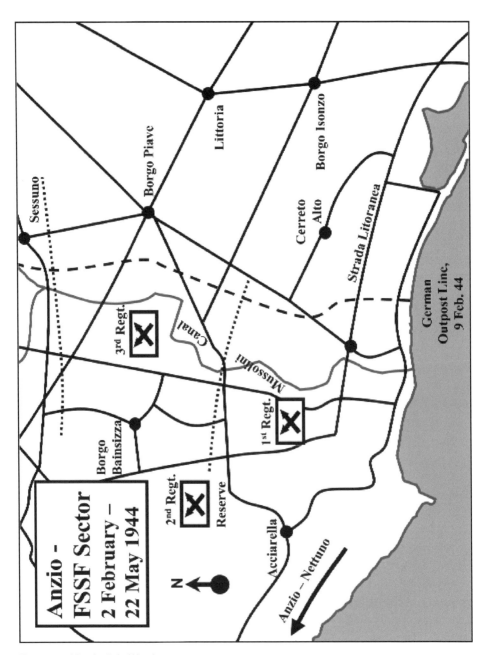

Figure 5.1  Map by Lyle Wood

While the fighting at Anzio during the last week of January had consisted of a series of attacks and counterattacks by Allied and German forces, resulting in few significant changes in the main lines of resistance, by February the VI Corps was on the defensive. In the Force sector, the first week of consolidating defences along the Mussolini Canal was not characterized by any major offensive actions involving the entire unit. All three regiments conducted numerous fighting and reconnaissance patrols to force the Germans back from the canal, occupying buildings and setting up observation posts on the "enemy side of the ditch," and establishing an area of no man's land between the two sides. "During the daylight this no-man's land looked like a peaceful Italian countryside. As soon as darkness fell, the area became a place of manoeuvre for the numerous patrols sent out by both the enemy and ourselves."[6]

Opposing the Force were elements of the Hermann Göring Panzer Division, consisting of former Luftwaffe personnel who had been reorganized and retrained for ground combat. With Force patrols pushing into no man's land during the first week of February, the night of 6/7 February witnessed a two-company assault by the 7th Luftwaffe Battalion, whose intent was to gain information and blow up footbridges across the canal. The attack fell against Third Regiment positions, but in a one-hour fight the raiders were stopped short of the canal by machine-gun fire. Mop-up operations secured two German prisoners. That same night, FSSF patrols continued pushing toward enemy positions at Littoria, and by the next day these efforts succeeded in establishing a buffer zone on the far side of the canal, with the "enemy forced to operate with extreme caution when within 1,500 yards of Canal."[7]

Though far removed from the type of warfare for which the Force had originally been organized and trained, this assignment to a defensive holding action along the Mussolini Canal probably saved the unit from being disbanded. On 9 February, Lieutenant-General Stuart discussed proposals for the withdrawal of the Canadian element with General Eisenhower in London. As expected, with the Force now engaged in active operations, Eisenhower thought it would be a mistake to withdraw the Canadians, and he assumed that the US War Department would probably agree. Pulling out the 1st Canadian Special Service Battalion would require reorganization of the entire force of which the Canadians formed an integral part, thereby burdening the Fifth Army with an additional manpower commitment at a time when VI Corps was already fighting for its life at Anzio. Agreeing with Eisenhower, though undoubtedly regretting the bureaucratic obstructions in January that had prevented him from raising this issue sooner, Stuart made his decision: if the Canadians were to remain with the First Special Service Force, they would be properly reinforced.[8]

Bringing the Canadian element back up to full strength represented a more difficult problem than simply sending more men. First, it would be necessary to find Canadians who were willing to serve in what was, for all intents and purposes, a formation of the US Army. What if there were no volunteers? Assuming that the required numbers could be scraped together and supplied with American uniforms and equipment, the reinforcements would then require training in new weapons and unfamiliar operating procedures.[9] "Obviously there would be objections to sending forward Canadian-trained infantry reinforcements … unless they were given some training on American weapons."[10]

Further, the recent expansion of the Canadian Army Overseas to five divisions organized in two corps imposed additional reinforcement commitments on the army as a whole.[11] In Italy, the 1st Canadian Division was still recovering from the Battle of Ortona in December 1943, where every battalion taking part in the fighting had suffered roughly fifty percent casualties in its rifle companies.[12] To request that the Canadian Army in Italy also shoulder the burden of reinforcing an "American" outfit— at a time when its own infantry battalions were still reeling from losses—was certain to meet with significant resistance from Canadian commanders in the theatre. In Canada, the memories of a conscription crisis in 1917 and the less serious, but similar, troubles in 1942 were still too recent to countenance any such waste of scarce manpower.

The elite status of the First Special Service Force imposed further difficulties as it required that special attention be devoted to the selection of volunteers. Confirmation that the US Army was providing regular infantry replacements to the Force without any specialist or parachute training came as some relief because it meant in turn that Canadian reinforcements sent to the Force need not be trained as parachutists.[13] Nevertheless, it might be necessary for the men to undergo parachute training at some time in the future. Therefore, to meet the immediate shortage, CMHQ decided that volunteers should be selected from existing Canadian reinforcement pools in Italy, but recommended a permanent solution if the unit were to be maintained on a long-term basis:

> The ultimate plan for reinforcing 1 Cdn Spec Serv Bn might well be the selection of suitable reinforcements in Canada [and] their despatch to USA for training with USA reinforcements for the Special Service Force. In this way, Canadian and USA reinforcements would intermingle and get to know each other at a much earlier date than if reinforcements are withdrawn from the general infantry pool, CMF [Central Mediterranean Force]. It follows that while we could reinforce immediately from CMF, there are strong arguments in favour of Canada immediately adopting the ultimate plan.[14]

Upon arrival at Anzio on 1 February, the Canadian element of the Force had numbered 27 officers and 339 other ranks.[15] Standing at roughly half their assigned strength, the Canadians represented less than one third of the combat element of the Force, which now included American replacements that had been received in January and trained at Santa Maria. Although personnel recovering from injuries suffered in December and January were beginning to filter back to the unit from American and Canadian hospitals throughout Italy, these returns were only slightly in excess of the numbers being killed and wounded on the beachhead.[16] With the Force still recovering its strength after the fighting in the mountains, the Anzio beachhead represented a less than ideal place for recovery.

Reports from this period recount an unending series of patrols into the disputed territory on the far side of the canal—a war of reconnaissance, ambush and raids intended to gather information and keep the enemy off balance. On numerous occasions these patrols were punctuated by short, violent engagements fought by sections and platoons on both sides of the waterway as the Force infiltrated enemy positions and the Germans responded in kind.

On the evening of 10 February, Second Regiment formed a provisional company under Captain Adna Underhill to capture the village of Sessuno, which lay beyond Third Regiment's lines on the far left of the Force sector. Following close behind a half-hour artillery barrage, assaulting platoons knocked out two German machine-gun positions with bazookas and grenades. Over the next three hours Underhill's company repulsed two counterattacks, withdrawing beyond the canal upon the approach of the enemy reserve force, which included eight vehicles. The raid resulted in the killing of forty enemy by actual count and an additional thirty estimated, with a loss of six Force dead and ten wounded.[17]

Throughout the next week, German "patrolling continued to press into the disputed zone while … harassing our own patrols. Towards this week's end it was clear that the [German] line had been reinforced."[18] In the early morning hours of 16 February a battalion-strength attack, with armoured support from four tanks and two self-propelled guns, struck at Third Regiment near the boundary between its 1st and 2nd Battalions. "All hell broke loose about 0600 hours when the Germans let loose all their artillery and mortars and ours replied. They attacked all along our line, most strongly on the left flank held by 1st Battalion, 3rd Regiment."[19] Initially forcing back Third Regiment's advance companies, the attackers made an attempt to dig in within 400 yards of the canal, but daylight allowed a combination of artillery, heavy machine-gun fire, and mortar fire to force their withdrawal. Two FSSF companies were considerably "banged-up" in the attack, though the wreckage of three panzers and one tank recovery vehicle beyond the canal indicated that the raid had not been without cost to the attackers.[20]

Between 17 and 24 February, the Germans did not venture too close to Force lines and turned instead to improving their defences. At night, Second Regiment patrols raided enemy outposts in no man's land. During the day, enemy artillery was a menace. "At the canal the Force is continually subjected to enemy artillery; they throw everything they have at our men for a few minutes and then quit while the Force get busy getting artillery support in for an infantry attack that does not develop. The men are beginning to get a bit tired and jittery as they have been in nearly 3 weeks with little sleep and continuous night patrolling".[21]

The nature of the fighting at Anzio weighed heavily upon the Force, as it did upon every unit engaged in the struggle to hold the beachhead. Night patrols were a dangerous, nerve-wracking business. The Force was relentless in carrying them out, but the strain this produced on the men was often enormous. "We used to cross the Mussolini Canal on a narrow footbridge," recalled one Second Regiment veteran, "I used to plot an accident to get me off the front and perhaps out of the war … If I slipped off the plank some frosty morning, the weight of the LMG and two or three boxes of ammunition that I carried should ensure a fracture of some kind. But, on the way over, I always felt guilty about trying it, and on the way back, the trouble was over for a few hours."[22] After the war, Canadian Lieutenant-Colonel J.G. Bourne said the Force was "punch-drunk" at Anzio. Worked beyond endurance during the assault on the Winter Line, it never fully recovered from the experience.[23]

On 19 February, newly promoted Brigadier-General Robert T. Frederick addressed these concerns in a letter to Lieutenant-General Mark Clark, commander of Fifth Army. In his letter, Frederick provided Clark with a detailed and rather blunt report on the difficulties facing the First Special Service Force almost three weeks following its arrival at Anzio:[24]

**19 February 1944**

**SUBJECT: First Special Service Force.**

**TO: Commanding General, Fifth Army, U.S. Army.**

Upon completion of the current phase of operations, it will be necessary to know the basic decisions that have been made for the future of the First Special Service Force. The combat strength of the Force has been so reduced that it cannot again take any major part in an operation, nor can it execute minor actions for any long period.

The possible decisions appear to be limited to the following:
a) Continue the Force as:
    1) A joint United States-Canadian unit.
    2) A United States unit without Canadian personnel.
b) Discontinue the Force.

To continue the Force with its characteristics is not possible under existing circumstances. The successes the Force has achieved in combat have been the result of special training and the development of certain qualities and spirit in the officers and enlisted men. This training and development required a comparatively long time under favorable training conditions. Comparable results cannot be accomplished by the Force if its casualties are replaced with men who are not specially trained, nor without its full complement of officers who have been indoctrinated with the spirit and combat methods of the command.

There is no existing source, either United States or Canadian, of trained replacements for the Force. A limited number of officers can be obtained by commissioning non-commissioned officers from the command, but this source is not great and officers without trained enlisted men cannot accomplish those missions considered normal for the Force.

If the Force is to be continued, it must be withdrawn from the combat zone to a place where suitable training conditions and facilities are available. After the arrival of new personnel, a period of four to six months should be allowed to accomplish their training.

The organization of the Force must be adjusted to the type of operations in which the Force is being employed. The present organization was created for a specific mission and was based solely on the conditions surrounding the accomplishment of that mission which was totally unrelated to the missions in which the Force has actually engaged.

Likewise, the equipment of the Force must be changed so that the Force will be properly equipped for the missions it is to be assigned, rather than to engage in combat with the handicap of unsuitable and inadequate equipment … Many essential functions, such as medical service, communications and supply during combat, have not been provided and create serious problems during the type of combat in which the Force has engaged.

Originally, the Force was to be made up equally of Canadian and United States personnel. This joint composition was agreed upon at the request of Allied officials who were neither American nor Canadian. It has no military basis, nor is it a sound arrangement.

The Canadian Army furnishes no service troops, and all overhead and administrative functions for the Force, except for Canadian records and pay, are performed by United States personnel. The Canadian officers and enlisted men are subjected to strange conditions and to policies and practices not encountered in the Canadian Army … The United States has, by necessity, furnished all clothing and equipment for Canadian as well as United States personnel. This has required the Canadians to use weapons and equipment with which they have no previous experience.

While the amalgamation of personnel of two armies into a single unit has worked successfully, it is basically unsound and difficult, and it has worked only because those intimately associated with the administration and supervision of the arrangement have made it work.

Another complication is that employment of the Force must be approved by Canada as well as the United States. In the past, this has resulted in the Force not being sent to a theater to which the War Department desired to assign it. In addition, because of the inclusion of Canadian personnel in the Force, the British Government has had to be consulted and its agreement obtained for the Force's employment.

The Canadian government has established a figure of seven hundred (700) officers and other ranks as the Canadian personnel to be assigned to the Force. This figure … was based on an early estimate of the personnel to be required for the original mission. It does not represent half the Force, nor even half of the combat echelon. As a result of training losses and losses that have occurred since arrival in this theater, Canadian officers and other ranks now assigned to the Force total slightly more than three hundred (300). The Canadian Army headquarters in Ottawa decided that no Canadian replacements were to be furnished for the Force, and this decision appears to be firm.

If the Force is to be continued as a joint United States-Canadian unit, the Canadian Army should furnish officers and other ranks to bring the Canadian strength up to half of the total strength of the Force. To absorb new Canadian personnel it will, of course, be necessary to withdraw from the combat zone for an extended period so that the Canadians can be given necessary training.

If the Force is to be continued as a United States unit without Canadian personnel, problems of organization, equipment, and qualified replacements and training still exist. In addition, other problems less tangible but more far-reaching are introduced. The international character of the Force has placed it in the position of representing the extent to which the United States and Canada can cooperate in an undertaking. It is an exceptional example of complete integration of personnel of two armies into a single unit. The Force has become well known as a joint American–Canadian force, particularly in Canada where knowledge of its existence has become widespread. For the Force to continue in existence without Canadian personnel might bring about serious repercussions, particularly in Canada where the elimination of Canadian participation in the Force may be misconstrued…

The elimination of Canadian personnel from the Force would deprive the unit of its key officers and men. When the Force was activated, the Canadian Army furnished, in general, better qualified officers and enlisted men than did the United States Army, and this has resulted in a large number of the key positions being filled by Canadians.

It is considered that, because of the possible unfavorable reaction, both official and public, that would arise if the Canadian participation in the Force is dropped, it is better either to continue the Force as a joint force, or to discontinue it…

The entire existence of the Force, until it was transferred to the North African Theater of Operations, was countenanced by the War Department only because of its international character and because of the interest of British officials, which no longer exists. The joint composition of the Force creates problems that must be solved without precedent or legal support. It is believed that the War Department would welcome the opportunity to discontinue this special unit, which has been a particular problem and unduly expensive.

Special units, such as this Force, are not looked upon with favor by other units of the Army. There is an intense feeling of dislike arising from the belief that special units are particularly favored and that they receive too much credit for their accomplishments. This feeling has been encountered quite generally, particularly in those normal units that have not been associated with this Force in operations. While this point is not of importance, it is worthy of consideration in deciding whether this and other units should exist.

Unless provisions are made for the reorganization, re-equipment and replacement of personnel losses with adequately trained personnel, the Force will soon become an ineffective combat unit. Because of the international interest in the unit, it would be better that it be discontinued before any strained feelings are created and while it is looked upon with favor by both interested nations. The whole project is delicate and has potentialities for international complications.

Should the Force encounter disaster in combat, it is possible that the Canadians at home may feel that their officers and men were unnecessarily sacrificed. Likewise, there is always the possibility of criticism for placing American soldiers under Canadian officers and non-commissioned officers should the fortune of battle be against them.

> For the sake of United States and Canadian relations, it may be best to let this unit pass out of existence while it is still in its prime, rather than to sustain it through a period when it will be remembered only for its faults and defects.
>
> [signed] Robert T. Frederick,
> Brigadier-General
> US Army, Commanding

In a word, the First Special Service Force was exhausted, and if the unit survived Anzio intact, Frederick believed it would require an extended period of reorganization in order to rebuild itself. Having made no provision for replacing combat losses, and with no existing source of trained replacements—either Canadian or American—Frederick was of the opinion that the FSSF should be disbanded at the earliest opportunity …"rather than to sustain it through a period when it will be remembered only for its faults and defects."

Frederick made it clear that should the Force be continued, the unit needed a chance to rest and rebuild in order to take any major part in operations or even continue in its present role. "To continue the force with its present characteristics is not possible under the existing conditions. The successes the Force has achieved in combat have been the result of special training and the development of certain qualities and spirit in the officers and enlisted men."[25]  Developing these certain qualities and the high standard of training, however, had required a comparably long period under favourable conditions at Helena. Frederick stated that if the Force were to be maintained as an elite formation, rebuilding the unit after Anzio would require its withdrawal from combat for a period of four to six months.[26] Being "special" was no easy task, claimed Frederick; hostility toward elite units was encountered quite generally, a factor which the Force commander felt must be taken into consideration when deciding the fate of the unit.

Concerning the bi-national composition of the Force, Frederick suggested that the time had come to end the experiment. The Canadian element imposed special difficulties and limited the usefulness of the Force because it required Ottawa's approval prior to any operational employment. In addition, "because of the inclusion of Canadian personnel in the Fo rce, the British Government has had to be consulted and its agreement obtained for the Force's employment."[27]

While Frederick viewed the Canadian element as a brake on the usefulness of the Force in general, he recognized that the withdrawal of the Canadians would absolutely cripple the unit. The catch for Frederick and the United States Army was that maintaining the Force as a bi-national formation required Canadian approval for any proposed employment of the unit, but withdrawal of the Canadian soldiers would go halfway toward decapitating the leadership by removing some of the best officers and NCOs. That being the case, Frederick strongly recommended that after Anzio the unit should be disbanded altogether. Though he was fully aware of the international difficulties involved, the letter leaves no doubt that Frederick now considered the bi-national composition of the Force to be a significant impediment that should be done away with as soon as possible. This, he felt, would be in the best interests of both nations.

For the officers and men at the front, Frederick's letter regarding the future of the First Special Service Force could not have had less impact on their daily lives—attacks and counterattacks up and down the banks of the Mussolini Canal continued throughout the remainder of February. A strong Third Regiment patrol pushed toward Borgo Piave on 25 February, running into a previously unknown minefield and newly constructed wire entanglements. The raid was called off when machine-gun fire erupted, sweeping across the field and blocking any approach to the objective. That night a German raid in platoon-strength attempted to cross the canal without success, and toward dawn a Force patrol fired rockets into an enemy-held canal gatehouse, killing six.[28]

Each night during the last week of February, the Germans were observed to be infiltrating the First Regiment sector, working towards one of the key bridges and often taking shelter in a row of houses north of Sabotino. On the night of 28/29 February, Colonel A.C. Marshall ordered a Force patrol to keep watch over the houses, taking prisoners if possible. The results could not have been more fortunate for Lieutenant George Krasevac's reinforced platoon, which was assigned to spring the trap. Moving up to attack FirstRegiment's bridge, small enemy groups we re seen going into the houses throughout the night, where they were met by Krasevac's troops and taken prisoner. The trap netted 111 prisoners, including four officers, at a cost of only a few wounded from First Regiment.[29] The enemy groups had been moving to force a crossing of the canal and a diversion in preparation for an attack further north.

By the end of Feb ru a ry the wiring and mining of the Force sector was nearing completion. The men were tired, but morale continued to be high; "they are continually on patrols and although they don't get a great deal of sleep, [they] like the work."[30] At the front the Force continued to hold, stretched thin with 1,296 officers and men along 12,000 yards of the Mussolini Canal. The Canadian War Diary records the situation at the end of February:

We have maintained the initiative by active patrolling all along the front. The 1st Bn., 3rd Regt., repulsed two very strong enemy attacks. Our orders are to 'Hold the Canal'. We have not enough strength to push past it and have to hold it by sitting on it and patrolling to the front. The enemy has high ground all around the bridgehead and can see all our ground and shell all our roads from at least two sides. The boys have done a wonderful job.[31]

At the end of February there were some indications the Force was beginning to recover from the weariness that had been brought on by the difficult mountain-fighting of the month before. Nevertheless, Frederick's letter of 19 February had insisted that the losses suffered on the Winter Line could not be overcome within the unit, owing largely to the same international complications that always characterized its existence.

"Matters Canadian" had drawn some fairly harsh criticism in Frederick's letter, and the Force commander had made clear his belief that the War Department would welcome the opportunity to disband the Force. For all that its officers and men had accomplished in the field, the unit remained the problematic and expensive "spoilt child" of the United States and Canadian armies. Better to let it disappear while it was still in its prime, a source of pride to Canada and the United States, rather than allow it to become a drain on the resources and patience of both countries.

Until such time as the unit could be withdrawn from the Anzio beachhead, however, Frederick insisted that the problem of Canadian reinforcements required immediate attention. To date, the American element had been provided with limited numbers of regular infantry replacements; the Canadians had received none at all. Neglecting to mention that NDHQ had offered in December 1942 to establish a permanent quota of Canadian reinforcements for the unit, Frederick also seems to have forgotten his own part in turning down Ottawa's offer and repeatedly assuring the Canadians that the Force would not require reinforcements upon commitment to combat. Passing the buck, as it turned out, did nothing to resolve the difficult situation now facing the Force.

Frederick's letter demonstrates that while the amalgamation of Canadian and American personnel had succeeded in establishing a fully integrated and effective military formation, the two countries failed to coordinate a means of maintaining the unit in sustained combat. On the ground, relations between soldiers within the Force were highly satisfactory—the men served together with little or no regard for nationality; indeed, they were often unaware which of their comrades were American or Canadian. From the perspective of higher headquarters, however, up to and including the US War Department and National Defence Headquarters in Ottawa, the arrangement seemed unnecessarily difficult and unwieldy. This was primarily the result of the failure to establish a coordinated system of providing replacements to the unit.

After two months of intense combat and mounting losses, these issues we re considered so serious that the American commander of the Force and the senior Canadian officer both recommended that the unit be discontinued, although it is unclear whether they colluded in making the suggestion. It is worth noting, however, that while both the US Army and Canadian Army official histories refer to the Canadian request to withdraw from the Force in February 1944, neither work mentions that Frederick was also recommending the unit be disbanded entirely.[32] In early February when Lieutenant-General Stuart had approached General Eisenhower and suggested the withdrawal of the Canadians from the Force, Eisenhower had told him that this would be impossible. Within the week, however, Frederick had also come to agree that disbandment was the best possible course. By mid-February, the matter had come to a head and was soon to be decided upon at the highest levels of the Allied command structure.

Members of 1st Company, 2nd Regiment awaiting lunch at a dugout kitchen, Anzio beachhead, 20 April 1944. Seen in this photo are: Lieutenant T.G. Gordon, Welland, Ontario; Staff Sergeant A.C. Mack of Pittsburgh, Kansas; Sergeant W.E.Watson, Hamilton Ontario; John Rose, St. Catharines, Ontario; Percy Crichlow, Bridgetown, Barbados; Sam Eros, Misatin, Saskatchewan; Joe Dauphinais, Starbuck, Manitoba; and Geoff Hart, Dawson Creek, British Columbia. Two are unidentified. *(C.E. Nye photo, LAC 128976)*

An aerial view of Anzio, Italy. After arriving at Anzio on 2 February, the Force took up defensive positions along the Mussolini Canal, 12 miles east of the town, and spent the next 99 days assigned to defending the right flank of the Allied beachhead. *(Grann photo, NA-CP SC 221447)*

An awards ceremony at Force headquarters. General L.K. Truscott, commander of US VI Corps, awarded the Silver Star to three men of the First Special Service Force. Nettuna, 14 March, 1944. *(Bell photo, NA-CP SC 244751)*

German prisoners in the Anzio beachhead are guarded by an MP with 3rd Division. In the Anzio beachhead, the First Special Service Force was attached to VI Corps and fought alongside the US 3rd, 36th and 45th Infantry Divisions and the British 1st and 56th Divisions. In one year of fighting in Italy and southern France, from December 1943 to December 1944, it is estimated that the FSSF took over 7,000 prisoners and killed 12,000 enemy soldiers. 16 March 1944. *(Leibowitz photo, NA-CP SC 212095)*

A mechanical smoke generator is shown here on the Anzio beachhead, 22 March 1944. A constant smokescreen was maintained during daylight hours to screen VI Corps operations from German observation. *(Blau photo, NA-CP SC 188968)*

Staff Sergeant Emil Bier of Omaha, Nebraska, and Sergeant W.E. Engel of Seymour, Wisconsin, both of 4 Company, 2nd Regiment, are milking "Blackie" the cow on the Anzio beachhead, 27 April 1944. *(C.E. Nye photo, LAC 183864)*

Forcemen preparing a meal on the Anzio beachhead, late April 1944. While fighting in the beachhead, the FSSF assimilated Canadian and American replacements into its ranks, restoring its strength before the final stage of the campaign. *(C.E. Nye photo, LAC 128973)*

Private Baptista Piccolomini (Leeminster, Massachusetts) and Private Paul Novembre (Union City, New Jersey) of 3 Company, 3rd Regiment, bury a German soldier on the Anzio beachhead. Both soldiers were Johnny Gunners, were later wounded at Anzio, and remained with the 474th Infantry Regiment after the Force disbanded. *(G. Ronald collection, CWM)*

An FSSF patrol invades no man's land to attack a German outpost in a farmhouse. Two members of the patrol are tossing grenades into the farmhouse as they run past, 14 April 1944. *(Gallagher photo, NA-CP SC 189583-S)*

This FSSF patrol hits the ditch and begins to fan out, on a mission to wipe out a German outpost in a farmhouse on the Anzio beachhead, 14 April 1944. *(Gallagher photo, NA–CP SC 189579-S)*

Two members of the FSSF firing Tommy guns at a German position located a few hundred yards away. Anzio beachhead, 14 April 1944. *(Gallagher photo, NA–CP SC 189582-S)*

FSSF patrol skirts a minefield along barbed wire while advancing on an enemy-held house in the Anzio beachhead. 14 April 1944. *(Gallagher photo, NA-CP SC 189580-S)*

An FSSF patrol passing a roadblock that identifies the end of the American minefields, at which point they are now entering enemy territory, 14 April 1944. *(Gallagher photo, NA-CP SC 189578-S)*

Second Regiment bazookas firing on a Cerreto Alto farmhouse, 14 April 1944. For raids, the Force used M-1 rifles, Thompsons M-1941
1JohnsonÀÚ

FSSF patrol firing their rifles from a ditch during an attack on a German outpost, 14 April 1944.
*(Gallagher photo, NA-CP SC 189581-S)*

Forcemen attack a German-occupied farmhouse, firing their rifles from the tall grass, 14 April 1944.
*(Gallagher photo, NA-CP SC189576)*

A group of German prisoners are eyed suspiciously by a "Force cow," one of several kept by the FSSF on the Anzio beachhead.
The prisoner in the centre appears to be quite pleased with his new accommodations.  *(Gallagher photo, NA-CP SC 189596)*

A group of prisoners captured by an FSSF patrol during a lightning raid await questioning at Force headquarters, 15 April 1944. Those lying in the foreground are Italian and the others are German. *(Gallagher photo, NA-CP SC 189597)*

## CHAPTER 6

# Reorganization Under Fire

The plan is that these Canadian reinforcements will be trained with the Unit at the Beachhead. Without in any way wishing to interfere with Gen. Frederick's prerogative as Commander of the Special Service Force … I am somewhat concerned that in the event of these troops being involved in combat, there is a possibility of loss of life because of unfamiliarity with weapons.

*Brigadier-General Ernest G. Weeks*
*OIC, Canadian Section, GHQ, 1st Echelon,*
*3 April 1944*[1]

IN EARLY FEBRUARY, Brigadier-General Frederick, the Force commander, and Lieutenant-Colonel Gilday, the acting senior Canadian officer, had considered disbandment of the First Special Service Force to be the best course of action. The Chief of Staff at Canadian Military Headquarters in London agreed, as did the Chief of General Staff in Ottawa and the Canadian Army authorities in Italy. All, however, recognized that the decision had international implications and that such a move required American approval. While Eisenhower had refused to consider such a course, General Jacob Devers, Commanding General of US forces in the North African

Theater, had also come to agree that the Force should now be disbanded. By mid-February, the matter had received serious consideration in American and British circles, as indicated by the following message from George C. Marshall to the British chiefs of staff:

> Some difficulties have arisen in connection with the PLOUGH Force. We can furnish replacements for the American part of the Force and are discussing the matter of Canadian replacements with the Canadian Mission here [CMHQ]. General Devers has recommended that this force be inactivated, the U.S. personnel therein to be reassigned to combat units, and the Canadian personnel (now about 300) to be turned over to the Canadian authorities in the Mediterranean Theater for assignment to the Canadian forces there.[2]

Marshall's telegram to the British chiefs of staff and Frederick's letter to Fifth Army started the wheels moving. On 21 February, Stuart reported to Ottawa that the entire future of the First Special Service Force "is apparently now in the melting pot. I was called by telephone on Friday by [the] Chief of Combined Operations, who told me that … the Americans were now proposing that the force be disbanded, but hesitated to make specific recommendations until they knew the Canadian reaction to this proposal."[3] The fact that they needed to ask indicates how much consideration Stuart's request of two weeks earlier had actually received.

The Force was now slated for discussion at the next meeting of the British Chiefs of Staff Committee. Informed of this by the British Chief of Combined Operations, Stuart discovered that the Americans were proposing to disband the Force, but felt it necessary to consult with the British prior to making a decision. The British chiefs of staff, in turn, wanted to check with Canada before making specific recommendations. Stuart assured them that there would be no objections from Ottawa.

Opposed to disbandment, however, were those commanders who remained more immediately concerned with the situation at Anzio, including General Eisenhower, General Alexander and Lieutenant-General Clark. "The whole affair," Stuart wrote, "seems to be travelling around in circles and I do not think that anything further can be accomplished by us until we know definitely what the future of this force is."[4] By the first week of March, however, the matter was settled between the British and the Americans, and a decision had been reached: Clark's Fifth Army was allowed to retain the First Special Se rvice Fo rce as a combined US–Canadian formation—at least temporarily.

While Allied planners continued discussing the long-term future of the First Special Se rvice Fo rce, both CMHQ and the US Fifth Army were considering short-term solutions aimed at maintaining the First Special Service Force for the immediate future and until it could be withdrawn from Anzio.

For Fifth Army, arriving at a solution proved relatively simple. With the disaster outside Cisterna on 30 January having destroyed Darby's 1st and 3rd Battalions and leaving only the 4th Battalion intact, on 17 February Clark recommended the inactivation of Darby's Rangers in order to provide replacements for the First Special Service Force. While recognizing that most of the 4th Ranger Battalion had undergone only a small amount of training, Clark pointed out that in joining the Rangers, these men had already volunteered for hazardous duty, and their dispatch to the First Special Service Force would serve to ameliorate the crisis outlined in Frederick's letter of 19 February.[5]

Frederick's letter to Clark also recommended that the organization and equipment of the Force should be brought in line with the missions to which it was being assigned. This was exactly what Clark intended to do. In an effort to rebuild the First Special Service Force, he decided "to increase its strength, revise its organization and equipment, and re-orient its mission to encompass essentially Ranger actions and, at least in part, paratroop capabilities."[6]

Although Fifth Army was able to resolve these issues without undue delay, in London the Canadians dragged their feet, torn between adopting an improvised solution to meet the immediate shortage and establishing a permanent system of reinforcing the 1st Canadian Special Service Battalion. In the last week of February, indecision produced relative inaction on both counts—which is hardly surprising given that the Americans and the British were now considering disbanding the unit altogether. While awaiting a decision, CMHQ inquired of the British and American authorities as to their respective methods of providing reinforcements to airborne formations.[7] Believing the incidence of casualties, or "wastage rates," in the Force to be higher than in a regular infantry formation, CMHQ sought to establish rates that were more in line with the special nature of the unit.[8] At the same time, these inquiries provided some bureaucratic stalling time while Canada awaited a decision from the British and the Americans regarding the future of the Force.

A decision came down on 28 February, when a telephone call from the British War Office confirmed that the Force would be retained for the present time: "As a long term project, it would seem that all concerned would agree to withdrawal but final decision would, of course, be made by CIGS [Chief of Imperial General Staff] at a later meeting."[9] Although this offered scant guarantee of the unit's long-term survival, for the time being the FSSF carried on with business as usual, pending an Anglo–American decision regarding its future.

On the last day of February, the Canadian War Diary recorded the situation at Anzio. While morale remained high, no doubt bolstered by the mass of German prisoners taken on the last of the month, the problem remained that "another month has gone but there is still no indication as to the policy of reinforcing the battalion."[10]

The absence of Canadian reinforcements was becoming a sore point. Further, owing largely to intricacies of British officialdom, the Canadians of the Force found themselves ineligible to receive the same awards as the rest of the Canadian Army. Canadian Forcemen received numerous American decorations, including the Bronze Star and the Silver Star, but British decorations, such as the Distinguished Service Order and the Victoria Cross, remained inexplicably closed to them. "This is probably the only unit in the Canadian Army that cannot recommend its personnel for these awards. The matter is felt very keenly by all ranks."[11] Together these issues were beginning to cause some resentment and a sense that the 1st Canadian Special Service Battalion had been abandoned by Ottawa.

On 4 March, CMHQ finally authorized the dispatch of reinforcements to the 1st Canadian Special Service Battalion. To meet immediate shortages within the unit, Stuart decided that volunteers should be selected from Canadian reinforcement pools in Italy and the Canadian element brought up to its authorized war establishment of 47 officers and 583 other ranks.[12] Subsequent battle casualties could then be met by drawing further reinforcements from the Canadian Army in the United Kingdom. This system could continue until the Force was disbanded or until the parachute training centre at Shilo was able to begin providing reinforcements directly from Canada.[13]

In Italy, action on providing Canadian reinforcements to the First Special Service Force paralleled the supplying of further attachments to the unit by Fifth Army. This was in keeping with Lieutenant-General Clark's orders that the Force be retained and its mission reoriented toward "Ranger" actions—operations requiring a revised organization and greatly increased strength. On 8 March, Fifth Army assigned the 456th Parachute Field Artillery Battalion as a permanent attachment to the FSSF and ordered the US 4th Ranger Battalion disbanded to provide the unit with roughly 20 officer and 500 enlisted man replacements.[14] In doing so, Clark intended to reorganize the Force and expand its current strength of 2,000 men to as many as 3,500—an organization that would "combine the best of Fifth Army's special troops into a hard-hitting, well-led unit which will be of even greater value to the Army Commander than its very excellent component parts."[15]

As it turned out, this was easier said than done. In March 1944, officers and men of the Ranger battalions and of the First Special Service Force were each convinced that theirs was the most elite formation of the United States Army. This created some degree of tension when Fifth Army opted to combine these "very excellent component parts" into an expanded First Special Service Force. Many of the former Rangers resented being assigned to the Force.[16] The latter, meanwhile, considered many of these replacements to be "Rangers in name only," because Rangers with more than two years of overseas service had been returned to the United States as instructors.[17] Overall, there were early signs that the integration of Ranger replacements into the First Special Service Force would not be accomplished as easily as Clark had hoped.

Canadian soldiers, on the other hand, literally lined up to volunteer for the Force, drawn by the unit's reputation and the promise of higher pay. From this number, approximately two thirds were turned away when they failed to meet the specified physical requirements of the Force. On 21 March, Lieutenant-Colonel Akehurst, having recently returned to the unit from the hospital to assume command as senior Canadian officer, learned that 15 officers and 250 other ranks were available as reinforcements; they were proceeding to Naples and then to Santa Maria, where they would receive training in US weapons and operating procedures before joining the unit.[18]

On the night of 21 March, the Rangers arrived as replacements for the Force, with the largest portion of the newcomers being assigned to First Regiment.[19] The unit was rapidly being rebuilt, although the exigencies of combat imposed certain difficulties that needed to be overcome. At Helena, American and Canadian soldiers had trained together for more than a year before being sent into combat. That long period of training had succeeded in establishing "certain qualities and spirit in the officers and enlisted men," an esprit de corps that Frederick regarded as absolutely critical to the combat effectiveness of the First Special Service Force.[20] At Anzio, Fifth Army adopted the expedient of attaching the remnants of other elite units to the First Special Service Force, reasoning that Rangers were already highly trained and could be integrated into the Force with a minimum of inconvenience. Canadian reinforcements, on the other hand, were selected on an individual basis and then sent for special training in American weapons and operating procedures.

Reviewing the situation at the end of March, Lieutenant-Colonel Akehurst hoped that the Force could be withdrawn from the line for a few months of reorganization and training.[21] This would provide some respite for the men at the front and allow an opportunity to integrate the new Canadians into the Force. It was the ideal solution, but unfortunately there were no other units available to relieve the Force on the Mussolini Canal. Instead, Frederick at first decided to rotate the First and Third Regiments off the front line in turns, withdrawing each for a period of refresher training in a rear area of the beachhead while Second Regiment kept up its program of raids and patrols across the canal. Canadian and American replacements, meanwhile, would receive training at Anzio with the Force headquarters detachment. While the conditions would be less than ideal, especially compared to those enjoyed at Helena, Frederick considered this the best solution in terms of training the newcomers and integrating them into the Force. As a result, on 1 April, Akehurst departed from the port of Anzio with instructions from Frederick to bring the Canadian reinforcements to the beachhead for training.[22]

At the Allied headquarters in Naples two days later, Akehurst met with Brigadier-General E.G. Weeks, who had recently replaced Brigadier Beament as the officer responsible for Canadian reinforcements in Italy. Already well familiar with the special circumstances of the Force, Weeks told Akehurst that 15 officers and 240 other ranks were ready and waiting. Up to this point, however, Weeks had understood that the Canadians would be trained at the Force depot in Santa Maria. Instead, Akehurst repeated Frederick's orders that they were to be issued US Army uniforms, equipped with American M–1 rifles and taken directly to the beachhead for training.[23] Upon hearing this, Weeks became somewhat alarmed that the men would be proceeding to Anzio carrying American weapons and not having the slightest idea how to use them. That afternoon he cabled Fifth Army, requesting a change of plans:

> Without in any way wishing to interfere with Gen. Frederick's prerogative as Commander of the Special Service Force, with the Canadian reinforcements totally unacquainted with American weapons, customs and methods of fighting, I am somewhat concerned that in the event of these troops being involved in combat, there is a possibility of loss of life because of unfamiliarity with weapons. I would like to suggest, therefore, that some assurance be given that these Canadian reinforcements will not be placed in combat until they have received sufficient training to become thoroughly familiar with not only USA weapons but also customs, methods of fighting, etc.[24]

Seeing the point, on 9 April, Fifth Army authorized the training of Canadian reinforcements to take place at Santa Maria under the supervision of NCO instructors provided by the Force, and assured Weeks, "Everything possible will be done to familiarize these reinforcements with the customs and methods of fighting of the 1st Special Service Force before they are committed to action."[25] While Frederick had hoped that training the Canadians at Anzio would provide the best means of integrating them into the Force, Brigadier Weeks could not allow this, seeing the potential for disaster should they become engaged in combat without proper training in US weapons. As a result, the Canadian replacements trained at Santa Maria from 11 April to 24 April prior to departing for the beachhead.

On the morning of 11 April, Captain Pat O'Neill left Anzio with orders to take charge of training the Canadian replacements at Santa Maria. At Helena, he had been the officer responsible for hand-to-hand combat training, and at Santa Maria he was to direct the instruction on a much wider range of subjects, emphasizing familiarity with

Force weapons first and foremost. The training was to be completed as quickly as possible, and the Canadians transferred to the beachhead at the earliest opportunity. With a group of four selected NCO instructors from Anzio, who were to be joined at Santa Maria by a group of Force officers and NCOs recently released from the hospital, O'Neill was given two weeks in which to conduct the training program.[26]

Before O'Neill left Anzio, Lieutenant-Colonel Wickham, the Force Executive Officer, provided him with a tentative training schedule. "You should use it as a guide in your training, but feel free to delete those subjects in which the replacements are already sufficiently well trained."[27] At Santa Maria, O'Neill had the Canadians divided into three training companies, which were rotated through a schedule that closely parallelled Wickham's suggestions, providing not only an introduction to Force weapons but also a crash course in patrolling, demolitions and small-unit tactics.

| SUBJECT | HOURS |
| --- | --- |
| FSSF Organization and Orientation | 2 |
| Close Order Drill, FSSF Regulations | 2 |
| M–1 Rifle | 15 |
| Light Machine Gun | 4 |
| Rocket Launcher | 4 |
| Johnson Light Machine Gun | 4 |
| Thompson Submachine Gun | 4 |
| Grenades, Hand | 2 |
| Grenades, Rifle | 2 |
| 60mm Mortar | 4 |
| Mine Warfare | 4 |
| Hand-to-Hand Combat | 4 |
| Defense Against Chemical Attack | 2 |
| Security Lecture | 2 |
| Scouting and Patrolling | 12 |
| Small Unit Tactics | 8 |
| Hygiene and Field Sanitation | 2 |
| Force Customs | 1 |
| Field Fortifications | 2 |
| AT and AA Defense | 2 |
| Demolitions | 8 |
| Extended Order Drill | 2 |
| Bayonet Training | 2 |
| Assault of Fortified Positions | 4 |
| House Clearing | 4 |

Table 6.1: Canadian Replacements Training Schedule, 10 April 1944.[28]

The Force conducted a similar program at Anzio for the Ranger replacements, which was aimed at familiarizing them with unit operating procedures and customs. This proved more difficult than might have been expected. As recalled by Kenneth Wickham, there was some trouble assimilating the Rangers into the Force, because "they also believed they were the best."[29] According to the Rangers, "We were amazed by the apparent lack of organization in the Force—we were also the outsiders coming into a new unit—we felt that we had been taken advantage of as we were never given the opportunity to join the Ranger Battalions forming in England."[30] Another former Ranger, James R. Metzger, recalls his introduction to the Force:

> This was our first contact with the half-Canadian, half-American outfit. Needless to say, we were not too happy with the thought of not continuing with the name of Ranger. We were all volunteers for the Rangers, and at the time we all felt sure that we would be regrouped and retrained and start another battalion. Much to our dismay, we found that this did not happen.[31]

The Canadian replacements, on the other hand, had eagerly volunteered for the Force and came with an open mind. The possibility of parachute pay provided some of the attraction, although the reputation the unit had won for itself on the Winter Line appears to have been the main draw. These victories became common knowledge in early April when censors lifted the ban on reporting Force activities and the first stories on the unit began to appear in Canadian newspapers:

**FROM *THE MONTREAL STAR*, 9 APRIL 1944, BY SHOLTO WATT**

**Crack Mixed Force Is Gradually Becoming American**
No parallel can be found for the U.S.–Canadian mixed force which has opened its fighting career in Italy with a series of brilliant victories. The past has known its mixed forces of mercenaries, but they were not the civilian soldiers of democracies … There was an International Brigade in Spain, perhaps the nearest approach to this organization, resting on an ideological unity. Canadians remain in their own army for pay and administration, Americans in theirs. The force has two armies behind it, two governments, two peoples.

**No Canadian Replacements**
As it exists at present the force is capable of effecting political benefits outside the scope of its military role. Wherever it is known it must be an inspiration in international goodwill. It could become an object lesson in concrete, human text to the so-long divided peoples of Europe … If it continues in the same

```
brilliant way, it may become a legend of this war that will exert
its influence in peace to no small advantage.
    But—there is a big but—the force at present receives little
or no Canadian replacements for the Canadian casualties, though
the policy is not unknown here [in Italy]. U.S. replacements
come in and Canadians are already outnumbered in a proportion
of seven to three, though they started even … The world has
certainly been informed enough about the unguarded frontier, the
long peace between our nations. This is another step from the
static to the active; from "We will not interfere with each
other" to "We will do big things together". The force is an
intensely dramatic embodiment of our common effort in a cause
that commands the faith of all of us.³²
```

In April the call for Canadian reinforcements resulted in nearly three times as many volunteers for the Force as there were vacancies. On 27 April the first Canadian replacements arrived on the beachhead, as recorded by the War Diary of the 1st Canadian Special Service Battalion:

> Our first overseas reinforcements, 15 officers and 234 other ranks, arrived today. Their L.S.T. docked at 0800 hours, was told to move about 15 feet and in doing so fouled their anchor chain in the propellers and spent 7 hours in the bay getting it clear; by this time the Hun had started his daily shelling of Anzio, and the boys had their first experience of being under fire.³³

An undignified entry, perhaps, but one that did nothing to dampen the welcome that these newcomers received in the unit, where the original Canadians had long awaited the arrival of these reinforcements as a sign of their continuing link to their own army.

In addition to integrating American and Canadian replacement personnel, the Force began preparing for a role in one of three possible plans for the upcoming breakout from Anzio, which would see the US VI Corps fight its way out of the beachhead and rejoin Fifth Army for an advance on Rome. Each of the scenarios under consideration required the Force to operate in conjunction with not only the conventional infantry units on its flanks but also the artillery, tanks and tank destroyers that would be attached to the Force itself. Although the FSSF, by this time, had gained extensive experience in working with artillery, tank–infantry cooperation remained a relatively new concept, the unit having been trained to operate alone and in mountainous terrain. In April, however, by rotating units off the front line during the hours of daylight, the Force was able to conduct some fifteen exercises in tank–infantry cooperation in preparation for the breakout.³⁴

Perhaps the most serious obstacle encountered during the training period was the exposure of the entire Anzio beachhead to German artillery fire from the surrounding hills. Training on the beachhead itself did offer a few advantages, however, including the possibility of conducting "live-fire" training exercises under extremely realistic conditions. In April, elements of the Force carried out two highly successful raids on enemy positions, which gave the unit valuable experience in working with tanks.

On the morning of 15 April, three companies from Second Regiment, supported by a company of medium tanks from 1st Armored Regiment and a number of light tanks, armoured cars and tank destroyers, attacked enemy strongpoints at Cerreto Alto. The attack resulted in 16 enemy dead and 61 taken prisoner for a loss of one man wounded, two medium tanks destroyed and three of the lighter vehicles damaged, all by enemy land-mines. Later that afternoon, Force observation posts noted considerable activity as the Germans moved to reinforce their hold on the village. "Our artillery fired on the enemy, inflicting casualties and forcing the enemy to withdraw." German artillery responded in kind that night, landing a barrage on forward Force positions near the canal.[35]

Capitalizing on the success of the earlier raid, Second Regiment and accompanying armoured support launched a second daylight raid against Cerreto Alto on 18 April. Light tanks from the 81st Reconnaissance Battalion created a diversion while a company from Second Regiment and four Shermans engaged enemy strongpoints at the main objective, destroying nine machine-gun positions.[36] A third raid, on the last night of April, encountered less success, running into a dense minefield before finding the objective abandoned by the enemy. In the counterattack that followed, Second Regiment suffered 25 casualties in addition to the loss of two light tanks and a recovery vehicle, once again to landmines.[37]

In the spring of 1944 there was a sense of optimism within the Force as the unit prepared for the breakout and advance on Rome. The weather had begun to improve, and on the far side of the canal the Germans had been relatively quiet for some time. The arrival of replacements indicated to the Canadians of the Force that they had not been abandoned to their fate. As of 30 April, these reinforcements brought the effective strength of the Canadian element to 49 officers and 595 other ranks. The Americans in the combat echelon numbered 56 officers and 1,361 other ranks. Although the Canadians had been reinforced to their original strength and occupied approximately half of the leadership positions in the Force, the concurrent expansion of the American element meant that Canadians still comprised only one third of the combat echelon.[38]

On 9 May, the 36th Combat Engineer Regiment relieved the First Special Service Force on the Mussolini Canal, after 98 days at the front. With detachments from

Second Regiment conducting nightly harassing patrols across the canal, thereby keeping up appearances in no man's land, the remainder of the unit moved to a bivouac area in the rear and began training for the breakout. In keeping with Frederick's earlier recommendation that the Force be properly equipped for the type of operations in which it was to be employed, attachments to the FSSF for the upcoming operation included the 463rd Parachute Field Artillery Battalion; D Company, 39th Combat Engineer Regiment; two companies of the 645th Tank Destroyer Battalion; A Company, 191st Tank Battalion; the mortars of B Company, 84th Chemical Battalion; and a collecting company from the 52nd Medical Battalion.[39] From 9 May to 20 May, much of the Force training program was devoted to tank–infantry cooperation in groups of various sizes, and included several regimental manoeuvres.[40] Intensive training in crew-served weapons was undertaken, "with particular attention being paid to the many replacements now being worked into the weapons crews."[41]

On the eve of the upcoming operation, Frederick addressed a message to his men, reminding them that "the Force has never moved backward" and offering a special greeting to those newcomers who had recently joined the unit. "We welcome you to our ranks knowing that you are the kind of soldiers who will fight with only the thought of victory in mind. We know that you will take the same pride in successful accomplishment of the mission as do the men you have joined." Frederick then gave a similar welcome to the unit's supporting attachments and closed with a final encouragement: "Our superior officers expect us to succeed as before. We shall prove to them that their confidence is not misplaced. The eyes of Canada and the United States are upon us. Let them see that, as in the past, we move only forward."[42]

The breakout from Anzio began at 0630 hours on 23 May, with the First Special Service Force moving forward on the right of the VI Corps advance and guarding the flank of the 3rd US Division attack on Cisterna. *(See map, Figure 6.1.)* As First Regiment set out in the lead of the attack, with two companies of tanks and a battalion of tank destroyers in support, German machine-guns laid down lines of fire. These were quickly overcome by the rifle sections, and by 0815 hours, First Regiment had advanced some two thousand yards beyond its line of departure and was approximately halfway to Highway 7, its initial objective.[43] Although small-arms fire was beginning to die down, the Germans started laying down mortar and artillery fire. Caught in the barrage, 2nd Battalion lost its commanding officer, Lieutenant-Colonel Walt Gray, who was killed along with several others as First Regiment charged through the curtain of shrapnel.[44] With forward elements of the Force reaching the far side of this artillery barrage, however, German resistance to the front began to collapse. By 1000 hours, First Regiment had secured Highway 7, and one of its battalions had advanced all the way to the railway.

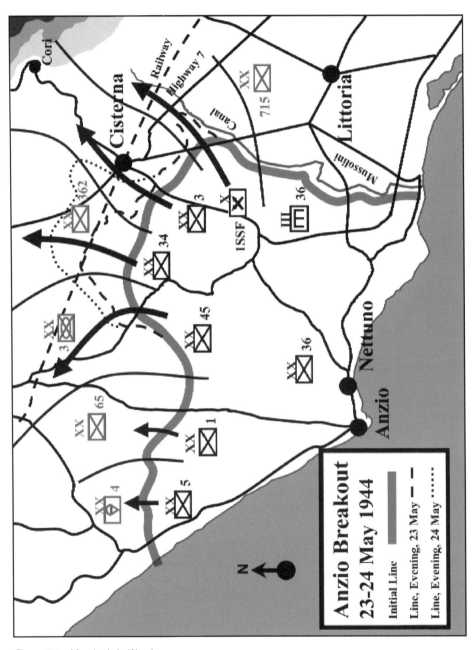

Figure 6.1   Map by Lyle Wood

"We advanced again," recalled William Sheldon, a former platoon commander, "the tanks giving us great support and several Jerries surrendering to them. I felt confident—ever so confident then. We had cracked Jerry's main line of resistance. With the tanks, it seemed easy ... We crossed the highway without opposition, and 200 yards beyond came to a high railroad bank where our company set up a defensive line— our final objective. It all seemed too terribly easy. I couldn't believe it."[45]

Glancing backwards, another Force officer remembers the moment differently: "We got out into the plains of high grass beyond the Highway 7 and ran into more artillery fire from 88s and began taking casualties. When we looked back, we saw a dozen of our Shermans, all of them burning and with smoke pouring out. It was a terrible feeling."[46] By advancing beyond Highway 7, First Regiment had created a salient for itself, one that now lay exposed to a crossfire of German 88s in Cisterna and Littoria. One by one, Shermans and tank destroyers attached to the unit began taking hits. To make matters worse, Paulick Force, the provisional unit formed to close the gap between the Force and 3rd Division, had been stalled by German small-arms fire, leaving the Force's left flank exposed. "Doesn't look good around canal," radioed First Regiment. "Two companies cut off on [far] side of Highway by heavy concentration of artillery coming from Cisterna."[47]

At noon an enemy counterattack was seen forming in the woods east of the Mussolini Canal. At 1230 hours, the two forward companies that were dug-in along the railway line began to see tanks—lots of them: five Tigers coming down the Ninfa road and another three from Littoria.[48] The tanks moved in to launch a violent counterattack, inflicting terrible losses, while the supporting Allied artillery radioed that they were unable to see what was going on beyond the highway. The two forward companies tried to withdraw but were pinned down. About half of 1st Company made it back, and 3rd Company was badly shot up. Although some had been able to withdraw to a line south of Highway 7 and suffered heavy casualties in doing so, others remained cut-off for two days before linking up with attacking elements of the 34th US Division.[49]

First Regiment fell back to Highway 7. By this time, Allied air and artillery were coming in with observed fire, but this did not prevent the Tigers from destroying much of what remained of the tanks and tank destroyers attached to the Force. Especially discouraging was the sight of a tank destroyer making a direct hit on a Tiger and seeing it bounce off, followed by a Tiger firing a round through a house, through a Sherman, and then watching the shell travel another thousand yards beyond the destroyed tank. The line held briefly at Highway 7, but according to Lieutenant Sheldon, "the big German tanks began moving in closer and then machine-gunning us. It was at once apparent that our fate would be the same as that of the Rangers ... Finally, the order came to withdraw and it was truly a wise move."[50]

The Force pulled back to some five hundred yards short of the highway, where it was able to link up with Paulick Force and close the gap. Steady air and artillery, along with the arrival of reinforcements in tanks and tank destroyers, broke up the German counterattack by 2100 hours. Once the situation had been stabilized, the 133rd Infantry Regiment relieved the Force on the front line, allowing the unit to prepare for a renewed drive against Monte Arrestino the next day.

Reorganizing for the next phase of the attack, on 25 May the Force moved against Monte Arrestino, occupying it, against light opposition, that afternoon in support of 3rd Division's push toward Cori. All across the VI Corps front the Germans were pulling their forces back in the direction of Rome. The breakout had succeeded. Following behind an attack by 3rd Division on Rocca Massima, the Force encountered no real resistance during its push toward Artena and the Valmontone plain. *(See map, Figure 6.2.)*

On 28 May the Force set out from the high ground above Artena, moving north in the direction of Valmontone in an attempt to sever Highway 6, the enemy's main east-west line of communications in the area. Moving to counter the threat to their escape route, the Germans sent every man available to defend this vital point. "The Jerries … brought up some high class troops and equipment," recalled John Dawson. "When we moved out of [Artena] to the plain below, I believe the small arms fire was the heaviest I have ever encountered … It was touch and go."[51] The fighting outside Artena lasted for five hours as the Germans rolled Tigers, self-propelled guns and flak wagons into the fight, inflicting heavy casualties before the forward companies of the Force were able to report that all objectives had been secured.[52]

Consolidating its defences in the last days of May, the Force suffered heavy casualties as the Germans kept up their shelling on the town of Artena and on FSSF front lines. On the night of 29/30 May, a German battalion, reinforced with tanks, launched an attack to regain lost ground but was driven back by field guns attached to the Force. The next night a second counterattack was broken up by artillery when an enemy force that was concentrating for the attack came under observation. On 1 June the Third Regiment held against one final attempt by the Germans, inflicting heavy casualties on the enemy.

That night the Force sent out a strong patrol, including tanks and most of the First Regiment, to reconnoitre the town of Colleferro. On the following day, Second Regiment led the attack to secure the town. Although the Germans were able to hold out for most of the day, especially on the northeast side of town across Highway 6, at 1500 hours the Force made contact with the 3rd Algerian Division of the French Expeditionary Corps as it made its way into town from the southeast. With Colleferro

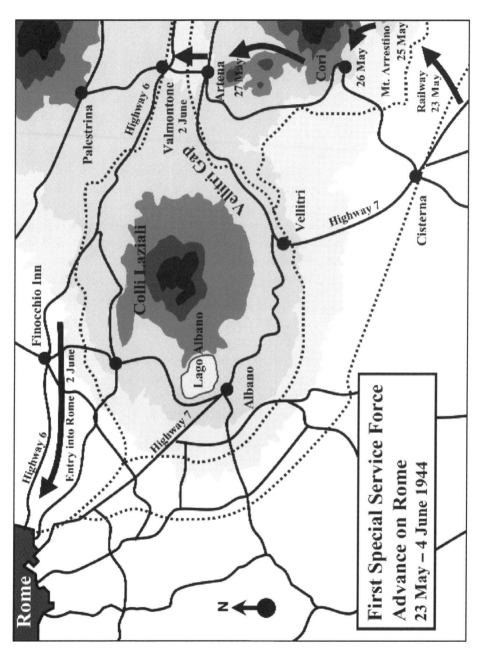

Figure 6.2   Map by Lyle Wood

secure and Highway 6 in Allied hands, the Force withdrew to Artena in order to join the final stages of Fifth Army's advance into Rome.

On the morning of 3 June the tanks of Task Force Howze were attached to the First Special Service Force to provide the unit with armoured support as it moved to secure six bridges across the Tiber. Although Rome had been declared an open city, rearguard elements of the German Tenth Army remained in place to delay the Allied advance while the remainder escaped. On 4 June, the First Special Service Force encountered strong resistance on the outskirts of the city, where the fighting lasted through most of the day. "Entrance of our troops into the city of Rome proper was made at approximately 1600, … the first permanent entrance of Allied troops into Rome. The six bridges were all secured by 2300 after further bitter street fighting."[53]

During this fighting, the Force lost many good men, including the First Regiment commander, Colonel A.C. Marshall, who was shot by a sniper just outside the city. Within Rome itself the fighting became somewhat confused, as described by J.G. Bourne, the officer commanding the 2nd Battalion, Third Regiment:

> There was little or no resistance at the outset and it was indeed thrilling to receive such a tumultuous welcome from the Romans. The cheering and happiness was quite moving. Every now and then, the crowds on the street would suddenly disappear and some die-hard Germans in an armoured car would turn a corner and start shooting. It was rather uncomfortable, as there was no cover to be taken—but skillful use of bazookas, grenades, and machine-gun fire quickly disposed of the enemy—then the crowd would reappear again.[54]

Sporadic fighting continued throughout the day as elements of the Force made their way through streets lined by civilians on both sides, scouted the unguarded routes, cleared resistance and posted traffic signs for the Fifth Army to follow into the city. By the evening of 5 June, Rome was in Allied hands. The next day, as the Allied landing went ashore in Normandy, the First Special Service Force was withdrawn from positions on the Tiber bridges and ordered to proceed to a Fifth Army rest area.

Reports indicate that the morale of the Force was excellent throughout the fighting in late May and reached its highest peak during the entry into Rome.[55] Reinforced and reorganized for the breakout, the men fought tenaciously in operations that differed in ve ry few respects from those assigned to a conventional infantry formation. After fighting its way from Anzio to Rome, the Force earned a position in the lead of Fifth Army's advance into the Eternal City. Victory came at high cost, however: in two weeks of fighting, the unit suffered an enormous number of casualties, leaving the Canadian element with only slightly more officers and men than there had been before the arrival of the replacements in April. Once again, the 1st Canadian Special Service Battalion needed reinforcements, prompting Akehurst to include a request in his monthly report to CMHQ: "The last reinforcements proved to be excellent men. We hope the next group will be just as good. Officers and men with battle experience would be preferred."[56]

As far as the officers and men of the First Special Service Force were concerned, the integration of Canadian reinforcements into the unit in the spring of 1944 was accomplished without any major difficulty. In this instance, the original plan of sending Canadian soldiers to Anzio without any training in the use of American weapons was avoided, and training the newcomers proved a relatively painless affair. Perhaps the ease with which these reinforcements were assimilated by the Force should not be surprising: from the earliest days at Helena, relations between Canadians and Americans in the unit had always been good. It was at the higher levels that the Force ran into difficulties, as evidenced by the exchange of telegrams and letters between various Canadian headquarters and, later, the discussions between American, British and Canadian planners regarding the future of the First Special Service Force.

If anything, the integration of Ranger replacements into the Force had actually proved more difficult than that of the Canadian reinforcements. Both the FSSF men and the US Army Rangers had their share of pride, tempered in the case of the Rangers by the memory of Cisterna and their subsequent disbandment. Prior to their arrival in March, the Rangers had had no experience in dealing with the First Special Service Force, and their first impressions of the unit were not entirely positive. Among two groups of elite soldiers there was bound to be a clash of unit personalities, although such antagonism was likely to fade over time. Keeping their Ranger flashes on the right sleeve, the newcomers were soon wearing a Force "Spearhead" patch on their left. As Force veteran Bill Story recalls, these men, upon joining the Rangers, had already demonstrated the same "volunteer attitude" that marked the officers and men of the First Special Service Force. In time, many would come to consider the US–Canadian Force to be their second home.

The Force, meanwhile, had adapted to Fifth Army's new vision of its role, reorienting toward what Clark described as Ranger actions. During the breakout, however, one would be hard pressed to differentiate Force operations from those regularly assigned to a conventional infantry formation. Beginning with the training period at Helena and continuing into 1944, differences in nationality, experience and training had served to create a unique spirit that complemented, rather than detracted from, the unit's fighting abilities. Given the nature of the fighting from Anzio to Rome and the character of operations to which the Force increasingly found itself assigned, success was coming to depend more upon attachments of tanks, armoured vehicles, mortars and especially artillery than it ever had in the past.

Brigadier-General Robert T. Frederick discusses the results of an FSSF raid with Lt. Col. Robert S. Moore, commander, 2nd Regiment. A US Fifth Army tank is burning in the background. Winston Churchill said of Frederick: "If we had a dozen men like him we would have smashed Hitler in 1942. He's the greatest fighting general of all time." 15 April 1944. *(Gallagher photo, NA-CP SC 437683)*

Sergeant Cyril Krotzer (Arlington, Virginia; HQ det. 3rd Regt) surveys the beachhead scene for the last time as the regiment prepares for the drive on Rome. His FSSF patch has been blacked-out in this photo by US Army Signal Corps censors. 15 April 1944. *(Gallagher photo, NA-CP SC 189497)*

Private Edward J. Wall
(Albany, New York; HQ det.
2nd Regt) enjoys a cigarette
while observing the beachhead
from beside a burnt-out tank.
15 April 1944. *(Gallagher photo,
NA-CP SC 189498)*

At a ceremony held at Fifth Army
headquarters in San Marco, Italy,
General Sir Harold Alexander,
C-in-C of Allied armies in Italy,
pins the ribbon decoration of the
honorary Knight Commander of
the Most Excellent Order of the
British Empire on Lt. General
Mark W. Clark, commander of
Fifth Army, 30 April 1944.
*(NA-CP SC 191384)*

Medium tanks of the US 1st Armored Division dug in 2 miles from the front awaiting the opening of the Anzio breakout. The First Special Service Force served with the US 3rd, 45th, 34th and 1st Armored Divisions, the 36th Division in reserve, and British 1st and 5th Divisions. They were given the task of driving north after taking Cisterna to sweep the right flank of VI Corps and capture Mount Arrestino. Facing them were the German 715th and Hermann Göring Divisions, the 7th Luftwaffe Battalion, and two battalions of the 1028th Grenadier Regiment of the 362nd Division. 20 May 1944. *(Gallagher photo, NA-CP SC 190900)*

Forcemen searching German prisoners taken near Cisterna, 25 May 1944. In the intense fighting of 23 May, FSSF dead numbered 39, with most casualties occurring in 1 Battalion, 1st Regiment. Enemy dead were scattered across the length of ground between the Mussolini Canal and Highway 7, and 61 prisoners were taken; 22 German and the remainder Italian. The American soldiers' unit insignias on their helmets and shoulders have been blotted out in the photo by US Army censors. *(Brinn photo, NA-CP SC 190738)*

On the right flank of Operation Buffalo, the Anzio breakout, VI Corps, including the US 1st Armored Division, 3rd Infantry Division and the First Special Service Force, took 400 prisoners in theCisterna area on 24 May 1944. *(Brinn photo, NA-CP SC 190739)*

German infantry trapped in Cisterna by the advancing VI Corps flee from a ruined building and attempt to surrender after their ammunition has given out. *(Bonnard photo, NA-CP SC 190740)*

The ruins of Cisterna. A street photographed after the town's capture on 25 May 1944. As the 3rd Division closed its front on the railroad line, the FSSF assembled for its successful drive on Mount Arrestino, and from there moved along mule trails to Artena and Rocca Massima. Under the command of the 3rd Division, the FSSF worked northward and fought for control of Highway 6, the major escape route for German units withdrawing from south of the beachhead. The "Anzio breakout" soon became the "road to Rome." *(Bonnard photo, NA-CP SC 190732)*

Some of the 2000 German prisoners captured on the Anzio beachhead over the last three days, 25 May 1944. *(Musser photo, NA-CP SC 191507)*

Motorized units of Fifth Army speed towards Rome, passing through an ancient arch on the Via Tuscolana on the outskirts of the city. At 0620 hours on the morning of 4 June, while attached to II Corps and Task Force Howze, the FSSF passed the city limits and led the way into Rome on a mission to secure the Tiber bridges and the main railway station. *(Edwards photo, NA-CP SC 191058)*

The first troops on the streets of Rome, 4 June 1944. Shown here, FSSF soldiers leave the protective cover of a burning Mark VI tank to move deeper into the city. The Force fought all day against the Hermann Göring rearguards, and by nightfall controlled all seven bridges over the Tiber. *(Gallagher photo, NA-CP SC 191061)*

Lt. General Mark Clark, commander of Fifth Army, rides through the streets of Rome on 5 June 1944.
*(Bell photo, NA-CP SC 191386)*

Lt. General Mark Clark accompanies General George C. Marshall, Chief of Staff, U.S. Army, north of Rome. Four days later the First Special Service Force at Lake Albano learned of General Robert Frederick's promotion and re-assignment to command the 1st Airborne Task Force in the upcoming invasion of southern France. General Clark's farewell message to Frederick congratulated the Force for its aggressive defence of the Mussolini Canal, where it held a front equal to that usually assigned to a full division, as well as their performance during the final breakout and the advance into Rome. 19 June 1944.
*(NA-CP SC 191518)*

Lt. General Mark Clark, Fifth Army, Major General John Coulter, commander of 85th Division, and Major General Geoffrey Keyes, commander of II Corps, check local position on a situation map, 19 September 1944. *(Thomas photo, NA-CP SC 437684)*

CHAPTER 7

# Disbandment in Southern France

This unit appears now to be submerged to such an extent with the U.S. Forces that the value to Canada of its retention is no longer apparent. I spoke to Eisenhower about this force some months ago but … he was not disposed to do anything about my proposal that the Canadian element might now be disbanded … I recommend that the Canadian element of the Special Service Force be disbanded and that the personnel be returned to the U.K. for reallocation.

*Lieutenant-General Kenneth Stuart*
*Chief of Staff, CMHQ*
*7 October 1944*[1]

Upon its withdrawal from positions guarding the Tiber bridges, the Force moved first to Tor Sapienza and then, on 7 June, to a bivouac area on the north shore of Lake Albano. "This is the best rest area we have hit in Italy," the War Diary recorded. "Lago Albano is an old volcanic crater, the steeply rising shore is well wooded; the lake is clear and grand [for] swimming. No living in dugouts or fox holes and no sound of artillery fire or bombing. The men are spending days in the water, lying in the sun, boating, fishing and getting laundry up to scratch."[2] As of 10 June, a rotation schedule came into effect, allowing some of the men to visit Rome each day while the remainder rested and trained at Lake Albano.

Three weeks of relaxation by the lake, near the site of Castel Gandalfo, the Pope's summer residence, provided the Force with a much-needed rest. In this time, officers and men began to recover from four months of uninterrupted fighting. Holding the Mussolini Canal had been a costly business, but the drive on Rome had proven particularly expensive, as indicated by the number of casualties incurred by the Force between 23 May and 4 June. Of the 2,061 soldiers in the combat echelon there were 749 casualties:

| | WOUNDED | | KILLED | | MISSING | | DIED OF WOUNDS | |
|---|---|---|---|---|---|---|---|---|
| | Officers | Enlisted Men | Officers | Enlisted Men | Officers | Enlisted Men | Officers | Enlisted Men |
| Force HQ | 1 | 11 | -- | -- | -- | -- | -- | -- |
| 1st Regt. | 11 | 274 | 5 | 46 | 2 | 28 | -- | 7 |
| 2nd Regt. | 7 | 111 | -- | 10 | -- | 19 | -- | 4 |
| 3rd Regt. | 4 | 132 | -- | 27 | 1 | 2 | 1 | 6 |
| Serv. Bn. | 1 | 32 | -- | 4 | -- | -- | -- | 3 |
| TOTAL | 24 | 560 | 5 | 87 | 3 | 49 | 1 | 20 |

Table 7.1: First Special Service Force Casualties, 23 May to 4 June 1944[3]

As of 10 June, the effective strength of the 1st Canadian Special Service Battalion stood at 32 officers and 396 other ranks, down from 50 officers and 590 other ranks at the beginning of May.[4] With the reduced strength of the Canadian element, Akehurst spent much of the second and third weeks of June at the Canadian headquarters in Naples discussing the Canadian reinforcements situation with Brigadier-General Weeks and his staff.

Upon his return to Lake Albano on 19 June, Akehurst talked with Frederick regarding the dispatch of further reinforcements from the Canadian Army. While Frederick, who was at this time recovering from wounds suffered during the advance on Rome, welcomed further Canadian replacements, both he and Akehurst agreed that replacement officers should be accepted only if they appeared especially well qualified, in keeping with the Force's practice of promoting officers from within the ranks whenever possible. On 22 June, Akehurst made the final arrangements for four Canadian officers and 206 other ranks to report to the Force's base camp at Santa Maria for training.

It was during his recovery at Lake Albano that Frederick had an opportunity to consider the lessons learned on the road from Anzio to Rome. First, it had not been possible in one month to train FSSF replacements to the standard of the original personnel, just as he had warned in his letter of 19 February. No amount of enthusiasm on the part of these volunteers could equal the full year of intense training provided at Helena, Montana. Second, it was immediately apparent that armoured and artillery support had been absolutely critical to the success of recent Force operations—just as such support was for any conventional infantry regiment conducting conventional, infantry battles. When the supporting armour had been knocked out during the breakout from Anzio, the advance had faltered and two of First Regiment's forward companies were overrun. Five days later at Artena, supporting artillery had been essential, both in preparing the ground over which the Force would advance and in repelling the German counterattacks that followed.

With these lessons in mind, on 22 June, Frederick sent his last letter to Fifth Army as commander of the First Special Service Force. Writing directly to General Clark, he detailed the difficult situation now facing his command:[5]

### HEADQUARTERS, FIRST SPECIAL SERVICE FORCE, U.S. ARMY

### TO: Commanding General, Fifth Army, U.S. Army

After deliberate consideration of the many factors involved, it is recommended that the First Special Service Force be organized and equipped in accordance with the Tables of Organization and Equipment for an Infantry Regiment, with the addition of one (1) battalion of light Field Artillery.

The non-availability of replacements specially trained for the Force, and the absence of facilities for training those replacements received to the standards of the original personnel, make it less desirable to continue the force under a special organization.

The present equipment of the force includes large quantities of parachute and winter warfare equipment. Such a small percentage of the present personnel of the force have received parachute or winter training that there is no necessity for maintaining this special equipment for the command.

The missions that have been assigned to the Force in combat have in most instances required the use of equipment normal to an Infantry regiment. This particularly applies to communication equipment. For each operation it has been necessary to make arrangements for the temporary use of necessary equipment.

> The operation for which the Force was originally organized
> did not require the medical personnel or motor transport that
> have been found necessary in the execution of missions assigned.
> Reorganization as an Infantry Regiment would correct these
> deficiencies.
>
>                    [signed] Robert T. Frederick
>                    Brigadier-General, U.S. Army
>                    Commanding

In this letter Frederick appears to have finally given up hope that the Force might be employed in a role similar to the one for which it had originally been organized and trained. In recommending reorganization as a regular infantry regiment, Frederick's letter recognized a process that was already taking place, owing to continuing attrition and the difficulties involved in training newcomers to the standard of the originals from Helena.

Mark Clark, in turn, respected Frederick and his opinions. On 3 July he endorsed Frederick's recommendations for reorganizing the First Special Service Force in a letter to the commander of the US Army's North African Theater. In this letter, he forwarded Frederick's suggestion that temporary attachments to the FSSF—field artillery, combat engineers and medical services—should be made permanent and the Force reorganized as an infantry regimental combat team.[6] From the Anzio breakout onwards, it had been necessary to make special arrangements for provisional attachments and the temporary loan of equipment. This was something that Frederick hoped an extensive reorganization of the First Special Service Force might correct and that General Clark's support would help to make a reality.

While Clark was willing to see the FSSF reorganized as a line infantry regiment—the unit would soon be leaving his command to join the Seventh Army in the invasion of southern France—he had no intention of losing a commander of Frederick's proven ability to an "ordinary" infantry formation. On 23 June, Frederick ordered the Force to assemble by the lake for the presentation of awards to the officers and men who had distinguished themselves during the fighting of the last few months. Canadians were awarded one Distinguished Service Cross, two Silver Stars and four Bronze Stars.[7] Frederick then addressed the gathering to announce his departure. "The General announced his re-assignment, that he was leaving the Force. A discernable, protesting gasp broke the hush in the ranks of men who normally withheld such sentiments."[8] Frederick explained that on several occasions he had turned down promotion to higher command in order to remain with the Force. Now, however, he was being ordered to a new appointment and had been given no alternative. He was leaving to take command of the

First Airborne Task Force (1st ABTF), a provisional airborne division being formed for the upcoming invasion of southern France. Colonel Edwin A. Walker, the officer commanding Third Regiment, would now assume command of the FSSF. On 23 June a saddened entry in the Canadian War Diary recorded Frederick's departure: "He has been the driving power behind the Force and its future is now in the air."[9]

Within days of Frederick's departure, Canadian Lieutenant-Colonel Gilday, the commander of 1st Battalion, Third Regiment, requested a transfer back to the Canadian Army. Months before, while acting as the senior Canadian officer of the Force, Gilday had recommended the withdrawal of the entire 1st Canadian Special Service Battalion. Now exhausted at the conclusion of recent operations, Gilday requested to join the Canadian company commanders and platoon leaders as they went on a short leave of absence. Walker turned him down, and a heated argument ensued, ending when Gilday told the Force commander that he would not serve under him and asked to go back to the Canadian Army.

By all accounts Gilday was an excellent officer. Only days before, Walker had even offered him a promotion despite the fact that the two men had never had much use for each other. In the past, Major Jack Secter, Third Regiment's Executive Officer, had always served as a buffer between Walker and Gilday. Now Secter was dead, killed at Artena, and on 28 June Gilday was on his way back to the Canadian Army after his personal transfer request was approved. Upon his departure, the Canadian War Diary recorded a rumbling of dissatisfaction among his comrades who remained with the Force:

> [Gilday] had reached the end of his tether at swallowing American Army methods. He has done an excellent job as battalion commander, and was offered command of a regiment recently, but wants no further part of the Force. He goes with the best wishes of those who served with him and no few Canadian officers will be envious of his getting back into his own army.[10]

Gilday left for Naples the next day, and returned to the Canadian Army with an unfavourable performance evaluation from Colonel Walker, a letter that remained in his personnel file to the end of his career. In the wake of Frederick's departure, the new Force commander was determined to prevent further transfers and was willing to use coercion if necessary. Referring to the incident in the Canadian War Diary, one of Gilday's fellow officers remarked: "This is one of the things that makes the Canadians wish they were back in their own army. It is the first official act of the new Force commander concerning the Canadians."[11]

While the majority of Canadian officers and men continued as they had prior to Frederick's departure, enjoying the surroundings of Lake Albano and the attractions of Rome, the recent upset over Gilday's departure prompted Canadian authorities to investigate the situation further. On 29 June, Brigadier-General Weeks flew in from Naples to meet with Canadian officers of the Force. Finding Canadian morale to be satisfactory on the whole, Weeks returned to his headquarters reassured by the results of his visit.[12] Although several Canadians requested transfer back to the Canadian Army while the Force was at Lake Albano, two of these men were clerks whose frustration with the unit may be traced to the convoluted administrative arrangements involved in dealing with two separate military bureaucracies on a daily basis.[13] For the most part, Canadians and Americans of the Force were happy with their assignment, and morale continued to be high, notwithstanding Frederick's departure.

On the last day of June the Force began moving to a new training area south of Salerno. Santa Maria di Castillabate, a southern Italian seaside village, became home for the next month as the Force underwent amphibious training in preparation for its next assignment. Force headquarters set up in a villa on the edge of town while the regiments encamped on the southern outskirts. In the vicinity of Salerno, thousands of American and French troops were arriving by truck convoy, train and ship as the US Seventh Army built up for the invasion of southern France.

The intent of Operation Anvil was to land an invasion force on the French Riviera and from there capture the Mediterranean ports of Toulon and Marseilles, before advancing up the valley of the Rhône in support of the Allied advance into Germany. At the beginning of July, Anvil was renamed Dragoon for security reasons. In the upcoming invasion, the First Special Service Force would land on the islands of Port-Cros and Levant and attack the German shore batteries that were guarding the left flank of the landing beaches. At Santa Maria di Castellabate, the First Special Service Force began a series of amphibious landing exercises emphasizing the use of rubber boats, cliff scaling and night operations.[14]

While the combat regiments reviewed their amphibious training and rehearsed for the landings, the Canadian and American replacements that had been received before July continued to train in groups within the regiments to which they had been assigned.[15] Their instructors reported that the officers and men appeared particularly well selected and quite keen on joining the Force.[16] By mid-July the new men had either begun training with their companies at Santa Maria di Castellabate on a regular basis or been sent for specialized training as radio operators or litter bearers.[17] While this arrangement continued for the replacement personnel who were already serving with the FSSF, Force headquarters decided to organize the replacement training centre at the old support echelon base in Santa Maria (Capua-Vetere) on a more permanent basis in order to train a continuing flow of replacement personnel from both the US and Canadian Armies.[18]

Organization of the training centre at the old Santa Maria represented an attempt to establish a regular system of providing replacements to the FSSF. Unlike his predecessor, Walker preferred an ongoing supply of replacement personnel over the improvised and somewhat irregular methods adopted during Frederick's tenure. On one occasion, which highlights the difference between Walker and Frederick, during the fighting outside Artena, Frederick had happened upon two unarmed British deserters who were intent upon joining the Force. Captain Pat O'Neill, then serving in the FSSF headquarters detachment, remembers Frederick's response: "Give them some rifles and let me know how they make out."[19] Colonel Walker, on the other hand, was determined to conduct business along more formal lines.

In July 1944, 191 American and 60 Canadian soldiers began a four-week training program at Santa Maria.[20] Training under a cadre of combat-experienced officers and NCOs sent to take charge of the group, the replacements were put through a strenuous program of weapons instruction, physical conditioning, patrolling and night operations.[21] As recalled by instructor Tom Zabski, "in two weeks we had them whipped into shape. [They became] tough and efficient fighting men. The officers of the 45th [Division, stationed in the vicinity,] couldn't believe this to be possible in so short a time and were amazed at the spirit between our officers and men."[22]

Walker also took steps to improve discipline in the Force, which he considered to have been notoriously lax under Frederick's command. He urged the officers to set an example for their men and, from this time forward, to take steps to deal with infractions immediately rather than turning a blind eye.[23] As if to punctuate the Force commander's concern over the growing indiscipline, the next night "3rd Regiment uncovered a clique of Canadians going AWL, presumably to return to Avellino and the Canadian Army."[24] Eight Canadians had already taken off before the officers had discovered what was going on and sent Major Jack Biscoe ahead to Avellino to have the others taken into custody and returned to Santa Maria. A certain degree of homesickness, however, was by no means restricted to the non-commissioned Canadians of the Force; on 21 July the Canadian officers requested two days' leave from the unit, during which time they intended to visit their old friends at Amalfi or Avellino. Arriving back at Santa Maria on 24 July, these officers reported having had "a grand time, really enjoying being back in Canadian Army surroundings."[25]

During the latter part of July, the Force conducted regimental training exercises covering all phases of amphibious operations, including beach marking, rubber boat landings, and cliff-scaling with full combat loads. These exercises were intended to replicate as closely as possible the conditions that would be encountered in the forthcoming operation. Amphibious training culminated on 7 August with a full-scale rehearsal on the islands of Ponza and Zannone. All three combat regiments took part in this exercise, which was conducted in conjunction with the naval units that had been assigned to the Force for Operation Dragoon. Four days later the Force embarked troopships, which departed from Santa Maria di Castellabate under escort, bound for the staging area on Corsica.

Arriving at the bivouac area on Corsica, the men received final briefings for their assigned mission of assaulting the islands of Port-Cros and Levant. Shortly before midnight on 14 August, FSSF boat groups began debarking from the infantry landing ships, HMCS *Prince Henry* and HMS *Prince Baudouin*, bound for the rocky shores where the landings would take place. Together Île de Port-Cros and Île du Levant formed part of the Îles d'Hyères group. Both islands were only lightly defended, presumably because the Germans considered their broken shorelines too steep for an amphibious landing. By midnight the regiments were en route to their assigned landing areas. *(See map, Figure 7.1.)*

On Île de Port-Cros, First Regiment landed unopposed and regrouped at an assembly area before advancing inland toward Fort de l'Eminence, the Napoleonic era fortress that now served as the key to German defences on the island. Meanwhile, Second and Third Regiments landed on Île du Levant and were also able to gain a foothold without firing a shot. Moving toward their objectives, Second Regiment met strong resistance as the German garrison withdrew toward a fort on the west side of the island. Initially Third Regiment met with better success, taking prisoners and meeting little opposition until it reached the German gun positions at the eastern end of the island. Unfortunately the enemy battery, which was the main objective of the Force landing on Île du Levant, was found to be wooden artillery manned by dummy Germans.[26]

By the end of 15 August, Île du Levant had been secured, and Second and Third Regiments withdrew to the Force bivouac area to await further orders. On Port-Cros, the Germans held out in Fort de l'Eminence until the afternoon of 17 August when naval fire-control parties attached to First Regiment began directing 15-inch shells from the battleship HMS *Ramillies* onto the stronghold. At 1315 hours, the German garrison surrendered, and First Regiment handed the island over to a French garrison company. On 19 August, the First Special Service Force again boarded landing craft, this time for a move to the mainland where it would be attached to Major-General Frederick's First Airborne Task Force (1st ABTF).

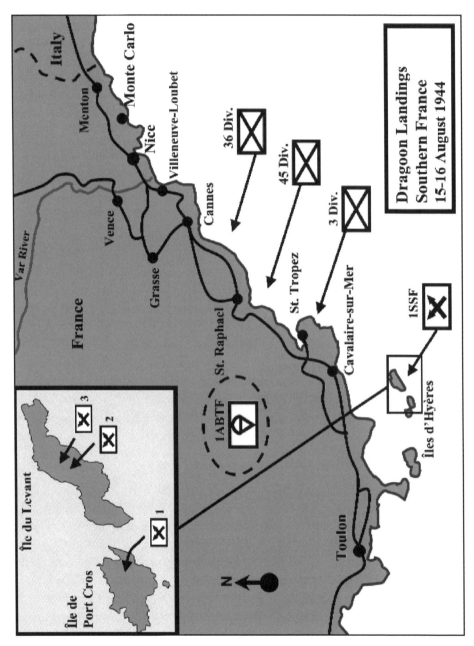

Figure 7.1   Map by Lyle Wood

In all likelihood, the First Special Service Force would have made the jump with 1st ABTF during the initial Dragoon landings were it not for the fact that the overwhelming majority of replacements received in previous months lacked any parachute training. Instead, the unit made its way to the front on foot. Taking its position on the line, the Force relieved the 2nd British Parachute Brigade on the right flank of Seventh Army. Fighting in rough terrain against scattered enemy resistance, the FSSF liberated a score of French towns and villages as the Germans withdrew toward the Italian border. By the end of the month, all three regiments were across the Var River and operating in the mountains outside Nice, advancing eastward in pursuit of the retreating German 148th Division. In many respects, the fighting in this sector represented a sideshow in the larger Seventh Army campaign, a "backwater behind the whirlpool" where the First Special Service Force, attached to Frederick's 1st ABTF, acted as a flank guard for the main advance up the Rhône valley.[27]

Casualties from the Îles d'Hyères landings had been lower than expected, and the Force was now receiving a regular stream of replacements from the training centre at Santa Maria. Upon completion of their training on 22 August, 191 American and 60 Canadian replacements embarked for France, arriving at Force headquarters toward the end of the month.[28] At Santa Maria, a further 225 American replacements provided by Seventh Army now underwent the rigorous training program in preparation for joining the First Special Service Force.

It is significant that no Canadians were included in this latest group of volunteer replacements for the unit. On 5 August, responding to a request for further Canadian reinforcements, CMHQ recommended that in view of the existing priorities between the Italian and Normandy theatres, along with the present shortage of infantry reinforcements in the Canadian Army, no further reinforcements should be dispatched to the 1st Canadian Special Service Battalion.[29] At this time the Canadian headquarters in London was beginning to take note of the impending shortage in infantry reinforcements, which was largely due to mistaken casualty forecasts and the heavy losses being suffered by Canadian infantry battalions, especially in Normandy. The situation was expected to continue until a recently-instituted program of remustering personnel from other arms, such as armour and artillery, could alleviate the shortage of infantry replacements in the Canadian Army.[30]

By mid-September, there had been no improvement in the situation. On 18 September, Walker again requested that the Canadian Army in Italy provide reinforcements. At this time, however, even Canadian infantry battalions in Italy were not receiving reinforcements, and several battalions were already considerably under-strength. For I Canadian Corps in Italy, the drive against the Rimini Line had proven a bloody and costly success—Canadian losses between 25 August and 22 September were heavier than for any period of equal length during the entire campaign in Italy.[31] Not surprisingly, Walker's request for additional Canadian reinforcements for the FSSF was turned down.[32]

In the autumn of 1944, the 1st Canadian Special Service Battalion was the only unit of the Canadian Army serving in southern France. For the time being, it continued to be administered through Canadian headquarters echelons in Italy, but this was becoming increasingly difficult due to poor communications between the two theatres. As a result there were endless problems. In Southern France, American hospitals were bewildered at the appearance of wounded Canadian soldiers wearing US Army uniforms. Not knowing what to do with these patients, some hospitals seemingly preferred to "return them to the unit to get them off their hands."[33] Reports travelled slowly back to headquarters, sometimes becoming lost in transit. At times, Canadian officers of the FSSF were sent to count graves in cemeteries and to search US hospitals in order to learn the fate of their men.[34] Communications with Italy were virtually non-existent, except by water, and Canadians noted, "It seems that as long as we are in this sector we are an isolated group and reports are bound to be slow getting to [Italy]."[35] To make matters worse, by the end of the month Walker intended to order the Force base detachment transferred from Santa Maria to France. "From now on it will be a different matter with no base in Italy," recorded a downcast entry in the Canadian War Diary, which now seems remarkably prescient.[36]

On 16 September the Canadian Army in Italy cabled CMHQ requesting relief from administration of the 1st Canadian Special Service Battalion. With Seventh Army and the Force no longer under the command of Allied Force Headquarters in Italy, the Canadian headquarters in that theatre wanted nothing more to do with the First Special Se rvice Force, hoping especially to be relieved of responsibility for providing replacements to the unit from its own depleted reinforcement pools.[37] CMHQ responded that so long as the Force stayed in its present location, Italy remained the closest Canadian theatre, and therefore the Canadian headquarters there would retain responsibility for the unit. For the time being, however, CMHQ agreed that current shortages rendered it inexpedient to divert reinforcements to the 1st Canadian Special Service Battalion until the situation in infantry reinforcement holdings had improved.[38]

As usual, Canadian and American authorities were not in communication with each other with regard to the First Special Service Force. If they had been, it would have become clear that the US Army was also in a quandary as to how to handle the unit. In June, Frederick had recommended that the Force be reorganized as a regular infantry regiment. With General Mark Clark having endorsed Frederick's suggestion, certain changes were under consideration, ranging from reorganization, to return of the Canadian element, to outright disbandment.

On 19 September, Colonel Walker responded to a suggestion by Seventh Army that the First Special Service Force might lose its Canadian component in the near future. Noting that Canadians occupied a large proportion of officer and NCO appointments in his command, Walker argued that the loss of these personnel would leave the unit without "a good basis for reorganization."[39] While recognizing that the missions assigned to the Force had not been those for which it was originally trained, Walker quoted an earlier letter to higher headquarters, written by Frederick, to argue his point:

> For the Force to continue its existence without Canadian personnel may bring about serious repercussions, particularly in Canada, where the elimination of Canadian participation in the Force might be misconstrued. The whole project is delicate and has potentialities for international complications.[40]

It is ironic to find Walker using his predecessor's own words to argue against a course of action that was recommended by Frederick himself. Walker's letter demonstrates genuine concern over the future of the Force, and in conclusion, the Force commander recommended that due to present operations, the lack of time for reorganization, and the special nature of the Force, no reorganization should be undertaken.[41] Aside from quoting Frederick's earlier letters, however, Walker presented no new arguments in favour of retaining the Force in its present status.

At the front the situation was becoming strained. German resistance remained scattered and entirely defensive in nature, and for the surviving originals of the Force, the men who had trained at Helena, the old spirit of the unit seemed to be disappearing. They found themselves assigned to a Seventh Army sideshow, and in mid-September the War Diary recorded, "Looks like the Force is getting another Anzio deal, being given a large front to hold by active patrolling ... The Hun seems to be fighting a holding war, though he has more troops than we and some really fine forts, built by the French as the southern portion of their Maginot line."[42]

By the end of September, reports noted that the Germans were "bringing in a great deal of artillery and have definite superiority numerically. Our men are confined to their fox holes and just have to take it. It is quite noticeable how many of the old original men are cracking—they have been through too much of this sort of thing, 99 days without a break at Anzio, over a month already here and no prospects of relief."[43] Simply stated, the upswing in cases of battle exhaustion in the Force was caused by the men having been in the line for too long without rest.[44] Overall, discipline and morale were described as "fair," notwithstanding a noted increase in absences without leave, with a number of these men disappearing for over three weeks.[45]

In Italy and southern France the First Special Service Force had become the unit that nobody knew what to do with, a fate hardly befitting the outfit that broke the Winter Line at Monte la Difensa and fought its way from Anzio to Rome. For Seventh Army, the issue had become whether or not to retain a specialized unit that, at this stage of the war, would be of greater value as a regular infantry regiment, complete with field artillery, motor transport and other supporting elements. At the Canadian headquarters in Italy, and CMHQ in London, the difficulty hinged on the provision of reinforcements to what was, for all intents and purposes, a formation of the US Army. In the last week of September, Brigadier-General Weeks, officer in charge of Canadian reinforcement units in Italy, again raised the issue of providing replacements to the 1st Canadian Special Service Battalion, this time voicing his concerns directly to the Minister of National Defence, Colonel J.L. Ralston.

Earlier in September, reports of an impending crisis within the Canadian Army owing to a shortage of infantry reinforcements had prompted the Minister to make a personal visit to the European theatres of war in order to discuss the situation with Canadian commanders in the field. Arriving in Naples on 26 September, Ralston discussed the plight of the Canadian Army in Italy with Brigadier Weeks and Lieutenant-General E.L.M. Burns, the commander of I Canadian Corps.[46]

On 3 October, Weeks provided the Minister with a memorandum outlining his position in regard to the 1st Canadian Service Battalion. To date, the Canadian Army in Italy had provided 24 officers and 494 other ranks to the First Special Service Force without any corresponding increase to the Army's own infantry reinforcement pools. On 18 September a request from the Force commander for further reinforcements had been refused on the instruction of General Burns, whose own infantry battalions in I Canadian Corps were already considerably under-strength. The Canadian Army had its own problems in Italy. In conclusion, Weeks presented what he considered to be the most serious difficulty in providing Canadian reinforcements to the FSSF on a continuing basis:

Reinforcements for 1st Canadian Special Service Battalion must come up to the specifications laid down for Canadian paratroops. The standard is very high and consequently the cream of the infantry reinforcements go to 1st Canadian Special Service Battalion. From the point of view of the General Officer Commanding I Canadian Corps, the divisional commanders, etc., this practice is highly repugnant as promising officers and potential NCOs are thus diverted from the fighting units of I Canadian Corps.[47]

While intended primarily for the Minister, this memorandum also circulated among the offices of CMHQ, where it crossed the desks of the Chief of Staff, Lieutenant-General Stuart; the officer in charge of administration, Major-General P.J. Montague; and Deputy Adjutant General, Brigadier-General C.S. Booth. All three officers were thoroughly familiar with the developing infantry reinforcements crisis in Italy and northwest Europe, and they were in full agreement with the arguments presented by Weeks in his memorandum.

After his visit to Italy, Ralston proceeded to London for the second leg of his tour. At CMHQ in the first week of October, Stuart confirmed in a conversation with the Minister that a shortage of Canadian infantry reinforcements existed throughout the European theatre. In reference to the 1st Canadian Special Service Battalion, Stuart strongly recommended disbanding the unit. His subsequent letter to Minister Ralston renewed old arguments in favour of a Canadian withdrawal from the First Special Service Force:[48]

**7 October 44**
**MEMORANDUM TO THE MINISTER**
**1 Cdn Special Service Battalion**

(1) I suggest that you discuss the future of 1 Cdn Spec Serv Bn with General Eisenhower when you see him next week.
(2) This unit is now serving with 7th U.S. Army in France. It is no longer under command of A.F.H.Q. and therefore should not be served by Cdn Sec GHQ 1 Ech.
(3) This unit is employed at present on the extreme right of the U.S. Group of Armies. It operates under the command of SHAEF but at such a distance from Cdn Sec GHQ 1 Ech AEF that effective Canadian administrative control is quite impossible.
(4) I would point out also that this unit appears now to be submerged to such an extent with the U.S. Forces that the value to Canada of its retention is no longer apparent.

(5)  I spoke to Eisenhower about this force some months ago but,
     as it was under command of A.F.H.Q., he was not disposed
     to do anything about my proposal that the Canadian element
     might now be disbanded. He felt also that there was great
     political value in the unique association of U.S. and
     Canadian forces as represented in the Special Service Force.
(6)  I recommend that the Canadian element of the Special Service
     Force be disbanded and that the personnel be returned to the
     U.K. for reallocation.

                              [signed] Lt-Gen K. Stuart
                              Chief of Staff
                              Canadian Military Headquarters

In accordance with Stuart's recommendation, Ralston decided to raise the possibility of disbanding the Canadian element of the First Special Service Force during his meeting with General Eisenhower on 12 October.[49] What Ralston did not know, but would soon find out, was that Eisenhower had already given the order for disbandment a week prior.

❖ ❖ ❖

Throughout September, Colonel Walker had fought to see the Force continued, arguing against Frederick's recommendation that the unit be reorganized as an infantry regiment. Nevertheless, on 4 October, Eisenhower made his decision and ordered the First Special Service Force disbanded on or before 15 November.[50] In Washington, General George C. Marshall, the US Army Chief of Staff, recommended that the reorganized all-American regiment be retained as a special operations unit, rather than wasting the extensive training and experience of the Force.[51] On 11 October, Jacob L. Devers, the commander of US Seventh Army in southern France, suggested to Eisenhower that the Canadian personnel be withdrawn and returned to their own army and the American component of the Force be retained for operations in the mountains.[52]

Post-war histories of the First Special Service Force have sometimes attributed the disbandment of the unit to a decision made by the Canadian government. On 17 October, Eisenhower wrote to Walter Bedell Smith, his Chief of Staff: "Devers [Commanding General, 6th Army Group] wants to use US Spec. Service Force in mountains. He should have it! Canadians want their men back. Col. Ralston informed me of this."[53] While this letter suggests that the Force was disbanded at the request of the Canadian government, Eisenhower had already made the decision to do so several days before Ralston even raised the issue, as indicated by his disbandment order of 4 October. The time for small, specialized units was past—Eisenhower was dealing in armies and army groups now. In light of this, the disbandment of the First Special

Service Force may best be described as an American decision that coincidentally accorded well with Canadian interests.

On 12 October the US War Department approached the Canadian Joint Staff Mission in Washington to informally suggest the disbandment of the First Special Service Force, citing a recommendation from the commander of US forces in the Mediterranean as the reason for the decision.[54] In Ottawa, NDHQ wasted no time on deliberation. The next day, the Deputy Chief of General Staff summarized the Canadian Army's position:

> The continued employment of this Special Force on operations detached from those upon which the main forces of the Canadian Army are employed constitutes a dispersement of our resources for which there is no special necessity.
>
> The reinforcement of this force constitutes an additional drain upon our best Infantry reinforcements and, in view of the heavy demands for this type of reinforcement from the Canadian Army Overseas, I suggest that we would be well advised to agree to this opportunity of minimizing our Infantry commitments.[55]

That same day, in a letter to Minister Ralston, Lieutenant-General J.C. Murchie, the Chief of General Staff, endorsed his deputy's recommendation, adding that the matter should be treated as urgent and that Washington should be advised of Canadian approval for disbandment at the earliest opportunity.[56] On 21 October, Major-General Letson of the Canadian Joint Staff Mission in Washington officially conveyed his government's approval for the disbandment of the First Special Service Force.[57]

The last weeks of the First Special Service Force serve as a depressing contrast to the unit's distinguished history up to this point. On 8 October, Lieutenant-Colonel Akehurst, the senior Canadian officer of the Force, requested and received approval for transfer back to the Canadian Army. Although both Colonel Walker and Akehurst seem to have been unaware that the Force was slated for disbandment, various disagreements between the two commanders had necessitated the Canadian's departure.

> Col. Akehurst will be missed both in the [Battalion] and the Force. He is a most capable officer and highly regarded by all ranks but he could not see eye to eye with the Force Commander and felt it was in the best interests of all concerned if he asked to be returned to the Canadian Army. The feeling of dissatisfaction within the Force is increasing rather than decreasing and involves Americans as well as Canadians.[58]

The dissatisfaction noted in the War Diary for October 1944 manifested itself in a number of ways, including a serious breakdown in the morale of the unit:

> Discipline has reached a very low plane. Men are not returning on discharge from hospital, others are taking off right from the lines. [This] is reaching rather serious proportions … The Canadians still feel their own country has let them down and written them off to the U.S. Army. They did not volunteer to become American soldiers but to join a [half and half] outfit. There is little Canadian about the Force.[59]

In October and November the number of disciplinary cases in the First Special Service Force actually began to interfere with operations in the field, as Canadian and American officers were repeatedly recalled from the front to conduct the courts martial.[60] Daily entries in the War Diary record an unending procession of disciplinary cases in these last two months in southern France, representing a disappointing final chapter in the history of the Force:

> Two more cases for F.G.C.M. [Field General Court Martial] today making nine to date, Court convenes at 1300 hrs tomorrow, 5 cases are ready for trial. The Yanks have about 40 cases for Court Martial. Although no excuse for breach of discipline, the men are getting pretty fed up and tired sitting up in the mountains day after day, it's over a month now and nearly two months steady fighting.[61]
>
> Two Canadians broke out of the stockade this evening about 2130 hrs, one had just been tried by our recent F.G.C.M., the other awaiting the next. They were able to charge the guard and get away. Our M.P.'s have never been what we consider M.P. calibre.[62]
>
> Another prison break this evening, 2 Americans, both apprehended in their old hangout down town with the same girls as well. On their return they beat up the one who gave them away, necessitating his admission to the hospital.[63]

Between January and April 1944 the First Special Service Force had conducted only 30 courts martial, but between 1 April and 13 November some 236 trials were conducted, representing an increase of nearly four hundred percent.[64] A report by the unit's assistant adjutant indicates that nearly one third of all trials involved former Rangers transferred to the Force.[65] Referring to disciplinary infractions in general and the trial of four Canadians from Third Regiment on 14 November specifically, the Canadian War Diary records: "A good many of these men do not want to be defended, preferring to take their sentence rather than go back in the line. It is noted that practically every case is from [the] reinforcements and not among the originals that came overseas with us."[66]

In spite of these difficulties, in November, Colonel Walker engaged in an almost desperate struggle to save the First Special Service Force from disbandment. To the commanding general of the Sixth Army Group, Walker described the Force as a successful experiment in inter-Allied cooperation. "The combining of American and Canadian soldiers has proved more than successful," he wrote, providing "the organization and the individual an esprit de corps which is non-existent in other organizations."[67] Disbandment would have a severe effect on the morale of the men, severing the ties of loyalty and fellowship.[68] As evidence of the destructive effect that disbandment might have on the morale of the individual soldier, Walker pointed to the experience of the Ranger replacements received by the Force:

> In confirmation of the [morale implications], the case of the remaining Rangers who were transferred to the First Special Service Force in April, 1944, is cited. The Rangers openly expressed their resentment and were very dissatisfied as a group. Of the 961 which were transferred to the Force, only 477 still remain and 84 have been tried by Court Martial.[69]

Rather than disbanding the Force and potentially losing all that had been gained in the experiment, Walker made a final plea for the unit to be returned to the United States for deactivation if there was no further need for it. "There, its mission is accomplished, the story is ended, and the individual, after his period of leave in Canada or the States, is readjusted and available for reassignment."[70] This, however, was simply not going to happen.

On 22 November, Lieutenant-Colonel Akehurst, then serving in a temporary assignment at the headquarters of Frederick's 1st ABTF, boarded a flight to London in order to protest the proposed plans for the 1st Canadian Special Service Battalion upon its return to the Canadian Army.[71] Having learned that the unit was slated to be broken up as reinforcements for the 1st Canadian Parachute Battalion, Akehurst "represented strongly" that the Canadian Special Service Battalion should be retained for a commando role similar to that for which it had been originally trained.[72]

Bringing his concerns before Major-General Montague at CMHQ, Akehurst was told that although the unit would be disbanded, "every consideration would be given to the individuals concerned."[73] To this end, Akehurst recommended that the 238 Canadians who had trained at Helena be kept together until they were needed to reinforce the 1st Parachute Battalion.[74] Integrating them into the new unit as a group, he realized, would be impossible due to the fact that approximately two hundred of the original Canadian other ranks personnel were now serving in the rank of sergeant or higher, a ratio that was far too high to allow its incorporation into the receiving unit.[75]

As for the reinforcements received in Italy, none of whom had received parachute training, Akehurst recommended: "Every effort should be made to keep these men together, except perhaps those who express a desire to return to reinforcement of that particular unit from which they were taken to come to the 1st Canadian Special Service Battalion."[76] In all of his recommendations, Akehurst acted to keep his men together in their new assignment. While CMHQ supported this idea, feeling that keeping the men together would result in the least hardship for all concerned, the commanders of the Canadian formations destined to receive the new reinforcements had other ideas.

On 1 December, Major-General Charles Foulkes, the new commander of I Canadian Corps in Italy, cabled London, informing CMHQ of his intention to employ the Canadians of the Force as individual replacements rather than attempting to attach them as a complete company to another battalion. "I would like to spread this advantage throughout the Corps," wrote Foulkes, adding that the men would make a valuable addition to tank-hunting and scout platoons in his command.[77] In the UK, similar arrangements were being made for the parachute-qualified Canadians who were earmarked for the 1st Canadian Parachute Battalion.

Meanwhile, the First Special Service Force was resting at its final bivouac area near Villeneuve–Loubet, France. At the beginning of December, rumours flew about Force headquarters regarding the impending disbandment. At this late date, however, Walker knew nothing for certain regarding the break-up, and inquiries to higher headquarters brought evasive answers from staff officers, who seemed to shy away from the question.[78] Then, on the afternoon of 5 December, Walker ordered his men to assemble for a final parade and memorial service for those killed in France. He also read aloud an official order that the Canadians of the Force were to be withdrawn to another theatre.

At this time Lieutenant-Colonel R.W. Becket, the acting senior Canadian officer, offered a few words, saying that the Canadians had enjoyed serving with the Force and that his thoughts and good wishes would always be with his American comrades. "Then the Force Commander spoke saying there was now no longer a First Special Se rvice Force, that he was sorry the break-up had to come but that it was far better to break-up with a really good reputation rather than being wiped out like the American Rangers, and that Special units were being broken up all over."[79] At this point, the order was passed for the Canadians of the Fo rce to fall out and form as a separate battalion. With that, the Canadians marched off, and the experiment of the First Special Se rvice Fo rce came to an end.

As the Canadians departed, bound for reinforcement pools in Italy and the UK, many seemed to view disbandment as the only logical result of the crippling losses sustained since the unit had entered combat almost a year before. "News of the break up of the Force was met with mixed feelings. It was a great surprise to all and it can only be estimated that 50% were glad and 50% sorry to leave."[80] For many of the surviving originals, it seemed that somewhere in the course of losing more than four hundred men killed and nearly two thousand wounded, the Force had also lost the fighting spirit that had made it unique. "I had a mixed feeling when the Force was disbanded," recalls one veteran. "There were few of the original men left that had come over with us. I would go to the various companies and perhaps find ten or twelve of the original men left."[81] Another remembers: "I hated to see the First Special Service Force disbanded, but it was almost impossible to get replacements that could fill in the gaps that came about. Replacements didn't have the spirit of the Force that we obtained during our training at Fort William Henry Harrison, Montana."[82]

The varied sentiments reflect what may be considered the mixed success of the First Special Service Force as a combined US–Canadian military formation. When the experiment came to an end on 5 December 1944, the men could look back with a great deal of pride upon their accomplishments. This sense of pride was entirely justified—the string of victories at Difensa, Anzio, Rome and southern France serve as evidence of the unit's combat effectiveness. It was at higher levels and in communications between the national military bureaucracies involved that the Force suffered its most significant setbacks. Here, administrative entanglements were encountered in legion, and the solutions enacted came too late to save the Force from disbandment.

The First Special Service Force memorial at Helena, Montana, where the American flag flies alongside the Canadian Union Jack at the monument's unveiling ceremony in 1947. The First Special Service Force is remembered for its range of skills, magnificent fighting record and spirit, and as a symbol of wartime cooperation between the two countries. *(CWM 19900261-019 #2)*

# More Men, More Guns, No Solutions

Ties of good will and fellowship became more binding by the loss of 401 Canadians and Americans killed in action, 1,805 wounded in action. The Mothers of these men know the First Special Service Force as the organization of their Sons. An ill-advised or premature de-activation would immediately give rise to questioning the soundness of the original plan for the formation of such an organization.

*Colonel Edwin A. Walker*
*Commander, First Special Service Force*
*15 November 1944*[1]

In his letter of 19 February 1944, written almost three weeks after the FSSF had arrived at Anzio, Robert T. Frederick suggested that the time had come to let the Force "pass out of existence while it is still in its prime, rather than to sustain it through a period when it will be remembered only for its faults and defects."[2] Four months later, upon his departure to command the 1st Airborne Task Force, Frederick remained convinced that the FSSF could not continue as a special organization, and he recommended that it be reorganized as a regular infantry regiment.[3] After deliberate consideration of the factors involved, Frederick, the man who had built the Force, departed with the certainty that the inherent "faults" and "defects" of the unit could not be ove rcome. Key among these difficulties, the Force commander cited the impossibility of finding suitable replacements for the Force and then training them to the standard of the original men.[4]

In hindsight, Frederick's warnings that the Force might someday be remembered only for its faults and defects seem depressingly exaggerated. Today the First Special Service Force is remembered both in Canada and the United States as an outstanding combat unit and a symbol of the lasting partnership between our two countries. In January 1944, Canadian war correspondent Sholto Watt found it difficult to describe the soldiers of the First Special Service Force: "You would not know if you were talking to an American or a Canadian from outward appearances. They all wear the same uniform … They look alike and behave alike." After speaking with these men and following them in combat, Watt explained that they were justifiably proud of their achievements, yet, "They do not brag. They are not 'tough'; they are soft-spoken, with gentle manners—and sometimes the mildest and meekest are fiercest in action. They are buoyant after a harsh and costly baptism in fire."[5] In a testament to the bravery and determination of these soldiers, the Force is today remembered as the "North Americans" who broke the Winter Line atop Monte la Difensa and continued on to become the first Allied formation to cross the Tiber bridges in Rome. The Force is not, as Frederick once predicted it would be, remembered for its faults and defects. Nor should it be.

Such recognition should not, however, preclude acknowledgement of the significant difficulties encountered in connection with the First Special Service Force. To ignore these faults would serve only to detract from the achievement of the men who built an unprecedented and remarkable Force and then held it together despite all manner of difficulties. Many of these difficulties were of an administrative nature and therefore posed no insurmountable obstacles within the Force itself, where the tendency was to ignore bureaucratic complications and defer them to higher headquarters. It was in its dealings with higher headquarters, however, that the First Special Service Force encountered more serious obstacles.

Operational histories, such as *The First Special Se rvice Force* by Robert D. Burhans, tend to overlook the unit's troubled relationship with the military bureaucracies of the United States and Canada. This is understandable given the intent to provide a detailed account of the unit's actions in the field. However, there have been a few works that consider the Force from a top-down perspective, including Stanley W. Dziuban's *Military Relations Between the United States and Canada* and James C. Nixon's *Combined Special Operations in World War II*. Both these works present brief accounts of the First Special Service Force and arrive at similar conclusions:

Th roughout its combat history, the First Special Se rvice Force engaged but little in the highly specialized types of operations for which it had been trained … Furthermore, the ve ry nature and status of the force required frequent attention of the Combined Chiefs of Staff to proposals for employment of this group of less than 2,000 men, as well as diplomatic exchanges to obtain Canadian acceptance of proposals—all in all an inordinate amount of high-level consideration in relation to the size of the force. But from the point of view of Canadian–US relations, the unique experiment was a re ma rkable success.[6]

Unfortunately, the Force could not exist without the high-level political involvement that created it. Problems with replacements, awards, and pay continued to create work at high levels and a 2,000 man unit conducting conventional operations did not warrant the attention … The inability of the Force to divorce the need for high-level involvement to solve problems was its downfall. The unit's small size, and its use in conventional operations, prohibited continued involvement by politicians and generals. The Force simply became more trouble than it was worth.[7]

On the ground, the First Special Service Force repeatedly proved itself in combat and demonstrated that Canadians and Americans could be molded into an extremely effective fighting unit. Viewed from above, the Force was a frustrating exercise in military cooperation, especially for the Canadian Army. In the American official history, Dziuban states that "complications [on the Canadian side] were handled so competently by the Canadian administrative personnel that they were hardly apparent to U.S. members of the force staff, and they had no practical impact on the force's fighting capabilities."[8] An examination of Canadian sources demonstrates, however, that these "complications" were far more difficult than previously recognized.

The amount of paperwork generated in connection with the 1st Canadian Special Service Battalion seems completely disproportionate to that of any similarly sized formation of the Canadian Army. The sheer volume of the correspondence—passing between Force headquarters, the Canadian Army in Italy, CMHQ in London, NDHQ in Ottawa, and the War Department in Washington—indicates that the problems were no minor inconvenience.

Of all the difficulties encountered by the Canadian Army in connection with its participation in the First Special Service Force, issues of manpower and the provision of Canadian reinforcements proved most problematic. From the early days at Fort William Henry Harrison to the disbandment in southern France, the question of Canadian reinforcements defied all efforts at a permanent solution. While the Force remained in Italy, proximity to Canadian reinforcement channels allowed temporary arrangements to be made, but these did not survive the move to southern France. From beginning to end, securing adequate reinforcement personnel on an ongoing basis remained the foremost problem for the 1st Canadian Special Service Battalion.

In hindsight, it becomes possible to trace these difficulties to the lack of a decided system of providing the Force with trained replacements after it entered combat. This problem, in turn, stems largely from the original nature of Operation Plough, the proposed sabotage mission in Norway, which was intended as a one-shot strike with no reinforcement implications. After October 1942, however, the cancellation of Plough had led the Force to be reorganized as an assault infantry formation. Noting this shift, the Canadians commented on Frederick's decision not to establish a system for replacing casualties in the Force: "With the nature of operations envisaged, there would appear to be a distinct possibility that the Force would be used more than once, in which case … it [seems] highly probable that further reinforcements will be required. However, the Americans do not appear to be making provision in this direction."[9] Upon the Force's reorganization for a role in sustained combat and before the unit proceeded overseas, there should have been a corresponding effort to arrange for replacing casualties. Primary responsibility for this oversight belongs to the Force commander, Robert T. Frederick, though the fact that the Canadians adopted an "ostrich policy" in December 1942, ignoring the problem and making not the slightest effort to sway Frederick from his chosen course, also deserves mention.

Without adequate means of replacing losses suffered in combat, within six weeks of its first action atop Monte la Difensa the First Special Service Force encountered serious problems, and the Canadian element was on the verge of a crisis. By the second week of January, those left standing on the front lines were forced to fight shorthanded, with one-man machine-gun "crews" and half size platoons becoming standard operating procedure.

Under these circumstances, with the Canadian element reduced to half strength, Lieutenant-Colonel Gilday recommended the withdrawal of the 1st Canadian Special Service Battalion while it could still be of service to the Canadian Army. In his reasoned opinion, some of Canada's finest soldiers were being squandered by the US Fifth Army in a conventional infantry role. Both the Canadian Army in Italy and CMHQ in London supported Gilday's recommendation. It was due only to bureaucratic procrastination and the opposition of NDHQ in Ottawa that the Canadians were not withdrawn from the Force before the unit proceeded to Anzio.

NDHQ's opposition stemmed from its concern over the potential impact on US–Canadian relations should the Canadian element be withdrawn from the Force. Had there been full communication with the American authorities, however, it would have been realized that the United States was also considering disbandment of the Force in February 1944. "It is believed," wrote Frederick on 19 February, "that the War

Department would welcome an opportunity to discontinue this special unit which has been a particular problem and unduly expensive."[10] Toward the end of the month, this possibility was being discussed between the American and British chiefs of staff, much to the annoyance of Canadian Lieutenant-General Kenneth Stuart, who concluded that the whole affair was "travelling around in circles." Writing to the Chief of General Staff in Ottawa, Stuart advised, "I do not think that anything further can be accomplished by us until we know definitely what the future of this Force is."[11] In this letter he gave voice to what often seemed official policy.

Although the future of the First Special Service Force seemed doubtful at the end of February 1944, American and British planners remained hesitant to disband the unit while it was actively engaged at Anzio. Disbanding the Force would leave the encircled Allied forces in the bridgehead even more shorthanded than they already were. Therefore, General Mark Clark, commanding the US Fifth Army, opted to increase the Force's strength by attaching remnants of the 4th Ranger Battalion as reinforcements. Rangers, Clark reasoned, were already highly trained and highly motivated volunteers and would make ideal candidates for assimilation into the Force, allowing the unit to maintain its elite status. At the same time, Clark also ordered field artillery, tanks and tank destroyers to be attached to the Force, reflecting his intent to employ the First Special Service Force in a more conventional infantry role.

The Canadians at this point also took steps to provide reinforcements to the Force, but faced additional difficulties in doing so. First, it was necessary to secure volunteers for the unit from Canadian reinforcement pools in Italy. Second, in order to maintain the elite status of the Force, it was necessary to devote special attention to the selection of these volunteers. Finally, the reinforcements had to be trained in the use of American weapons and operating procedures, a necessity that precluded their being trained in close proximity to the front lines. As Brigadier Weeks pointed out in his letter to Fifth Army, should Canadian troops unacquainted with the use of American weapons become engaged in combat, the results could be disastrous. Despite these hindrances, however, the first draft of Canadian reinforcements arrived in April 1944, just as the Force was preparing to break out from Anzio and rejoin the Fifth Army for a drive against Rome. All that had been lacking to this point was an official decision by the Canadian Army to send them.

At Anzio, Canada and the United States each adopted separate methods of bringing the FSSF back up to strength. For Fifth Army, the expedient solution was to attach the remnants of another elite unit to the Force. The Canadian Army, on the other hand, had to select replacements on an individual basis and then send these men for special training in American weapons and FSSF operating procedures.

These contrasting methods of providing reinforcements represented the best options available to each army, but they were no substitute for training men over a long period, as had been the case with the original men prior to the unit's departure for overseas in 1943. At Helena and other training facilities, soldiers from Canada and the United States had trained together for more than a year before being sent to Italy, not to mention their full-dress rehearsal at Kiska. This long period of training succeeded in establishing what Frederick referred to as "certain qualities and spirit in the officers and enlisted men," an esprit de corps that was absolutely critical to the combat effectiveness of the Force.[12] Similar results, Frederick argued, would be impossible to achieve without a comparably long period of training in which the newcomers could be indoctrinated with the spirit and trained to the standard of the original men. The experience of integrating replacements from the 4th Ranger Battalion provides some indication of the difficulty involved in attempting to do so.

Upon his departure in June 1944, Frederick recommended that the Force be reorganized as a conventional infantry regiment, noting that "the non-availability of replacements specially trained for the force, and the absence of training facilities for incoming replacements, makes it less desirable to continue the force as a special organization."[13] The last months of the unit's history bear this out, as disciplinary problems became increasingly serious in the Force as a whole and among the replacements in particular.

By October the Canadian War Diary recorded that the number of courts martial being conducted was actually beginning to interfere with operations in the field because of the number of officers required to preside over the trials.[14] Reports from the period identified an especially high incidence of AWOL among Ranger replacements to the Force, with the Canadian War Diary adding that "practically every case requiring disciplinary action is from the reinforcements, and not from among the originals that came overseas with us."[15] These reports indicate that either the replacements provided to the Force were exceptionally poor human material or, far more likely, the unit had not been allowed sufficient time to integrate these newcomers into the Force. Both Canada and the United States, however, took pains to ensure that only selected soldiers were sent as replacements, either individually or as formed units, such as the Rangers. That being the case, it seems likely that these new men were not properly assimilated into the Force. Given the limited time available for training the newcomers, it is difficult to envision how it might have been otherwise.

Upon assuming command in the summer of 1944, Colonel Edwin Walker made a concerted attempt to replace the earlier methods adopted by Frederick with more formal arrangements. In July he ordered the formal establishment of a replacement training centre at the old Force headquarters in Santa Maria, hoping to replicate what had been achieved at Helena. It cannot be certain whether his reforms would have succeeded, however, because upon the unit's departure from Italy, the First Special

Se rvice Force received no further reinforcements from the Canadian Army. All attempts by Walker to secure additional Canadian personnel were met with point-blank refusals from the commander of I Canadian Corps in Italy, whose own infantry battalions we re already fighting shorthanded. Though Walker continued his efforts to save the First Special Se rvice Force through the autumn of 1944, in October the unit was ordered disbanded.

Upon the Force's disbandment, the Canadian administrative staff of the unit offered the following in its final report to CMHQ: "The administration of the Force was no doubt a headache to all concerned from the top down, with the result that nothing was ever done to satisfactorily straighten out the problems that arose."[16] Certainly this was true in regard to replacing casualties in the Force. Veterans of the First Special Service Force point to the high rate of casualties, citing these losses as one reason the unit was disbanded. On the one hand, these men hated to leave the Force. Some expressed bitter disappointment, while others were saddened beyond words at being separated from their comrades, American and Canadian. At the same time, however, the surviving originals recognized that the Force simply could not continue as it had once been. From the Winter Line to the Mussolini Canal, Artena and Rome, the Force had established an enviable combat record—and did so despite the many difficulties encountered along the way. The problems had been of an administrative nature, pa rticularly in regard to planning and communication, between the nations involved. They should not, and have not, overshadowed the achievement of the Canadian and American soldiers who carried on in the field regardless of the events at headquarters.

# APPENDIX 1

## MONTHLY REPORTS OF THE 1ST CANADIAN SPECIAL SERVICE BATTALION

### MONTHLY REPORT OF 2nd CDN. PARACHUTE BN. (AF), WITHIN 1st SPECIAL SERVICE FORCE, 1–31 AUGUST 1942

The 1st Special Service Force is organized as follows:

- Force Headquarters;
- Three Regiments, each consisting of two battalions;
- Each Battalion consisting of three companies;
- Each Company consisting of three platoons;
- Each Platoon consisting of two sections of nine men each.

The above is known as the Combat Force. In addition there is what is known as the Service Battalion. This Battalion is responsible for the complete administration of the entire Force. There are no Canadians in this Battalion. It will be seen from the above set up that the Combat Force is entirely relieved of all fatigue, guards, etc., thus ensuring that all time of the members of the Combat Force is devoted solely to training.

The W.E. [War Establishment] of the Combat Force is 1157 all ranks. Canadian strength at 2359 hrs 30 Aug 42, 567 all ranks. From this must be deducted the fracture casualties of 31 as unlikely to remain with the Force. However, 150 Canadian personnel expected to arrive today and tomorrow will bring strength to a figure which on completion of parachute training will allow for normal wastage and ensure 50% of the Force being Canadian.

Allotment of Canadian Personnel

- Of the three Regimental Commanders one is a Canadian Officer.
- Of the three Regiment second-in-commands two are Canadian Officers.
- Of the six Battalion Commanders three are Canadian Officers.
- Of the six Battalion second-in-commands three are Canadian Officers.
- Of the eighteen companies within the Force ten are commanded by Canadian Officers.

Other Ranks are mixed throughout the three combat regiments on an equal basis with the United States Other Ranks.

It is pointed out that officer appointments are temporary, and the holding of these appointments is contingent upon their ability to capably perform their duties. When these appointments are confirmed after satisfactory performance, I [McQueen] will forward complete organization showing distribution of personnel by name.

Training

The training of the 1st Special Service Force during August has been concentrated on qualifying men in parachute jumping. This was due to the fact that the planes were only available to the Force until the 31st of August. However, permission has been granted to retain one plane for a further period to allow training of personnel who have been hospitalized and personnel who reported too late to complete training.

The following is an outline of parachute training received by each soldier:

On arrival, each man is given one week of parachute training before he makes his first jump from 1200 feet. The equipment for paratroop training is as follows:

a) Platform with three levels 2-4-6 feet above the ground. Students jump from different levels of this platform to practice proper landing and rolling. Practice from the platform also builds leg muscles.

b) Swing harness. This is a regular parachute harness suspended from a frame built 15 feet above the ground. A pulley arrangement makes it possible for a pupil to be suspended in the harness three feet above the ground. While suspended thus, the pupil can be taught how to control his parachute while going from plane to ground. He learns how to check oscillation, get his back to the wind, prevent oscillation, guide his chute to land.

c) The mockup. This is a frame structure built 4 feet above the ground and resembles the cabin of an aeroplane. In this the student is taught the proper exit from the plane.

d) The two cardinal points stressed during all phases of training are:
1. Proper exit from plane.
2. Proper landing attitude.
3. Training on all three of the above noted training devices progresses along with the long route marches and strenuous P.T. The student spends one period on each and then repeats until he is thoroughly trained in the mechanics of parachuting. When his training is complete he is tested on these training devices; if successful he is fitted to the harness of the parachute with which he will make his novice jump the following day.
4. Canadian personnel qualified as parachutists during period 6 August–31 August:

| | |
|---|---|
| Officers | 35 |
| Other Ranks | 436 |
| Total qualified | 471 All Ranks |

## Weapons Training

The force is at present issued with the following weapons:

1. Carbine, .30 cal.
2. Browning automatic rifle, .30 cal.
3. Automatic pistol, .45 cal.
4. Revolver, Colt, .45 cal.
5. Thomson sub-machine gun.
6. Browning machine gun.

All ranks who have qualified as parachutist are carrying out range practice at present with the Carbine Automatic. The remaining weapons are still in the stage of stripping-assembling and elementary handling. At present an Assault and Battle Practice Range is being constructed and will be in use shortly.

## Demolition

This subject is being stressed and at present is in the lecture and demonstration stage. The object is to train each soldier in use of demolition so that he would be capable of carrying out a task by himself if necessity arose. There is an abundance of training explosives and instructors are most competent.

## Unarmed Combat

The services of an expert from the Shanghai Police have been acquired in this subject. A class of instructors within the Force have been trained by him and several periods have been given to each regiment. The training is very popular with the troops and great keenness and interest is shown.

## Physical Training

After the soldier has qualified as a parachutist, ordinary calisthenics are stopped and physical training periods are being used in cross country runs and orientation marches, the object being to build up the legs and the arms for future ski-training. All movement between classes and return to sub-unit areas is at the double.

## Training General

As explained in a previous paragraph, members of the Force have no fatigues or duties to perform and this makes training conditions most satisfactory. The training is very rigorous and the training day commences at 0630 hrs. and lasts until 1630 hrs. In addition, Officers and N.C.O.s have classes every evening.

There is a very liberal supply of Equipment and ammunition. Each battalion has its own projection machine and lecture hall. Training films are being used to a great extent and cover practically all subjects. A chart is at present being drawn showing the complete training program, a copy of which will be forwarded on completion.

## Returned Personnel

During the period 6 August-31 August 42, 1 officer and 175 other ranks have been returned to District Depot 13. The majority of this number have been due to loss of nerve and absolute inability of the man to stand height. I have personally interviewed each man before returning and on the advice of the instructor concerned and the man's statement of his nervousness I have dispatched him to District Depot 13. It is imperative that such personnel leave this Force immediately in the interest of morale of the remainder of the troops.

## Casualties During Parachute Training

| | |
|---|---|
| Officers injured (fracture) | 5 |
| Officers injured (sprains) | 6 |
| Other Ranks injured (fractures) | 26 |
| Other Ranks injured (sprains) | 47 |

The above injuries are from a total of 1100 jumps.

Of those shown as sprains it is likely they will be able to resume training in a short period.

The figures shown as fractures are injuries which will likely preclude the personnel from further training with this force and the amount of time lost from training will set them too far behind the remainder of the Force. Also, at the time they would be able to return to duty, the training will be a standard that will require each man to be superbly fit. Therefore, Colonel Frederick and myself, in consultation with the medical officers, feel they must be returned to their former stations.

As was pointed out in my previous interim report, in this type of training we must be prepared to accept casualties of this nature and am convinced the training and instruction is of the highest quality and is in no way a reflection on the instructors.

## Morale and Discipline

The morale and discipline of Canadian personnel generally is good and individually improves as each man qualifies as a parachutist. As will be seen from Para 3. quite a number of men have been sent home as they have not had the nerve to jump. I am assured by experienced and expert United States parachute instructors that this is quite normal and to be expected. Rations and quarters are extremely good and receive favorable comment from all ranks. The relationship between Canadian and American personnel is very congenial and is most satisfactory to both Colonel Frederick and myself.

Plough Project

Owing to my injury and duties in connection with the Force, Colonel Frederick and myself have not had opportunity to discuss planning.

I am informed by Colonel Frederick that planning and collation of information is proceeding favorably in his Washington office and I will be given the complete "picture" in the near future.

In the interests of security, Colonel Frederick has ruled that the project will not be discussed at this station.

Pay

In telephone conversation with Lt.Col. Anderson I recommended that Canadian personnel be given American rates of pay. This recommendation was made after discussing the comparison of Canadian and American rates of pay with my Paymaster and Colonel Frederick and finding the American rates to be more beneficial. There has been a general feeling of dissatisfaction due to the fact the Americans receive more for doing exactly the same work. I feel that in the interests of morale it is necessary for personnel of both armies to receive the same rates of pay. I sincerely hope that an early settlement of this question can be reached so that I may inform the men what they are to receive.

Records and Administration

The paymaster and Records Sergeant have been experiencing certain difficulties obtaining accurate returns especially from the hospital. This is due to the newness of the organization and I believe that these difficulties are now nearly overcome and a satisfactory system for obtaining up to date information installed.

Administration has required a great deal of time particularly interviewing personnel wishing to return to Canada; there should be little of this in future and the time can be used for other matters that have necessarily been put aside.

## REPORT OF THE ACTIVITIES OF THE FIRST CANADIAN SPECIAL SERVICE BATTALION C.A. (A) FROM 16 DECEMBER 1943 TO 31 JANUARY 1944

Station

The Force is still in Santa Maria, Italy.

Strength

The strength of the Battalion when leaving Santa Maria for the front line on night of 21-22 of December was as follows: 44 Officers and 535 Other Ranks including 5 Officers and 125 Other Ranks in hospital.

The Force was relieved during the 16th and 17th of January, 1944 and returned to base at Santa Maria. Canadian casualties resulting from the operations were as follows:

Killed in Action: 1 Officer and 19 other ranks
Died of Wounds: 1 Officer and 1 other rank

Present strength of this Battalion is: 41 Officers (Colonel D.D. Williamson was S.O.S. [struck off strength] on January 2nd, 1944) and 516 Other Ranks. (Sgt. G.B. Gardner was S.O.S. in Africa, returned to the Unit and was T.O.S. [taken on strength]). This includes 15 Officers and 193 Other Ranks who are at present in various United States and Canadian Hospitals.

Total effective strength 26 Officers and 323 Other Ranks.

The total effective strength of Americans in the Combat Echelon of the Force is 33 Officers and 781 Other Ranks. There are 52 Officers and 616 Other Ranks in addition to the above in the Force Service Battalion. These figures do not include those in hospital.

Operations

During the period 21 December to 17 January 1944, the Force was engaged in two distinct and separate operations against the enemy.

The first operation was carried out by the First Regiment on Mount Sammucro. The top of the mountain itself was held by friendly troops. The First Regiment pushed forward by night through these friendly troops down the West shoulder of Sammucro and attacked Hill 720. The attack was made early Christmas morning. It was completely successful. Strong enemy opposition was encountered and the regiment was caught under very heavy shell fire which inflicted severe casualties. The weather was below freezing and snow covered the mountains.

The second operation consisted in taking Mount Majo. The main attack in this operation was carried out by the Third Regiment. The operation covered the 1st to 17th of January inclusive. The operation was divided into two phases:

Phase I – Push off through own troops … and seize high ground.

Phase II – Take Mount Majo and swing left (West) along high ground.

During the operation the Force was acting as flank protection for II Corps, 5th Army. The operation was a complete success and as a result of this operation and the previous operation of the First Regiment on Mount Sammucro the II Corps regained its mobility on the right flank and was able to use Mount Majo as a pivot of manoeuvre and proceed toward Cassino on a broad front from the high ground which the Force had taken …

The terrain covered by the Force in these operations was extremely difficult and mountainous. The weather was below freezing throughout and many casualties were caused by the result of frost bitten feet. Mules were used for supply and found very successful. Both Officers and men were wonderful and deserve high praise for the cheerful and efficient manner in which they performed all duties under most trying conditions.

Awards

The question of Decorations for Canadians was taken up by Colonel D.D. Williamson with Brigadier Beament. These recommendations went through to C.M.H.Q. Authority has been received to accept American awards. There are Canadians in the Force who have successfully carried out extremely hazardous tasks in the field. My position in this respect is rather difficult as Canadians naturally feel that their acts should be recognized by their own forces. It is also difficult for United States soldiers to understand why we are overlooked in this respect. The following American Gallantry Awards have been accepted on behalf of the Canadian Government as Authorized by Canmilitary Cable A 177.

Distinguished Service Cross

Lieut. Frederick Blake ATTO

Silver Star

|  | Lieut. John Donald MITCHELL |
|---|---|
| *H-205057 | S/Sgt. Leopold Henry RUDOLPH |
| *D-158509 | Sgt. Camille GAGNON |
| *M-31330 | Sgt. John Allison PARFETT |

| *M-102270 | Sgt. Ronald Alexander STIRLING |
| *D-109795 | Pte. Robert Bruce AITKEN |
| M-11122 | Sgt. (A/S/Sgt.) William C. BROTHERTON (Since Killed in Action) |
| G-60658 | Pte. (A/Sgt.) James Edward KELEHER |

\* These personnel received their decorations from Major-General Keyes,
Commanding Second Corps, Fifth Army, at a ceremony held in the camp.

## Administration

The large number of personnel in American hospitals who are spread from forward Field hospitals to General Hospitals in North Africa provide the principle [sic] administration problem. The hospitals are generally not reporting admissions, discharges, or diagnoses either to the Unit or 2nd Echelon despite instructions circulated to all concerned outlining the procedure to be followed. At the time of writing we have 222 hospital cases and of this total we are unable as yet to trace approximately 50. It is felt that some of these cases may be evacuated through American channels to the United States without the unit being advised. It is hoped that when Canadian Authorities are notified of these cases the unit may be advised in order that documents may be forwarded as soon as possible.

The Force is presently endeavouring to set up a system whereby all Force casualties will be concentrated in one general hospital. The procedure then would be for personnel on becoming fit for duty to return to the Unit direct. Canadians who are disabled or require a long period of hospitalization will be turned over to Canadian hospital Authorities for disposal through Canadian channels. This plan is meeting with a fair measure of success.

All information concerning casualties has to date been taken personally by the Administrative Officer to the 2nd Echelon as soon as it was received by the Unit. However it is anticipated that the Force may move forward shortly and this means of communication will no longer be possible. In this eventuality casualties will be reported by the most expeditious means.

## Discipline and Morale

The morale of the men after these operations is very high. They are being extremely well treated and receive ample food, cigarettes, candy and other necessaries. Their quarters are comfortable. Discipline has been excellent and no cases requiring disciplinary action have resulted from operations in the field.

The writer, whose battalion was the assault battalion on Mount Majo can personally vouch for the discipline and esprit de corps of both Canadian and United States soldiers of this Force.

## Reinforcements

In his monthly report dated 16th of December 1943, Colonel D.D. Williamson mentioned the matter of reinforcements. United States personnel in the force are being reinforced. Battle casualties have noticeably decreased Canadian personnel in the Force. Both men and Officers notice the decrease in strength and it is beginning to have a noticeable effect on Canadian morale. Rather than have the Canadian element waste away, I feel that the question of reinforcing the Battalion should be decided immediately. The Force is rapidly losing its character as the Canadian element decreases and morale is bound to be affected accordingly.

[signed] T.P. Gilday
Acting Officer Commanding
1st Canadian Special Service Bn.

## ACTIVITIES OF THE FIRST CANADIAN SPECIAL SERVICE BATTALION C.A. (A). FROM 1 NOVEMBER 1944 TO 9 JANUARY 1945

Station

The Force was relieved from the line 28–30 November 44 by the 442 Regtl Combat Team, American naturalized Japanese, and moved to a bivouac area near Villeneuve-Loubet. On 6 December the Canadian Bn. left the Force for Marseille port of embarkation and arrived Italy 9 Dec. Reinforcements received from AAI were left in Italy, the remainder originals who landed at Casablanca embarked 27 Dec 44 at Naples and disembarked Greenock, Scotland 6 Jan 45. Bn. ceased to exist on being turned over to #5 C.I.T.R. 9 Jan 45.

Strength

The strength of the Bn. on 1 Nov 44 was 49 Officers and 711 Other Ranks of whom 8 Officers and 105 Other Ranks were in hospital.

Other Ranks

Prior to our leaving Italy 31 Other Ranks who were qualified parachutists that had been [struck off strength] were [taken on strength], to accompany the U.K. draft.

Training and Operations

Training of a general nature was carried on for the week we were out of the line in France. In Italy a re-orientation training schedule in Canadian drill was carried out to be continued by #5 C.I.T.R.

Honours and Awards

The first British Decorations to be received by members of the Bn. appeared in Routine Orders in November.

| | |
|---|---|
| Lieut. (now Capt) J.A. Jennings | Military Cross |
| L86683 S/Sgt McAuley, M.F. | Dist Conduct Medal |
| M3328 S/Sgt (now Lt.) Wright, A.L. | Military Medal |
| H25272 Sgt. Prince, T. | Military Medal |

A number of recommendations that have been held pending a decision in this matter are now being submitted.

The following American Gallantry Awards were approved prior to our leaving the Force.

| | |
|---|---|
| Lt. Col. R.W. Becket | Silver Star |
| M106249 Pte. (A/Sgt.) Kineh, T.R. | Bronze Star Medal |

This makes a total of 43 U.S. Gallantry Awards to Canadians:

- 6    Distinguished Service Crosses
- 27   Silver Stars
- 10   Bronze Medals

In addition to recommendations for

- 7    Silver Stars
- 8    Bronze Star Medals
- 2    Croix de Guerre

had been submitted but not approved at the time of the breakup of this Force.

It is assumed arrangements will be made, when any of the latter are approved, to have them accepted on behalf of the Cdn Govt.

<u>Administration</u>

The period was a hectic one between moving from place to place and closing out Bn. affairs in Italy and the U.K.

The administration of the Force was no doubt a headache to all concerned from the top down, with the result that nothing was ever done to satisfactorily straighten out the problems that arose and what was done was always to the detriment of the Force.

The chief problems can be broken into two groups (1) Pay (2) Honours & Awards.

Such a Force composed of Americans and Canadians could be handled more satisfactorily if the Administration were handled by one or the other country but a joint administration did not work.

<u>Discipline & Morale</u>

The news of the break up of the Force was met with mixed feelings. It was a great surprise to all and it can only be estimated that 50% were glad and 50% sorry to leave.

Those left behind in Italy were certainly very bitter, they had volunteered to become parachutists but never got the chance and felt they were being ditched.

The U.K. draft on the other hand were very eager to get to England and to find out what was in store for them.

<u>General</u>

The last chapter of the Bn. was written at 1100 hrs on the 9 Jan 45. Major General E.G. Weeks arrived in camp and after a general salute, spoke to all ranks telling them the Bn. no longer existed, thanking them on behalf of the Chief of Staff for the work they had done, that he was sorry their exploits had of necessity always been cloaked in security but that some day the story could be told and they would get their just dues. He said he was sorry to have to tell them their para[chute] pay ceased that day and although a recommendation for its continuance had gone forward to NDHQ, he made no promises regarding its acceptance. He also stressed the need for security in so far as mentioning the disbandment of the Force in letters. The Bn. then had its last march past, Gen Weeks taking the salute, and were dismissed pending being officially taken over by #5 C.I.T.R.

# APPENDIX 2

## SELECTIONS FROM THE CANADIAN WAR DIARY

### August 5, 1942, On Train, Enroute

Wednesday — To-day across the prairies and exercise at Lethbridge. Had to make shift mess dinner tonight on board train in order to toast his Majesty the King for what may be the last time on British soil for some time. Major Keane explained the reasons and proposed the toast. God Save the King was sung. The toast in port, kindly donated by Mr. Douglass, drunk. It will certainly be the last dinner with the same personnel.

### August 6, 1942, Ft. William Henry Harrison

Combined parties at Fort William Henry Harrison, Helena, Montana, U.S.A. at 1200 hrs. Quarters are small square huts with tent tops, two or three officers to a hut. 4 other ranks, two Canadian & 2 Americans where possible. Camp has only been under construction two weeks but progressing rapidly. After a much needed shower Canadian Officers met their O.C. Lt. Col. J. G. McQueen who had come by plane the night before and officially took command. Also met Col. Frederick, O. C. Joint Forces who outlined briefly the plans for training etc.

### August 13, 1942
Lt. Col. McQueen made first jump of Canadians, got a broken ankle but enjoyed the experience of jumping. Too windy for any more to jump in afternoon.

### August 23, 1942
Pay seems to be coming to a head. A decision being required between pay at Can or American rates. Can rates only include para. pay of $60 and $30 American rates even less U.S. Income tax will be more favourable and will be suggested.

### August 24, 1942
Over 300 men were jumped this morning. Major Keane & Capt. Bourne left at 0630 by air to procure 6 officers and 150 other ranks. Major Keane to Debert. Capt. Bourne to Camp Borden.

### August 25, 1942
A bad day for jumpers, an unusually large number balked at the door. Casualties were also high compared to previous days. 37 admitted to hosp. Of 17 Canadians interviewed who wished to go back 15 had not been able to make the jump. They are now all given a second chance to try if they wish. Decided by phone today that Canadians will receive American rates of pay and pay U.S. income tax, mechanics to be worked out & paymaster advised of procedure.

### August 26, 1942
Finishing up the jumping over 400 Canadians have qualified & will now commence regimental training and shooting on the ranges. 19 other ranks returned to #13 D.D. Most of them so scared they could not leave the plane.

### August 28, 1942
All companies in force were instructed chiefly in all three American weapons mainly (1) Machine Gun (2) The Garand M 1 rifle (3) The Browning Automatic Rifle. One regiment finished up their basic work on the rifle range and other company finished work on the pistol range. All Canadians were fitted for the new American uniform and all personnel of the force were shown several army instructional films.

### September 4, 1942
Lieut. Storrs, A. T. made his first jump this morning receiving knee injury. Three O/Rs who had stated they couldn't jump to Capt. Ellis their instructor found themselves unexpectedly in the air over the training field. They all jumped successfully.

### September 5, 1942
Telegram from Adj. Gen. selects Lt. Col. McQueen for special duty in Washington and appoints Major Williamson Commanding Officer and Lt. Col. effective date of Transfer. Transfer of command took place in the afternoon.

### September 15, 1942
The regular Canadian Mid-Month pay parade was held after supper as yet no word received on the new proposed pay procedure. Dissatisfaction general over non-receipt of parachute pay.

### September 21, 1942

Training this week will for the most part be reviewing the last 7 weeks, preparatory for examinations to be held next week. There will be in addition night schemes and a march and climb to the top of Mt. Helena.

### September 24, 1942

Instructions in the use of Foreign weapons being given. The whole force was paraded to the ranges at 2030 hrs. to see the firing of 3 rounds of tracer bullets from a German Anti-Tank Gun.

### September 29, 1942

Lt. Col. Spink called Capt. Biscoe this morning and advised him that no additional pay had yet been authorized for this Battalion and that American rates had not been authorized. Lt. Col. Williamson phoned Lt. Col. McQueen but nothing definite to report so it was arranged to call all Canadians together before pay parade tomorrow and explain the situation to them. They are expecting parachute pay and it is going to be pretty tough trying to explain that nothing has been authorized after eight weeks down here.

### September 30, 1942

All Canadian personnel were paraded to the theatre at 1645 hours and Lt. Col. Williamson explained the whole pay situation to them, all that had been done and reminded them of the form they signed before coming here that they would accept Canadian rates of pay and that he could make no promises as to what if any additional pay would be authorized or when.

This is probably one of the finest groups of men ever assembled, their morale has been extremely high. Despite the arduous training they came into the theatre singing and laughing but left a very sullen and sober bunch. There were very few complaining but their morale has been very obviously shaken ...

It is earnestly hoped that this situation will be rectified and in this connection it is strongly recommended that Parachute Pay at the rate of $100.00 per month for officers and $50.00 per month for other ranks be authorized at the earliest possible date to be retroactive to the date personnel were taken on strength of the 2nd Cdn. Parachute Bn. — The Lord help us if the situation is not cleared up before the mid month pay.

### October 5, 1942

This week will be mostly on demolitions for a group of picked officers who will later act as instructors. There will be radio instruction given to nine men per Company.

Parachute jump training for about 36 who had not yet jumped will be given.

There will be instruction of flame thrower, the prevention of forest fires and throwing of hand grenades.

Some night practice placing and exploding charges while controlled charges were set off near by to give the effect of active conditions.

Everyone must go over the obstacle course each day.

### October 6, 1942

The officers, picked for advance study in demolitions, left at 0700 hours to blow a bridge near Butte returning for dinner and left again at 1300 hours by truck for Libby, about 300 miles north west of here, where they will blow an old bridge about 3,150 spans ... The first regiment left at 0700 hours on a force march 36 miles — to Marysville and return — full equipment plus two improvised ski poles.

**October 7, 1942**

The second regiment left at 0700 hours for forced march to and from Marysville. The officers' demolition class returned late, had good experience as they were able to try a different method of placing charges on each of the three spans of the bridge. Some damage was caused to nearby houses and a number of windows were broken in Libby.

**October 9, 1942**

The best group of the officers' demolition class left to blow an old smoke stack this morning. The mill caught fire after the demolition and required guards all night to see that it did not spread.

**October 11, 1942**

Cooler, with occasional thunderstorms. The Second Regiment left by truck at 1600 hrs for Adel Montana, to return by a cross country foot march about 45 miles over very rugged country, to be done in five days.

**October 13, 1942**

An unlucky day. An American soldier was shot through the head on the range this morning during section combat problems and died this afternoon.

**October 15, 1942**

The First Regiment left this afternoon by truck to Adel for their march to Nelson tomorrow.

Another pay day and still no word of additional pay. The men took their pay without saying a word, but it is quite evident that they are really mad and a few paraded to their Company Commanders wishing to be returned to Canada. They are quite satisfied with other conditions but it again reverts to the fact they cannot work in exactly the same things and receive different rates of pay; it's contrary to human nature and this situation cannot go on much longer.

**October 18, 1942**

A perfect day, hardly a cloud to be seen. A number of officers out hunting deer and elk. Lt. Col. Scott and Capt. Martin from the Battle Drill School in British Columbia arrived by plane to compare ideas and look over the set up.

**October 21, 1942**

Colonel Frederick addressed all officers at 1830 hours in the theatre regarding discipline and difficulties occurring in differences of Canadian and American procedure in drill, discipline etc. He praised the Canadians for the way they had fallen in with American ways, especially since they were obliged to adopt more American customs than Americans had to adopt Canadian customs. Discipline was not up to the standard and the onus of correction was placed on the platoon commanders.

**October 24, 1942**

At 1430 hours a demonstration in Battle Drill was put on for all officers by a platoon especially trained by Capt. Martin. Captain Martin having returned to Vernon B.C., the demonstration was directed and explained by Lieut Cotton. It showed methods of attack and infiltration by platoon and section and reorganization on the completion of assignment. It finished with the attack on and capture of a pill box by means of torpedo, smoke, gun cotton and grenades and reorganization beyond the pill box.

**October 27, 1942**

The First Regiment left at 0440 hours for the vicinity of Nelson. One Battalion will be given the task of defending York Bridge at all costs until sundown, the other Battalion will try to dislodge them and capture the bridge.

## October 30, 1942

Captain Biscoe received a telegram from the Paymaster General approving parachute pay at the same rate as flying pay. It was a ve ry great disappointment especially from the men's point of view as they get less than half their American friends' parachute pay. We now have Canadian Staff Sergeants drawing less money than the American privates under them. These men were sent down here to work and live under exceptional circumstances and there seems to be a lack of understanding in this regard some place.

Lt. Col. Williamson decided to have all Canadian personnel assembled and tell them what they were to receive, and in order to try to ease their expected disappointment all acquittance rolls were destroyed and new ones prepared giving each man an additional $25.00 as tangible proof that something had at last been done.

## November 2, 1942

A record number of A.W.Ls and several charges of drunkenness. This seems more a result of having a little extra money at their disposal than disappointment at the amount of parachute pay authorized. On the whole the men accepted the extra .75 cents a day very well but are keenly disappointed that it was not equal to the American parachute pay.

Training this week will cover bayonet drill, firing of L.M.G., Thompson S.M.G., pistol, rifle and motor school. Ski training (8 hours by the end of the week for eve ryone) the daily run of the obstacle course.

## November 23, 1942

Training continues with a view of developing all units from the section to the regiment into a highly mobile organization prepared to accomplish successfully the following types of combat MISSIONS:
   a) Operate against vital military and industrial targets.
   b) Operate as an overland training force infiltrating, penetrating or encircling deep into enemy territory to destroy important targets.
   c) Operate as a spearhead in forcing strongly fortified localities with the expectation of early support from friendly troops.
   d) Operate in cold or mountainous regions to accomplish any or all of the possible missions.

## December 4, 1942

The inspecting officers left by plane this afternoon. They remarked favourably on how Canadian Officers had adapted themselves to existing conditions. At 1830 hours the Rev. W. A. Eckel, who has spent 10 years in Japan talked to the officers on the Japanese, their ideas, hopes of world domination, their plans and preparations for war and methods of fighting. He concluded by stating that their foremost General Yamitsa was in command of their northern division and might be contemplating attacking the United States through Alaska, Alberta and into Montana. His talk included much flag waving but was very entertaining.

## December 10, 1942

97 O/Rs arrived from the 1st Cdn Parachute Bn, Ft. Benning, Capt. Becket in charge, at about 1400 hours. A good looking group of boys and really looked smart marching through camp. All but one are qualified parachutists, some qualified in both England and U.S.A.

## December 14, 1942

Training for the two regiments in camp will continue as in the last few weeks. A new and rather elaborate combat range is being constructed at the back of the fort, it will have many moving targets and is about 3 miles long.

### December 26, 1942

14 Canadians, formerly of the 1st Canadian Parachute Bn who had previously qualified as parachutists in England, jumped to-day in order to qualify the "American Way".

Training continued as per schedule with some companies starting outdoor living exercises by going on overnight bivouacs, building their own shelter and cooking own rations.

### January 11, 1943

Training this week includes for the 1st and 2nd Regiments, Combat principles on skis with motors. They will also stage a three day field exercise. The 1st Regt. taking the offensive, the 2nd Regt. the defensive, the problem to be issued by the training officer. Platoon Commanders are to take their platoons over the combat course and will be examined on how they handle themselves and their men under the various conditions with which they will be faced.

### January 18, 1943

Really cold, the temperature almost forgot to stop falling last night, 38 below here and 46 below at Blossburg. The person who said you don't feel cold in a dry climate won't be appreciated here.

### January 21, 1943

This morning started at 22 below with an increasing wind, much snow and falling temperature. This afternoon the warning went around that the temperature would go to 35 below with a high wind, personnel being warned to watch their hut fires and fasten down any loose equipment. Training is practically at a standstill as the men haven't the equipment for this severe weather. A 100 yards into the wind is enough to produce many frost bitten faces. The next Yankee to refer to Canada as a land of cold, ice and snow is likely to be shot.

### January 26, 1943

In the evening Col. Adams spoke to the officers regarding the planning required in preparation to our moving out so that when the warning order is issued everyone will know what must be done and will waste no time doing it.

### February 1, 1943

Continues mild. Training for the week will cover: 1st Rgt., Field Fortifications in the snow, Rifle, L.M.G., Mortar, and Antiaircraft firing, platoon combat proficiency tests, instruction on anti tank rocket; 2nd Regt. will have field exercises from Tues to Sat inclusive; 3rd Regt., Field Fortifications in snow, a field exercise, marksmanship with Rifle, L.M.G. and Mortar.

### February 13, 1943

Bright and mild. Ranges in use all morning. Some very heavy demolitions back of camp that really shook the building. The regular afternoon inspections and so to town.

### February 15, 1943

Cooler but continues bright. Training like last week is general brushing up. The ranges are controlled by the 2nd Rgt, which will use them very consistently throughout the week; they will have over 100,000 rounds of ammunition mostly rifles, L.M.G., pistol (.45) T.S.M.G.

### February 25, 1943

A few more companies off for their 15 miler this morning, others went over the obstacle course, the first time it has been used since last fall. Morale has been noticeably low lately probably entirely due to our in-action, everyone expected to have been far from here by now.

### March 1, 1943

Bright and cold. Major Becket phoned from Ft. Benning that ve ry few men and no officers volunteered to come to this Bn from the 1st Bn. Apparently the last lot that came have not been writing very favourable letters back. Our inaction is getting everyone down.

### March 7, 1943

A very quiet day in camp. Major Becket arrived from Ft. Benning with 12 O/Rs, the only volunteers for this unit. Since he expected to get 6 officers and 125 O/Rs the result was very disappointing. A report as to the reasons for failure was submitted to Lt. Col. McQueen.

### March 23, 1943

In the afternoon the 3rd Co. 1st Regt put on an attack on and capture of a pill box for all Force personnel. They used about 13,000 rounds of ammunition, flame-thrower and 60 mm mortars. Lt. Roll again took the officers conference talking on characteristics of German military tactics.

### March 24, 1943

The 1st Regt was out all day on a battle problem. Everyone is busy packing having boxes built etc to be ready for the long hoped for "alert".

### March 31, 1943

Col. Adams had a meeting of staff officers and told them a definite move was pending soon but unlikely to go beyond the continental limits of the U.S.A. All personnel must be prepared to leave on short notice and therefore all preparations must be completed immediately.

### April 3, 1943

In the morning a rehearsal of the guard of honour for Brigadier Weeks, G. S. who arrives from Ottawa tomorrow night for a few days. The 2nd Coy, 1st Regt commanded by Lieut Shaw, Canadian Army, was chosen for the guard of honour. Regimental inspections in the afternoon. Col. Adams inspecting the Service Bn.

### April 5, 1943

Brigadier Weeks inspected the various phases of training and at 1300 hrs addressed the Canadian officers asking for any questions of a general nature that required to be cleared up. He said that the General Staff were well aware of the difficulties that had arisen and been surmounted and he was ve ry pleased with what he had seen and knew much work must have been put in to achieve the results. All officers were introduced to him by Lt. Col. Williamson. He then gave a short talk to all Force officers Canadian and American. Colonel Frederick then took over to say we were to move to the east coast, the tentative date for moving being Monday April 12. We would undergo Amphibious training and would likely have 3 or 4 moves before going overseas.

### April 7, 1943

Bright and warm, everyone putting the finishing touches to their packing and movement preparation generally. Loading of freight begins tomorrow. Each company is required to furnish two men for each of the remaining three nights to act as special M.Ps in town. The Force does not want to leave a bad reputation as it has been good to date, but apparently fear is held that the boys may really cut loose. They made a very good start last night after the parade.

### April 24, 1943, Camp Bradford, Norfolk, Virginia

The Force colours made their first appearance, a good looking flag, red background, a spread eagle in the centre with a shield in its crest with a dagger on it. One claw clutches an olive branch, the other a number of arrows. A ribbon underneath with First Special Service Force, another in the eagles beak for the Force motto when decided upon. Passes were from 1600 hrs to midnight.

### May 7, 1943

Very warm. Training mostly at the beach for swimming and rubber boat drill. The 3rd Regt. went to Fort Story this morning to examine their coast defenses.

### May 25, 1943

Lieut Colonel Williamson left with Colonel Frederick for Ottawa at 1200 hours today to keep an appointment with the Chief of the General Staff to iron out some ve ry pressing problems of the policy of the 1st Canadian Special Service Bn.

### May 26, 1943

Cool and damp. A number of Americans repoted for duty with the Force, they are mostly parachutists who were on a draft overseas, missed the boat and have been reassigned to the Force.

### May 27, 1943

Col. Williamson and Col. Frederick returned at 1600 hours having been grounded nearly 24 hours in Montreal. Their mission considered most successful, having also conferred with Major General Letson and Brigadier Weekes D.C.G.S. The C.G.S. introduced both Col. Williamson and Col. Frederick to the Prime Minister who called while they were present. Col. Williamson brought back the authority changing our designation from 2nd Canadian Parachute Bn to 1st Canadian Special Service Bn.

### May 28, 1943

Cool and dull. An officers meeting at 1830 hours. Col. Frederick explained the reason for the many changes in training had been the changing of the mission for the Force. He said that one day in Washington within 14 hours the Force had been assigned to 6 different missions. At present the Force was not assigned to any mission but it was sufficiently trained that it must expect to be alerted at any time and leave with little notice. He also said that some officers were working by the clock and that they must remember they are on duty 24 hours a day 7 days a week and should not head to town as soon as training was finished if they had any unfinished work, or preparation to do.

### July 1-3 1943, Enroute

All trains arrived in San Francisco Saturday, the 2nd Regiment arrived first at noon, the Service Bn last about 0200 hrs Sunday A.M. Trains went down to the pier, troops and equipment unloaded and loaded onto a ferry which took them to Angel Island where they were bedded down at Camp McDowell.

### July 4, 1943, Fort McDowell, Angel Island

Reveille at 0600 hrs and a full days work got under way at 0700 hrs. Angel Island rises steeply out of San Francisco Bay. It is near Alcatraz and we can see both San Francisco and Golden Gate Bridges. The camp is built on one side and is quite comfortable although the Force rather overcrowds it. After dinner Major General Corlett spoke to the officers telling a bit about our mission. He commands the expedition which will also include a Canadian Infantry Brigade, good news to our officers.

### July 11, 1943, San Francisco

Still at the pier this A.M. leaving about 0830 hours, circled Alcatraz a couple of times and instead of going out went up the bay under the Oakland-San Francisco bridge and anchored. The convoy of 7 transports and 4 destroyers weighed anchor at 1730 hours passed under the Golden Gate bridge about 1900 hours and by 2100 hours were beginning to roll and the beginning of the seasickness.

### July 16, 1943, At Sea

At 2100 hours Lt. Col. Burhans S-2 (Intelligence) discussed the attack on Attu. The big point was inability of the invaders to find out where the Jap fire came from due to their excellent camouflage.

### August 5, 1943, Amchitka, Alaska

Foggy and fairly cold. Training for the period 5th to 14th August has as its objective,

- a)   Improve ability for sustained operation in the field under adverse conditions.
- b)   Improve ability to operate over terrain typical of this locality.
- c)   Improve combat firing technique.
- d)   Improve amphibious technique.

### August 16, 1943

Speculation is rampant as to whether any Japs other than a handful are still on the island. If there are not, the navy, who have claimed to have such a tight ring about Kiska, will have some explaining to do.

### August 18, 1943

This must just about wind up the Kiska invasion as it is quite evident there are no Japs left in these parts. The Administration sections were warned to be ready for a move back to the U.S.A. probably before the end of the month. There is no further need for the Force to remain here and the original plan was to relieve the Force as soon as the Commanding General A.T.F. #9 thought it was safe. It certainly seems safe enough now. Radio Tokyo asked tonight why Secretary Knox was so quiet about the invasion of Kiska. As if they don't know. All are waiting for Washington's announcement and Tokyo's reply.

### September 14, 1943, Ft. Ethan Allen, Vermont

The holiday makers continue to return and are busy sorting their equipment and settling down. Lt. Col. Williamson and Capt. Biscoe returned from Ottawa at night having seen Major General Letson, Major General Murchie, Brigadier Gibson, Brigadier Roome, Brigadier Mortimore, Brigadier Noel, Colonel Chesley, Colonel Delalanne, Colonel Spink and Colonel Coleman. Arrangements were made to get as many reinforcements as possible from the transit camp at Windsor, Petawawa, Camp Borden, and M.D. #4, those available to be transferred to D.D. #4 for selection. A request was made to have existing pay arrangements apply in the U.K.

### September 21, 1943

Four officers, Capt. McWilliams, Lieuts D'Artois, MacDonald and Tomlinson were returned to #4 D.D. this afternoon. Also Pte. Long who was injured on Kiska and will only have partial use of his hands. Lt. Col. Morrisey phoned from Ottawa that a maximum of 90 O/Rs were available as reinforcements. Arrangements were made to have them assembled at #4 D.D. for selection Sunday. Lt. Col. Gilday to be selecting officer. There are still about 175 absent without leave, 50 Canadians. This is getting to be a habit and little done to get the causes cleared up.

### November 5, 1943, En Route

A grand morning bright warm and calm. We caught up to and passed a convoy of about 12 ships including a small aircraft carrier at 0800 hrs. At about 0900 hrs above a low hanging mist the tops of buildings at Casablanca began showing up; as the sun cleared up the mist the whole city came into view.

### November 6, 1943

The 2nd Regt and Service Company to proceed to Oran tomorrow, the 3rd Regiment the next day. The train was quite a sight, there were 2 day coaches for officers, one fairly modern European style aisle down the side, and 12 compartments off it, supported by 2-4 wheel trucks the other smaller same style and only 4 spoked wheels, 4-8 officers per compartment. The cars for the men attracted the most attention; they are called 40 and 8s from a statement on each car reading 32-40 Hommes or 8 Chevaus; 24 men assigned per car plus equipment.

### November 19, 1943

Bright and quite warm, saw the Isle of Capri and in the distance Mt. Vesuvius at 0730 as mist hung low over Naples and did not see much of the city until we passed Capri; it is very spread out all about the bay … Our destination was an Italian Military Academy built in 1935 sponsored by the Bank of Naples in memory of Costenzo Cianno, father of Count Cianno. The Germans had used it for the past 3 years and did a very thorough job of willful destruction before leaving all windows broken, plumbing destroyed and walls smashed but even so one could see it had been a very fine school.

### November 22, 1943, Santa Maria, Italy

A patrol made up of representatives of regiments and Force H.Q. left in the afternoon to operate over the hills assigned as our mission to clear of German opposition. These hills are strongly and stubbornly defended, are holding up the progress of the 5th Army.

### November 24, 1943

Bright and cool in the morning, rain and raw by noon. Col. Williamson was at the front in the afternoon [close to] the hill his regt. has been assigned to capture. It is very high and rugged and promises real difficulties in getting up even without German opposition. The Artillery are throwing a great number of H.E. shells at it.

### November 27, 1943

Wet and raw, the Force was scheduled to leave to-day on their mission but was put off until Monday. The 1st and 2nd. Regts have been assigned one hill each to capture. The 1st Bn 3rd Regt. is reserved, the 2nd Bn 3rd Regt to carry supplies and evacuate the wounded.

### November 29, 1943

Dull and wet and warmer, a 24 hour delay announced at noon which will give everyone time to get their breath. The operation order did not come down from Force H.Q. until this morning making it almost impossible to be ready by 1600 to-day. Hard to understand why it should be so late being distributed other than this is the First Special Service Force, and things are done that way.

### December 3, 1943

Reports from the front advise that the 2nd Regiment took their objectives one and one half hours ahead of schedule but lost one hill during a counter attack during the day. Casualties are fairly high.

### December 5, 1943

Bright and warmer. Reports from the front seem to confirm the rumour that Lt. Colonel MacWilliam was killed, a very popular officer and a real loss to the Battalion.

### December 7, 1943

Bright and fairly warm. Another list of wounded received. It is known that 115 have been evacuated through one advance evacuation hospital to Naples, others being brought in as fast as they can get them down. It takes 10 men to bring down one stretcher case and takes them the best part of a day, the mountain is so precipitous, all able bodied men are needed for combat. The Air Corps has made one or two unsuccessful attempts to drop supplies of food, water and ammunition to advance groups who are right out and the supply lines can't get to them.

### December 9, 1943

The 2nd Regiment began to arrive about 0200 hours, the showers were in operation as were the kitchens. The men though extremely tired perked up considerably after getting cleaned up and a hot breakfast. The 3rd Regiment and Service Battalion arrived during the morning and by noon practically everyone who was not a casualty had arrived …

The chief stories were: 1. The spirit and determination of the men on the attack and their superiority man to man over the Germans, 2. The large number of German shells that were duds, and 3. Their respect for the machine pistol which was used more as a signal for laying of deadly mortar fire than as a killing weapon although it was used a lot by German snipers.

### December 10, 1943

Rain during the night, a fair day. The last patrols arrived in the evening and a Force muster was called, also pay for those present to receive it. The result of a muster from a Canadian point of view disclosed 26 killed (2 officers and 9 other ranks buried, 15 other ranks seen killed), 86 wounded, 1 missing, 41 suffering from fatigue, a total of 154 casualties; some fatigue and lightly wounded are already returning to duty. At this rate the Canadian element which is not being reinforced will not survive many like missions; the Americans have requested reinforcements from 5th Army.

### December 11, 1943

Colonel Williamson left with Major Biscoe in the afternoon to inquire about the possibility of acquiring reinforcements and if a decision had been reached re honors and awards. Brigadier Beament was away, both matters to be taken up on his return.

### December 14, 1943

Bright, warm in the sun. Another trip to Naples, Brigadier Beament was away and Colonel Williamson explained our position re honors and awards and reinforcements to Colonel Tow; the former has created an embarrassing situation in so far as the Americans are ready to award theirs and we can give no answer regarding our own. Some Canadians in hospital have been given Purple Hearts, these can only be souvenirs at present. The latter is a problem to be referred to the Brigadier. Brigadier Beament returned later in the afternoon from the 8th Army front, said he expected an early discussion on awards and would have no part of the reinforcement angle in view of the C.G.S. decision not to reinforce. It now becomes a matter to be taken up through Washington for N.D.H.Q. to decide whether we are to be reinforced or continue to be a wasting asset and withdraw from the Force when the Battalion peters out.

The Brigadier approved Colonel Williamson's recommendation, appointing 8 of our men to the rank of Lieut. They all did a fine job through the operation and would fill vacancies created by officer casualties.

**December 19, 1943**

Bright and warm. News brought in from the front reveals the Germans are retreating toward Cassino, Mt. Sammucro is now in our hands as is S. Pietro which means a new mission, the Force is warned for 2200 hours but not likely to move before tomorrow night, they are to establish an advance base at S. Pietro; however all decisions await the return of a recce party that went out this A.M. and are due back late this evening. The recce party reported part of our bivouac area still in enemy hands very hard to tell where the front line is and there is heavy artillery fire all around this area.

**December 20, 1943**

Bright and fairly warm. The Force will not move before to-morrow morning. Our mission is a spear head to a general 5th Army advance, the hill assigned is higher than the last one. The Force is operating on the right flank of the 36th Division. The 6th Corps are on our right. The objective will provide O.P.s for the area right up to Cassino, but are presently believed to be right to the sphere of enemy artillery fire. Our ability to hold the objectives is very much dependant on other elements of the attack, taking out Germans O.P.'s.

**December 21, 1943**

The Germans are raising hell with their artillery and mortar fire, and also employing some dive bombers. The fight for Cassino will be a tough one for us. The Regiments moved off on schedule in the pouring rain.

**December 24, 1943**

Rain continues and cold. One hundred men from the Service Battalion were sent to the front in response to a phone call this morning. They are required for pack duties.

Christmas eve spent at the front preparing for an early morning attack. All the men's rucksacks with dry underwear, shelter halves, etc have been taken to the front, they must be expecting to be there for some time.

**December 25, 1943**

Two German prisoners were taken a day or so ago, by other troops. Under the influence of Vino, one, a Pole, was quite talkative, said they hated their officers and pointed out the officers' billets on the map, a good artillery barrage was laid on the spot just in case.

**December 26, 1943**

Ve rywindy, wet and raw. Unconfirmed reports from the front, 1 U.S. officer approximately 20 other ranks killed in yesterday's engagement. Tremendous quantities of Christmas parcels and mail have been arriving during the last few days. The letters are going on to the front, the parcels kept for the men's return.

**December 31, 1943**

A miserable wet cold day. The new U.S. reinforcements went on a route march this afternoon. A quiet and sober New Years eve.

A request for 50 men from the Service Battalion to be pack carriers was received during the evening from the forward base. The 3rd Regiment should be starting off on their mission very soon now. This ends another year, it has been a very eventful one for the Force which covered a good 20,000 miles during the past 12 months, a long way before getting into real combat, and at that finds itself in a definitely secondary theatre being used as glorified infantry and all the special training going by the boards, except possibly for mountain climbing. The question that can only be answered in the new Year is "Will the Force be permitted to peter out here, which it is doing rapidly, or will it be employed in a new theatre where some of its specialized training can be used to advantage?"

**January 1, 1944**

Colonel Williamson came in from the front in the afternoon, he had been called into the Force Commander's C.P. in the morning, shown statements signed by some of his regimental officers, declaring lack of confidence in him as a result of the La Defensa operation four weeks ago. Not one officer said a word to him about it and he was given no intimation that they lacked confidence in his leadership until he was handed the declarations four weeks after. He felt that he might have been told. He was asked how quickly he could be packed and leave as he had been relieved from his command. He had no opportunity to defend himself — a most unfair way to handle the case and especially to treat the man who had helped to create the Force and who has been at the helm through its many turbulent and trying times.

**January 3, 1944**

Colonel Williamson left the Force at noon to report to Brigadier Beament, Lt. Colonel Gilday assumes temporary command until Lt. Colonel Akehurst is released from hospital unless instructions to the contrary are received from N.D.H.Q.

**January 5, 1944**

Bright and cold. The Force is in action with some casualties although the opposition is not so severe as formerly and they only have one objective left to take, this action is expected to-night.

**January 7, 1944**

Bright and cool. Casualty returns from the front include a number of frost bitten feet. There is no information of the fighting other than everything is going satisfactorily.

**January 8, 1944**

Continues bright and cold. Today's casualty return from the R.A.P. lists nearly 100 names half of them frost bite and exposure, the rest battle casualties. The weather in the hills is very cold, high wind and snow. German resistance is quite severe, artillery and mortar fire still taking its toll.

**January 9, 1944**

Warmer, some rain in the morning, snow in the hills. Today's Force casualty return has 122 names again nearly half are frost bite and exposure. There soon won't be much left of the Force if casualties keep on at this rate. Captain Perry is reported killed, Lieutenant Atto seriously wounded.

**January 10, 1944**

Mild and damp. News from the front is bad, the Force commander now commands Task Force B of which the First Special Service Force forms a part. The Force is being thrown into one action after another with only a handful of able-bodied men left and no sign of their being relieved. Seventy-three names on to-days casualty report, 40 frost bitten feet. Those returning to camp on light duty say it is really rugged and they are all played out. Three weeks to-morrow since they left here.

**January 13, 1944**

Bright and warm. Lt. Colonel Gilday returned from the front to find out what was going on, he had heard of Colonel Williamson's release, but had no particulars. What's left of the Force continues to do a good job, but all are thoroughly tired out.

**January 15, 1944**

Bright, and cool wind. Lt. Colonel Gilday discussed with Brigadier Beament our status in view of our greatly depleted strength, we have nearly 300 in hospital and on light duty and hard to say how many of the rest are really fit. A cable was sent to General Stuart for consideration.

### January 20, 1944

Clear and cool. A final list of deceased personnel from the last missing was taken to Avellino.

At 1400 hours, Major General Keyes, commanding 2nd Corps presented American Gallantry Awards to both Canadians and Americans of the Force and in a short address, commended the Force on the excellent job it did and hoped to have it attached to his Corps on another operation. The following Canadians received the Silver Star:

Lieutenant J. D. Mitchell
H-205057 S/Sgt. L. H. Rudolph
D-158506 Sgt. C. Gagnon
M-31330 Sgt. J. A. Parfett
M-102270 Sgt. R. A. Stirling
D-109795 Pte. R. B. Aitken

Four American, 1 officer and 3 other ranks completed the list.

### January 23, 1944

Cool, and cloudy, a little rain. A memorial service was held for those who died during the last operation, all personnel attended at 0900 hours. Passes were issued to the nearby towns in the evening, the officers had quite a party, a good quantity of liquor was presented for use in officer's clubs, rather a change of policy for the U.S. Army which is a "dry" army. There was also a turkey dinner.

Most of the remaining deceased's effects were taken to Avellino.

### January 25, 1944

Partly cloudy and raw. Lt. Colonel Akehurst, Lt. Colonel Gilday and Major Biscoe went to Forino to say good bye to Colonel Williamson who expects to leave for U.K. in a day or two.

It is sincerely regretted that he should be leaving the Force and certainly under conditions which he did not deserve.

### January 30, 1944

Bright, and cool wind. The Force left by truck convoy for a staging area in an olive grove 2 miles above Pozzuoli, pitched their pup tents and bivouacked over night.

The Force Commander was promoted to Brigadier General today.

### January 31, 1944

Bright and warm. Movement by foot began soon after noon with full pack to Pozzuoli, where the Force embarked on 4 L.S.Ts. and 7 L.C.Is. These craft left port at 1800 hours, joined a large convoy in the bay and set out for the Beachhead during the evening.

### February 5, 1944, Anzio Beachhead, Italy

The enemy advanced two kilos, then retired to their original positions. Our boys made an unsuccessful attempt to blow a German O.P. Three patrols went out, one with explosives was turned back, the others were to cause a diversion. One officer and 5 other ranks did not return. We have had several missing to date.

### February 7, 1944

Enemy artillery hit one L.S.T. and one L.C.I., sinking one, also set 5 trucks on fire and hit an ammo dump at Nettuno. 68 of our men arrived for duty, being discharged from hospital, had to wait 4 days for shipping space out of Naples. One Canadian officer and 6 other ranks amongst them, they left for the front as soon as they had sorted their equipment and clothing.

### February 16, 1944

All hell broke loose about 0600 hours when the Germans let loose all their artillery and mortars and ours replied. They attacked all along our line, most strongly on the left flank held by 1st Bn., 3rd Regt. It was apparently a diversion for a main attack against the British, all attacks were repulsed and settled down to the regular artillery and air attacks.

### February 18, 1944

At the canal the Force is continually subjected to enemy artillery, they throw everything they have at our men for a few minutes and then quit while the Force get busy getting artillery support in for an infantry attack that does not develop. The men are beginning to get a bit tired and jittery as they have been in nearly 3 weeks with little sleep and continuous night patrolling. The 3rd Regiment are taking the brunt of the thrusts.

### February 20, 1944

Two platoons of the service battalion are to be alert all night, till further notice, in readiness to go to the canal. A further group of 20 men and 1 N.C.O. are assigned permanently to the combat echelon to patrol the beach at the entrance to the canal for defence against parachute attack or beach landing.

### February 29, 1944

Another month comes to a close with no decision regarding reinforcements or British awards for our personnel. The lack of action on these two subjects is felt very keenly throughout the battalion.

Morale of all ranks continues to be very high. The men are very tired as they are either digging or fighting 24 hours a day. The main question is "When will we be relieved?"

The portion of the Mussolini Canal which the Force holds is 11,000 metres long. This is very close to being 1/4 of the bridgehead. It is a very thin line to hold with 1296 Officers and men.

We have maintained the initiative by active patrolling all along the front. The 1st Bn., 3rd Regt. repulsed two very strong enemy attacks. Our orders are to "Hold the Canal." We have not enough strength to push past it and have to hold it by sitting on it and patrolling to the front. The enemy has high ground all around the bridgehead and can see all our ground, shell all our roads from at least two sides. The boys have done a wonderful job.

### March 2, 1944

Bright and warm in the morning. Several hundred heavy and medium bombers hit all along the front and enemy supply lines. Cloudy and showers by afternoon. More troops and supplies arriving from the old base, they had a number of shells land in the area as the Hun laid down a barrage directed at the road which is the only supply line to the central sector of the front. Intelligence reported the enemy planned throwing 200 rounds every hour at the road from the bridge above us to Nettuno.

### March 4, 1944

Dull, some rain and raw. Q.M. property coming all day. About a dozen men discharged from hospital returned to duty and were sent to the front after dusk.

Colonel Marshall, officer commanding 1st Regiment was in, said his men were very elated at capturing 111 prisoners since they only expected to get about 30. This Hun company was apparently the forerunner of a major attack, since it was made up from many units and had engineers and artillery observers. He added however that the men were getting tired after over a month of continuous night patrolling and little time during the day for sleep.

**March 8, 1944**

German artillery in this sector very active, seemed to be trying to hit the main road between here and Nettuno. At 1900 hours about 12, 88 mm shells came in close, directed at the castle on the point which we used as an OP, all shells landed in the water.

**March 9, 1944**

Bright, but cool. Routine patrolling, the enemy on the Force front appear to have withdrawn, likely for rest and reorganizing for a further offensive.

**March 11, 1944**

Cloudy and cool. A bit of air activity last night and early this morning, some good shows of A.A. during the night, some heavy bombs dropped during the night on Anzio.

Our combat echelon is very indignant and feel insulted to find an Italian Marine unit is being used opposite them instead of the all German units encountered to date.

**March 12, 1944**

Received advice that Lt. Colonel Akehurst assumed command of the Battalion effective 27th January 1944.

In the evening we were warned that starting in the morning and there after from 6 to 9 the area will be included in a large scale smoke screen of the harbour. Were also warned that the Huns might start shelling when they see the smoke.

**March 13, 1944**

We were advised unofficially that Canadian reinforcements were being considered. Lt. Colonel Akehurst, Lt. Colonel Gilday and Major Biscoe had a meeting at the forward C.P. re, reinforcements and decorations. When these two questions are cleared up we should have some clear sailing, we hope. If the Force is to continue it will need a complete reorganization taking 2 or 3 months, this will be ample time to train any replacements in both specialized Force training and American weapons.

**March 15, 1944**

Cool and overcast. Some heavy German shells came in a bit too close rocking the trees and ground. Their artillery is increasing in both quantity and caliber. This morning an American officer who was captured the night before last, returned to the Force, he had been near Littoria and soon after a German officer started questioning him our artillery opened up, the Huns beat it and he escaped. He had been beaten on the neck with a rubber hose when he failed to answer questions. Hun prisoners can expect some rough treatment from here in.

**March 21, 1944**

Another dull and cool morning clearing by noon. No enemy air activity during the night or day, some shelling of the port and roads leading in. A large duck park between our area and Nettuno got a lot of shelling, but keep very busy going out to ships and bringing their supplies in.

Lt. Colonel Akehurst was advised that 15 officers and 250 other ranks are available as reinforcements, and he will likely go to Naples to arrange for training in the U.S. weapons etc, before they join the Unit.

The 509th Parachute Battalion (U.S.) is expected to be attached to the Force tomorrow. What is left of the Rangers were attached to-night, those having served overseas 2 years are to return to the U.S.A.; there are very few left; of 19 officers eligible to return, only 2 are alive.

**March 27, 1944**

Clear and cool. The usual harassing fire in these areas. Have been told the Hun is really pasting Nettuno and Anzio these days with 270 mm shells (10 inch), the buildings go up in a cloud of dust when hit. Quite a heavy raid about 1630, a least 10 planes bombed the harbour, the R.A.F. shot down 5, no further raids during the night.

**March 28, 1944**

Bright, and cool wind. An increase in Hun artillery fire, some men in the first regiment were hit, one killed when an 88 came in a window and exploded in the room they were in, the man sitting under the window was untouched.

Lt. Colonel Akehurst and Lt. Colonel Gilday were in during the morning concerning Canadian matters generally and reinforcements in particular. It is sincerely hoped the Force can be withdrawn from the line and taken off the Beach Head for a few months reorganization and training of reinforcements. They have been in the line for nearly two months and a good many men are getting very jittery from lack of sleep and continual patrolling. They are rapidly getting out of condition, particularly the forward element who are pinned in their foxholes all day.

**March 31, 1944**

We have been advised that 15 officers and 250 other ranks were reporting to our old bivouac area to-day as reinforcements. Lt. Colonel Akehurst is leaving to-day for Naples to arrange for their coming up after they are equipped with U.S. clothing and weapons etc. The month closes with the Beach Head in a relative state of inactivity.

The month of April, apart from bringing mosquitoes and the danger of Malaria should bring better weather and we hope either the Beach Head can be considerably expanded or the Force can be relieved and return to the rear for a rest and reorganization. The question of honours and awards remains unanswered.

**April 2, 1944**

Captain Fletcher, who just returned from hospital yesterday was again wounded and admitted to hospital today jinxed. Two Canadian other ranks have been killed within the last two days as Jerry seems to be stepping up his activity, he is doing much shelling along the front and an increase in the rear areas.

**April 10, 1944**

Our reinforcements are to receive their training in Santa Maria instead of up here, a much better idea as this is no place to come equipped with strange arms and equipment and no knowledge of the way the Force operates. They will get approximately 2 weeks training. One officer and four other ranks to go down to help train; there are four officers and several other ranks just out of hospital who will remain at Santa Maria as instructors.

**April 27, 1944**

Our first overseas reinforcements, 15 officers and 234 other ranks arrived today. Their L.S.T. docked at 0800 hours, was told to move about 15 feet and in doing so fouled their anchor chain in the propellers and spent 7 hours in the bay getting it clear; by this time the Hun had started his daily shelling of Anzio, and the boys had their first experience of being under fire. They arrived at the bivouac area at 1600 hours and unfortunately missed the Seaforth's pipe band which had come over from the British front to play for their arrival but had an engagement in the afternoon; they did play for a short time for a group of 500 officers and men assembled for a tank-infantry lecture.

**May 1, 1944**

The second regiment raid was not a success. The group that went to Cerreto Alto, where most of the prisoners in the last successful raid were taken, ran into a minefield of the wooden box variety that mine detectors can't pick up. Casualties were very high and mostly serious … The final casualty count was two killed, 19 wounded, of whom 12 are definitely lost to the Force.

**May 5, 1944**

Rumours that we will be relieved soon are rampant, only hope it will be off the Beachhead, but that seems unlikely.

Five Canadian and five American other ranks are recommended for commissions, most of them have commanded platoons for some time and appear good officer material.

**May 20, 1944**

A quiet day with a few scattered artillery exchanges. The Force has been continuously on manoeuvres in conjunction with tank outfits since being withdrawn from the line and final plans for attack are now being contemplated.

**May 23, 1944**

Heavy artilleryfire broke out at 0500 hours indicating the start of the long awaited Beachhead push. An early report states that the Force has cut highway number 7 and advanced beyond. Later were forced to fall back to highway 7 when expectedreinforcement from U.S. infantry division did not arrive.

**May 29, 1944**

The Force is digging in around Artena under heavy shelling and an imminent threat of counterattack. Casualties have been high, there is no communication with the unit and we are not allowed to go into the area which means reporting of casualties will be held up at least temporarily.

Captain Atto's loss is felt keenly, he was one of the most popular officers in the Force and a very capable chap. Lieutenant Fortune was the second officer, was one of our recent replacement officers and in Captain Atto's company. Lt.-Colonel Gray, the commander of 2nd battalion, 1st regiment was killed and his battalion virtually wiped out. It has also been learned that Major Secter has been seriously, if not mortally wounded, we can get no confirmation of this.

**May 31, 1944**

The Force C.P. is situated in a castle high up in Artena. The town is built on the face of a cliff overlooking highway number 6 and facing the German lines 300 yards north. It is a really hot spot and no place for a peace loving citizen. It is continually under artillery fire as the Huns have the commanding heights across the valley and are sniping with 88's every time one of our men shows himself.

**June 5, 1944**

Bright and warm. Fifth Army reports they are beyond Rome so the Force supply officer has gone up to try to locate the Force and arrange to move the Base forward as we are now much too far back to establish contact. Received orders after supper to move first thing in the morning to Ost Finocchio on highway six about six miles this side of Rome. A busy evening packing.

Colonel Marshall O.C. 1st regiment was killed by a sniper just outside of Rome, one of the finest officers and a serious loss to the Force.

### June 6, 1944

Bright and cool. Breakfast at 0600 hours, advance party left at 0700 hours, destination changed to Tor Sapienza, halfway between highways 6 and 5, 4 miles from Rome. On arrival found that 8th Army had taken over sector and the Force to be moved below highway 6, bivouac area not decided upon and a good many left to see Rome.

The 2nd battalion 3rd regiment was relieved from guarding eight bridges in Rome over the Tiber this p.m. The Force now at rest in the Fifth Army reserve. The Force was given credit as being the First into Rome. There was considerable Hun rear guard activity by small groups well armed with tank support and the men found themselves being embraced whole heartedly by the populace one minute and engaged in heavy street fighting the next.

### June 7, 1944

Bright and warm. Air raids of one hour duration in Rome this a.m. What could be rounded up of the Force moved to our new bivouac area on the north shore of Lake Albano below Castel Gandalfo last night. It will likely take a day or two to get them all assembled as they don't all know our new station. This is the best rest area we have hit in Italy. Lago Albano is an old volcanic crater, the steeply rising shore is well wooded, the lake is clear and grand swimming. No living in dugouts or fox holes and no sound of artillery fire or bombing. The men are spending the days in the water, lying in the sun, boating, fishing and getting laundry up to scratch.

### June 19, 1944, Lago Albano, Italy

Dull, cool wind and rain. Lt. Colonel Akehurst returned from Naples at 0800 hours. He was advised this evening that he could request reinforcements to be brought up here for training and is flying to Naples in the morning to arrange for their selection.

The mission planned for the Force has been cancelled and so long as the Fifth Army keeps rolling it is unlikely to be called upon. The mission was a ship to shore behind the first wall of resistance the Hun put up.

### June 20, 1944

Dull, cool and some rain. Lt. Colonel Akehurst left by plane for Naples, hoping to get 250 other rank reinforcements. Officers will only be taken if they appear especially good.

Our casualties from the 1st of May to and including the capture of Rome were 18 officers, 194 other ranks (including killed, missing and wounded), approximately 30% of our strength.

### June 21, 1944

Major Harrison, Historical officer from 1st Corps came in this afternoon to compile a complete history of the battalion to supplement and enlarge upon our war diaries and monthly returns. The main point of view from an Historical interest seems to be the feeling of Canadians serving in the American Army, and the fundamental differences in the administration and discipline of the two armies.

### June 23, 1944

Dull and cool. A parade at 0900 hours for presentation of awards to 15 officers and other ranks.

The Force commander spoke to the personnel present on the pleasure it gave him to present these awards, which were all well deserved. He then expressed disappointment that he had been ordered to leave the Force, effective to-day. This was a stunning announcement to all present and entirely unexpected. He apparently has been offered the command of the 36th Division on several occasions and turned it down each time until order to take it now. He has been the driving power behind the Force and its future is now in the air. Colonel Walker officer commanding 3rd regiment assumes command of the Force.

Lt. Colonel Akehurst returned from Naples about noon. The Canadian reinforcements arrived about 1700 hours, 4 officers and 206 other ranks, they were assigned to the regiments and will receive their training with the companies to which they are assigned.

### June 28, 1944

Lt. Colonel Becket is to command the 3rd regiment, replacing Colonel Walker, now Force Commander. Lt. Colonel Gilday's request for transfer back to the Canadian Army was approved today. He had reached the end of his tether at swallowing American Army methods. He has done an excellent job as battalion commander and was offered command of a regiment recently but wants no further part of the Force. He goes with the best wishes of those who served with him and no few Canadians will be envious of his getting back into his own army.

### June 29, 1944

Mostly bright and hot. Lt. Colonel Gilday left to report to 1 echelon to-day with an adverse report made out by the new Force commander, who only a few days ago saw fit to give him command of his old Regt.

This is one of the things that make the Canadians wish they were back in their own army. It is the first official act of the new Force Commander concerning Canadians. Brigadier Weeks came out to the camp in the afternoon, met all the Canadian Officers and left soon after supper.

### July 8, 1944, Santa Maria Castillabate, Italy

Colonel Walker had an officers meeting at 1930 hrs in the Officer's Club. He first expressed his pleasure in assuming command of the Force which had already made such a good name for itself. He then went into a long talk giving constructive criticism on many points, particularly discipline in which the Force has been notoriously lax. The officers were asked to set an example and to look for breaches in discipline and not shy away from them. The talk was well received.

### July 10, 1944

Last night 3rd Regt uncovered a clique of Cdns going AWL, presumably to return to Avellino and the Cdn Army. 8 had already taken off. Major Biscoe left at 2000 hrs to arrange to have any picked up in Avellino taken into custody and returned immediately to the unit.

This morning he received the usual prompt and excellent co-operation on many points, including the lining up of 30 reinforcements for Colonel Akehurst's selection tomorrow.

The transfer of Major Mair to the Bn approved.

### July 21, 1944

Plans were made to allow Cdn. officers of the Force to go on a two day leave to Amalfi or Avellino. They have been two years in the outfit without meeting any of their friends in the Cdn Army and they hope to run into at least a few of them.

### July 30, 1944

Colonel Akehurst left this morning for Avellino to look over the reinforcements and arrange a F.G.C.M. for a few cases we have pending and training makes it difficult to make up our own court.

It is understood that Gen. Frederick is taking Lt.-Colonel Wickham, the Force Executive Officer. Pretty tough on the new Force Commander to have his executive yanked out right before the first operation since the change of command.

**August 2, 1944**

Bright and hot. At 1630 hrs 7 Officers and 65 O.R.s left Avellino to begin training at the Base Detachment, Santa Maria.

Some of the ships to be used in the operation have arrived and are anchored in the bay at Agrololi, one of them, Prince Henry, is Canadian …

Lt. Col. Wickham, Force Executive Officer, returned from Hospital and left to be General Frederick's Chief of Staff.

**August 7, 1944**

Bright and hot, a very calm sea. Troops embarked during the morning, completed before noon. Weighed anchor at 1400 hrs, and along with the French Commandoes Force put to sea. French Force turned in near Gaeta. Ours arrived at the islands of Ponza and Zannone at about 2200 hrs. A great deal of difficulty was experienced getting away from the ships, units being up to an hour late in getting away. A bright moon, alright for an exercise, but not for an operation.

**August 8, 1944**

Bright and hot. All troops had embarked by 1200 hrs and the ships got underway. Some went into Naples for refuelling and supplies. The 1st Regiment returned direct to Santa Maria and had another exercise getting to shore by rubber boats. More successful than the previous night.

**August 15, 1944, Santa Maria, Capua Vetere**

Bright and very hot. "D" Day, and everyone is wondering how the Force and the invasion generally is making out. 15th Cdn General Hospital will admit our men who are returned to unit as fit but are not ready for combat. After all the time we have been here and all the circulars issued to U.S. Hospitals re the handling of Canadian personnel, there are still some that don't know what to do, and seems to return them to the Unit to get them off their hands.

**August 16, 1944**

Bright and very hot. Only news is that the Force took their two Islands with little opposition and went on to take a town on the mainland before dawn yesterday. (The Force did not reach the mainland until D day plus 2)

**September 5, 1944, Nice, France**

Bright and warm. Contacted Lt. Col. Akehurst at his C.P. in Bougheas. The Force is in the hills, not much action but flares up every now and then. They have walked all the way from St. Rafael and are on the tired side. The French Forces of the Interior are doing a good job bringing in information and prisoners, besides their own warring.

First Regt is opening an advance C.P. in Peillon tonight. Everyone is always on the move and hard to find, one never knows when they may overshoot their mark and be in enemy lines. The Germans have some very powerful forts all through these parts that must be knocked out one by one.

**September 9, 1944**

Bright and warm. Third Regt is running into stiffer resistance in the hills although the Jerry seems to be falling back to the M.L.R. across the Italian border. Our patrons have been across the border.

**September 14, 1944**

Clear and cool. Major Biscoe spent the day at Dragingnon checking with the 51st Evacuation Hospital for Cdn admissions, discharges and transfers. They handle all personnel evacuated from this sector and either return them to duty when recovered or send them to a convalescent Hosp or evacuate them to the interior (at present Italy). They send all their returns to 7th Army but as yet the unit has been given no information except for 1 D.O.W., and also checking with the American Military Cemetery for Cdns buried there, found one officer who had been buried 27 Aug. No information had been sent by the hospital in which he died and burial returns always take a long time to come through. The Br. Graves Registration were going to send the effects to Cairo, having no other instructions. They were asked to obtain authority to send them to 2 Ech and the effects they had were brought to the unit for shipment to 2 Ech.

### September 16, 1944

Clear and cool. The Frenchman was turned over to French Intelligence today. Artillery still scattered along front lines and taking its toll on our personnel. Looks like the Force is getting another Anzio deal, being given a very large front to hold by active patrolling with its high rate of casualties. The Force is completely committed with no reserves and for that matter there are no troops to speak of between here and Marseilles, but the Hun seems to be fighting a holding war though he has more troops than we and some really fine forts (built by the French as the southern portion of their Maginot Line)

### September 17, 1944

Bright, warm and windy. 3 more Cdn O.R's killed when a shell hit their fox hole. Force Commander is requesting more Cdn reinforcements. O.C. requests we be brought back up to strength while the Base Det is at Santa Maria, Capua Vetere. It is proposed the Base will move out by the end of the month and come up here. If the reinforcements can be selected in time they will come up with the Det and get their training here. From now on it will be a different matter with no base in Italy.

### September 18, 1944

Cool, dull and wet. Little activity along the line, some artillery. A push is planned to straighten out the line, to take place possibly today. It is unlikely there will be any offensive action in this sector, both sides digging in. It is hoped the French will take over and relieve the whole of the 1st A.B.T.F.

### September 24, 1944

Bright and warm. The 1st Convoy of U.S. reinforcements and personnel returned from hospital arrived at 0100 hrs. As many as possible will go to their companies today. The rest from Marseilles should arrive late today or early tomorrow. 3rd Regt came in for some very heavy shelling this A.M., no casualties reported.

### September 25, 1944

Bright and warm. All personnel from Marseilles have arrived and those ready for combat are being equipped to return to their coys or be assigned to coys. Those who require more training are being billeted in the hotel near the Var river and a training centre has been selected; if Cdn reinforcements arrive they will receive their training there also.

### September 30, 1944

Bright and cool. The enemy are bringing in a great deal of artillery and have definite superiority numerically. Our men are confined to their fox holes and just have to take it. It is quite noticeable how many of the old original men are cracking, they have been through too much of this sort of thing 99 days without a break at Anzio, over a month already here and no prospects of relief.

### October 7, 1944, Field, Southern France

Cool rain and still a high wind. Major Biscoe returned this afternoon. All hospitals visited were most cooperative and seemed very glad to be advised what reports were required and how to handle Canadian patients. Despite the instructions that are supposed to be circulated not one hospital had any idea what to do about Cdn personnel nor had they seen any instructions pertaining thereto. All promised to send reports to 2 Echelon.

### October 8, 1944

Cloudy some rain, quite warm. Lt. Col. Akehurst's request to return to the Cdn Army has been approved by the Force Commander and went into effect to-day insofar as the Force is concerned as he left his Regiment and returned to the base pending advice from 1 Ech as to his next move. Lt. Col. Becket is recommended to command the Bn. Lt. Col. Whitney, Force Adjutant assumed command of 1st Regt, a big assignment for an administrative officer. Col. Akehurst will be missed both in the Bn. and the Force; he is a most capable officer and highly regarded by all ranks but he could not see eye to eye with the Force Commander and felt it was in the best interests of all concerned if he asked to be returned to the Cdn Army. The feeling of dissatisfaction within the Force is increasing rather than decreasing and involves Americans as well as Canadians.

### October 10, 1944

Cool and showers. Little artillery activity, our patrols were active. Cases for our Court Martial are increasing as some long time AWLs return. Discipline has reached a very low plane. Men are not returning on discharge from hospital, others are taking off right from the lines, and is reaching rather serious proportions. The feeling of dissatisfaction within the Force is again increasing both among Canadians and Americans. The Canadians still feel their own country has let them down and written them off to the U.S. Army. They did not volunteer to become American soldiers but to join a 1/2 and 1/2 outfit. There is little Canadian about the Force.

### October 12, 1944

Bright and cool. Two more cases for F.G.C.M. to-day making 9 to date, Court convenes at 1300 hrs tomorrow, 5 cases are ready for trial. The Yanks have about 40 cases for Court Martial. Although no excuse for breach of discipline the men are getting pretty fed up and tired sitting up in the mountains day after day; it's over a month now and nearly two months steady fighting.

### October 14, 1944

Clear and cool after a wet night. A new Court convened at 1300 hrs to hear 4 more cases, they will be busy for some time, although the officers on the Court must be drawn from the line; the low state of discipline requires immediate and severe disciplinary action.

### October 15, 1944

Exigencies of the service required the F.G.C.M. to continue to-day. It has been authoritatively reported the German General Commanding the line across from us uses a white staff car with a red cross, another German violation of the Geneva Convention.

### October 16, 1944

Cool and rain. The front seems fairly quiet. The Force now going into its third month of uninterrupted fighting. F.G.C.M. in session all day.

**October 17, 1944**

Cool dull and heavy rain. A First Regiment raiding party captured 11 POWs in a house, the first Hun out looking for a fight was cut in two by our automatic rifle fire; the others, all German "supermen", were more reasonable. Court Martial tried its tenth and last case to-day finishing after 2100 hrs.

**October 20, 1944**

Cool and clear. The Force Cannon Company had a field day catching a Heinie Bn moving down a hill into a woods, they estimate they threw 300 rounds at them, results unknown.

**October 24, 1944**

Mostly dull and cool. First Regiment are expecting the French to relieve one Bn, but as they are completely green troops only 2 Coys will come out and 1 Coy remain to get them established. What few French troops we have seen here to date do not impress one favourably, they are inexperienced untrained and undisciplined. Two Canadians broke out of the stockade this evening about 2130 hrs, one had just been tried by our recent F.G.C.M., the other waiting the next. They were able to charge the guard and get away. Our M.P.s have never been what we consider M.P. calibre.

**October 25, 1944**

A raw wet day. American General Court Martials getting underway at A.B.T.F. HQ. They have over 30 cases. One of our last nights' escapees was apprehended today.

**October 29, 1944**

Heavy rain and storm last night, mostly cloudy today with rain in the morning. Our patrols continue to advance without resistance, have occupied Sospel. Enemy harassing with artillery and mortar fire. Menton received some shelling this evening and it's pouring rain again. These people that told us it never rained in Nice.

**November 2, 1944**

Dull and wet. The myth about sunny Italy is being carried on in Nice where it never rains?? The Natives say this weather is unprecedented. We never miss unprecedented weather. Lt. Colonel Akehurst returned from Rome this afternoon, had a successful trip including an interview with General Burns who instructed him to go to London to see General Stewart [Stuart] re: the Force. He continues meanwhile in command of the Battalion.

**November 5, 1944**

Bright and cool. Regular Church Services at Regt'l C.P's and rest hotel. Two more of our deserters apprehended in Marseilles. Another prison break this evening, 2 Americans both apprehended in their old hangout down town with same girls as well. On their return they beat up the one who gave them away, necessitating his admission to hospital.

**November 7, 1944**

Bright and cool. A 3rd Regt. patrol got caught in an enemy minefield, another patrol went out to help them and got in another. There were 2 killed and 7 wounded, a rather disastrous evening. Patrolling is at a minimum as there is little to be gained for the risks taken.

**November 13, 1944**

Cloudy and cool. F.G.C.M. convened at 1300 hrs and tried, three cases of A.W.L. all 1st Regt. all pleading guilty. The convoy that came in is the 100th Bn composed of American naturalized Japanese, they are relieving a Parachute Bn.; they have just come down from the Belfort Gap area.

**November 14, 1944**

Dull wet and raw. A 2nd F.G.C.M. convened at 1300 hrs to try four 3rd Regt cases. A good many of these men do not want to be defended preferring to take their sentence rather than go back in the line. It is noted that practically every case is from reinforcements and not among the originals that came overseas with us.

**November 15, 1944**

Clear and cool. The U.S. Admin are trying to account for 4 missing prisoners who escaped from the stockade last night (1 Cdn sentenced by F.G.C.M. Monday). No one knows when they left, they got under the barbed wire fence a few feet from a sentry post. Each of 3 sentries on that post last night swear they did not leave during their tour of duty.

**November 16, 1944**

Clear and cool. The Cdn escapee on Monday night turned himself in this morning and all 3 of Monday's sentences were promulgated. Lt. Col. Akehurst has accepted a temporary job working for Major General Frederick until his instructions from 1 Cdn Corps come to make his trip to England.

**November 17, 1944**

Clear and cool. Our 3rd and we hope last F.G.C.M. convened at 1300 hrs to try the second of our 2 AWLs apprehended in England. A total of eight cases have been tried this week.

**November 21, 1944**

Lt. Colonel Akehurst received a telegram from 6th Army Group re the Cdn element of the Force and plans to leave for London tomorrow to protest the proposed plans.

**November 28, 1944**

Col. Dunn O I/C 2 Ech arrived this morning. He was able to give the Force Cmdr a good deal of information regarding the next move, apparently the cables covering administration instructions have not been sent on from 6th Army Group yet. Plans are being made to be in a position to move as soon as possible, after the information is passed to the troops.

**November 30, 1944**

Bright and cool. Muster parades and check on Next of Kin for 1st and 3rd Regiments. All Cdn Officers were advised by the Force Cmdr of the segregation of Cdn and US personnel in the Force and Colonel Dunn gave some particulars that move to another theatre was to be made forthwith, the disbandment is Top Secret and no mention is to be made in correspondence.

**December 1–4, 1944**

A very busy period. Force Commander knows nothing on the Force break-up from U.S. channels and the wires are being kept hot trying to get the information. All higher headquarters are shying from it and we are getting nowhere. It is definite that the Bn. is being withdrawn from the Force and sent to Italy for disbanding and is to be done soon but no shipping space or definite instructions as yet.

**December 5, 1944**

Mostly bright and cool. Colonel Dunn was advised this morning that A.F.H.Q. were to handle our move and he left by air for Italy to tie in that end. At 1400 hrs the Force was assembled near Villeneuve-Loubet for a farewell parade and memorial service for those who fell in France. The official Order was read advising that the Canadian element was being withdrawn and moved immediately to another theatre. The Bn. Commander spoke, saying the Canadians were now returning to the Cdn Army, that they had enjoyed their being with the Americans and hoped the Americans would remain as a unit and continue to carry the Union Jack with the Stars and Stripes as our thought and good wishes would always be with them. Then the Force Commander spoke saying there was now no longer a First Special Service Force, that he was sorry the break-up had to come but that it was far better to break-up with a really good reputation rather than be wiped out like the American Rangers and that Special units were being broken up all over. The Roll of the fallen was then read and prayers by both Chaplains and the last Post. The Force flag was sheathed. The Canadians were then asked to fall out forming into a 3 Company formation and marched past the American element while the band of 442 Regt. an all Japanese (Naturalized Americans) Regt played. Again forming up while the Force Commander shook hands with every Officer and man.

### December 6, 1944

Bright and cool. The balance of the Pay Parades were held during the morning and early afternoon. Everyone busy packing and saying their farewells. The convoy of 36 trucks left Villeneuve-Loubet 2315 hrs to start the long cold trip to Marseille.

### December 8, 1944, At Sea

Rain and raw. Sailed at 0630 hrs rough and a very top heavy ship, many were sea sick. The Bn was given all the ship's details as our officers were senior and we were travelling as a unit.

### December 9, 1944, Field, Italy

Rain and raw. Italy again, we had all hoped we would never see it again after we left some 3 months ago. Arrived Naples 0830 hrs. Disembarked at 1000 hrs over the same sunken hospital ship we did on our first arrival over a year ago. Cdn Officials met us at the dock and the Bn moved to a transit camp where dinner was served from mobile kitchens. The Bn. was split for the move, the 1st draft left at 1230, entrained at 1330; the 2nd draft left at 1300, entrained at 1340. At Nola troops detrained and entrucked for Avellino, arriving at Canada Barracks between 1700 and 1830 hrs where we all received a good reception back into the Cdn Army.

### December 13, 1944

Mostly bright and cool. Things are really hectic getting changed over into Cdn clothing and customs. Our efforts to draw a liquor ration for officers and men has been successful. Col. Akehurst left for Rome at 0930 hrs.

### December 14, 1944

Dull and wet, real Italian weather. Bit by bit our people are getting into Cdn uniforms and turning in American clothing.

### December 27, 1944

Mostly bright and windy. Reveille at 0500 hrs, breakfast at 0530, mustering at truck positions at 0640. Trucks arrived shortly after 0700 hrs and moved outside town when loaded. The convoy moved off at 0745 hrs for Naples. Embarkation began onto the Arundel-Castle about 0930 hrs. Ptes first, Sgt WOs and Officers. All the Cdn draft was embarked by approx 1100 hrs. Quarters good, a noon meal was served and the afternoon was spent organizing duties, details etc. Lt. Col. Akehurst finally got off for England from Naples Airport at 0830 hrs and arrived England 1445 hrs.

### December 28, 1944

Raw, mostly clear. Due to leave at 0839 hrs but held up, getting away from dock about 1100 hrs putting to sea with two other transports. No escort. A very quiet running ship, good meals and looks like a good trip. Quite a change to be under British discipline. Many details required but is a very well run ship.

### January 9, 1945, Field, England

Dull and raw, heavy blizzard early and off and on during the day. A few rehearsals early. The M.G.A. arrived at 1100 hrs. He spoke to all ranks telling then that the Bn was now finished, that Para Pay ceased to-day although recommendations had been sent to N.D.H.Q. for a period of continuation but he gave no promise. He thanked the Bn on behalf of the Chief of Staff for a job well done, that the Cdn Army would be proud of them when security would permit publishing the full story. The Bn then marched past in review order, the M.G.A. taking the salute. General Weeks spoke to the Officers in the Ante room afterwards and left before dinner. All ranks preparing for a 4 day leave starting tomorrow and promised a 10 day leave after their course. Considerable number of movies and photos of this parade were taken which will probably never be released. It is doubtful if any other Force has been as frequently photographed and yet neither its members nor the families at home have ever seen any of them.

# ENDNOTES

## INTRODUCTION

### The First Special Service Force

1   Sholto Watt, "Crack Mixed Force Is Gradually Becoming American," *Montreal Star*, 9 April 1944, 13.
2   Letter, Col C.P. Stacey to M-Gen Robert T. Frederick, 10 Dec 1947, Hoover Institution Archives, Stanford University, California (hereafter HIA), Robert T. Frederick Papers (hereafter Frederick Papers), Box 3, File: FSSF, History, Correspondence.
3   Sholto Watt, "Real American Force: Joint U.S.–Canadian Unit Gets Canadian Reinforcements," *Montreal Star*, 25 May 1944, 13.
4   J.L. Granatstein, "The American Influence on the Canadian Military, 1939-1963," *Canadian Military History 2*, no. 1 (Spring 1993), 63.
5   Stanley W. Dziuban, *Military Relations Between the United States and Canada, 1939-1945* (Washington, DC: Department of the Army, 1959), 264.
6   C.P. Stacey, *Arms, Men and Governments: The War Policies of Canada, 1939-1945* (Ottawa: Department of National Defence (DND), 1970), 392.
7   G.W.L. Nicholson, *The Canadians in Italy, 1943-1945* (Ottawa: Queen's Printer, 1956), 671.
8   Activities of the 1st Cnd Sp Serv Bn (First Canadian Special Service Battalion), 1 Nov 1944-9 Jan 1945, DND Directorate of History and Heritage, Ottawa (hereafter DHH), 145.3009 (D7), File: Monthly Reports.

## CHAPTER ONE

### The Talented Mr Pyke

1   Memorandum, M-Gen J.C. Murchie to the Minister of National Defence (MND), 23 June 1942, Library and Archives of Canada, Ottawa (hereafter LAC), RG 24, Series C-1, Reel C-5436.
2   M-Gen Maurice Pope, "Canadian Services Representation in Washington," in Diary, 29 July 1942, LAC, MG 27 III F4, Vol. 1 (hereafter Pope Diary).
3   Memo, Col L.M. Chelsey, 27 April 1942, LAC, RG 24, Series C-1, Reel C-5481; Wilfrid

Eggleston, *Scientists at War* (Toronto: Oxford University Press, 1950), 98.
4   Pope Diary, 30 May 1942.
5   Forrest Pogue, *George C. Marshall: Ordeal and Hope, 1939-1942* (New York: Viking Press, 1966), 312.
6   Bernard Fergusson, *The Watery Maze: The Story of Combined Operations* (London: Collins, 1961), 150.
7   Ibid., 145.
8   Ibid.
9   David Lampe, *Pyke: The Unknown Genius* (London: Evans Brothers, 1959), 9.
10  Commentary by Mr. Pyke re North Norway, Large Scale Operation, 15 April 1942, US National Archives at College Park, Maryland (hereafter NA-CP), RG 165, Entry 21, Stack 390/30/16/4, Box 968, Folder 319.1 (6-13-42).
11  Ibid.
12  One of Pyke's other well-known schemes, Operation Habbakuk, was to construct massive, oversized aircraft carriers using an experimental mixture of ice and sawdust. With Mountbatten's support, Pyke's scheme received serious high-level consideration before field testing demonstrated it to be impracticable. See Fergusson, *The Watery Maze*, 145.
13  Michael J. King, *Rangers: Selected Combat Missions in World War II* (Fort Leavenworth: Combat Studies Institute, 1985), 5.
14  Memo for the Deputy Chief of Staff (DCS), 21 April 1942, NA-CP, RG 165, Entry 21, Stack 390/30/16/4, Box 968, Folder 381 (4-10-42).
15  Ibid.
16  Ibid.; Steven E. Shay, *"From Braves to Black Devils: The Activation and Battles of the First Special Service Force, 1942-1944"* (Master's thesis, Washington State University, 2000), 17-20.
17  Lampe, *Pyke*, 111.
18  Ibid.
19  Janet G. Valentine, *"The North Atlantic Triangle and the Formation of the First Special Service Force, 1942-43"* (Master's thesis, University of North Florida, 1995), 60.
20  Ibid.
21  Memo, Col Chelsey, 27 April 1942; memo re Capt T. Gilday, 30 April 1942, LAC, RG 24, Series C-1, Reel C-5481.

22    Eggleston, *Scientists at War*, 98.

23    Robert D. Burhans, *The First Special Service Force: A War History of the North Americans, 1942–1944* (Washington, DC: Infantry Journal Press, 1947), 7.

24    Valentine, *"The North Atlantic Triangle,"* 61.

25    Lampe, *Pyke*, 120.

26    Ibid., 121.

27    Richard Alexander Hough, *Mountbatten* (New York: Random House, 1981), 151.

28    Robert H. Adleman and George Walton, *The Devil's Brigade* (Philadelphia: Chilton Books, 1966), 29.

29    Carlo D'Este, *Eisenhower: A Soldier's Life* (New York: Henry Holt, 2002), 306.

30    Adleman and Walton, *Devil's Brigade*, 28.

31    Philip Ziegler, *Mountbatten: The Official Biography* (London: Collins, 1985), 181.

32    Adleman and Walton, *Devil's Brigade*, 17.

33    Letter, Robert T. Frederick to Robert D. Burhans, 10 Sept 1946, HIA, Frederick Papers, Box 8, File: Burhans Manuscript; Adleman and Walton, *Devil's Brigade*, 31.

34    "Major General Robert T. Frederick: Remarks by General Paul D. Adams," First Special Service Force (FSSF) Association Pamphlet, 17 August 1973.

35    Catherine C. Yeats, *"The Worst Was Yet to Come: The Genesis and Evolution of the First Special Service Force, 1942–1943"* (Master's thesis: University of Idaho, 1995), 19–20.

36    Alfred D. Chandler, Jr., ed. *The Papers of Dwight David Eisenhower*, vol. 1, *The War Years* (Baltimore: Johns Hopkins Press, 1970), 333.

37    Letter, Frederick to Burhans, 10 Sept 1946.

38    Note for File, Col Chelsey, 9 June 1942, LAC, RG 24, Series C-1, Reel C-5481.

39    Memo re Geoffrey Pyke's visit to Ottawa, 12 June 1942, LAC, RG 24, Series C-1, Reel C-5436.

40    Min of mtg, June 12th, 3 p.m. in H.Q. Royal Canadian General Staff [sic.], 19 June 1942, NA-CP, RG 165, Entry 21, Stack 390/30/16/4, Box 968, Folder 381 (6-12-42).

41    Ibid.

42    Memo, Lt-Col W.A.B. Anderson to M-Gen J.C. Murchie, 13 June 1942, LAC, RG 24, Series C-1, Reel C-5436.

43    Letter, Frederick to Burhans, 10 September 1946.

44    Ibid.

45    Memo of Conversation, Lt-Col Anderson, 15 June 1942, LAC, RG 24, Series C-1, Reel C-5436.

46    Ibid.

47    Conversation between Geoffrey Pyke at Ottawa and Col Frederick in Washington, 15 June 1942, NA-CP, RG 165, Entry 21, Stack 390/30/16/4, Box 968, Folder 319.1 (6-13-42).

48    Memo, Lt-Col Anderson to M-Gen Murchie, 13 June 1942.

49    Memo, M-Gen Murchie to MND, 23 June 1942, LAC, RG 24, Series C-1, Reel C-5436.

50    Memo, Lt-Col Anderson to Lt-Gen Stuart, 20 June 1942, DHH, 112.3S2009 (D255), File: Org & Mob, 1st Cnd Sp Serv Bn, Jun/Dec 42. (Hereafter DHH File: Org & Mob)

51    Memo, Lt-Gen Stuart to MND, 11 July 1942, DHH, File: Org & Mob Jun/Dec 42.

52    C.P. Stacey, *Six Years of War: The Army in Canada, Britain and the Pacific* (Ottawa: Queen's Printer, 1955), 105.

53    Adleman and Walton, *The Devil's Brigade*, 33.

54    Burhans, *The First Special Service Force*, 12.

55    Stanley W. Dziuban, *Military Relations Between the United States and Canada, 1939–1945* (Washington, D.C.: Office of the Chief of Military History, 1959), 260.

56    James C. Nixon, *"Combined Special Operations in World War II"* (Military Arts and Science master's thesis, U.S. Army Command and General Staff College, 1993), 41.

## CHAPTER TWO

# Being Special in Helena, Montana

1    Speech to FSSF Officers, Robert T. Frederick, Helena, Montana, 22 Oct 1942, Frederick Papers, Box 5, File: Speeches and Writings, 1942–1950.

2    Burhans, *First Special Service Force*, 19.

3    Interview, Kenneth Wickham, 16 Dec 1963, HIA, Robert H. Adleman Papers, Box 12, File: Interviews, Miscellaneous; Memo for File, 11 July 1942, DHH File: Org & Mob Jun/Dec 42.

4    Memo for File, 11 July 1942, DHH File: Org & Mob Jun/Dec 42.

5    Telegram, Lt-Col Bud Drury to Lt-Col Anderson, 11 July 1942, LAC, RG 24, Series C-1, Reel C-5436.

6    Ibid.

7    Memo for Dir of Staff Duties, General Staff, Ottawa (hereafter Wickham–Williamson agreement), 15 July 1942, DHH File: Org & Mob; Memo, Lt-Gen K. Stuart to Lt-Col J.G. McQueen, 9 Sept 1942, ibid.

8    Wickham–Williamson agreement, 15 July 1942, ibid.

9    Ibid.

10    Requisition for Enlisted Personnel, FSSF, 6 July 1942, HIA, Robert D. Burhans Papers, Box 6, File: Personnel Requisitions.

11    Interview, Kenneth Wickham, 16 Dec 1963, Adleman Papers, Box 12, File: Interviews, Misc.

12    It is worth noting here that the portrayal of American Forcemen as thugs and misfits in David Wolper's film, *The Devil's Brigade*, which was based on Adleman and Walton's book of the same title, provoked an outcry from American and Canadian Force veterans alike.

13   Memo re 2nd Canadian Parachute Battalion (2nd Cdn Para Bn), 18 July 1942, DHH, 168.009 (D43), File: Org & Adm, 16 Jul 42–20 May 43.

14   Burhans, *First Special Service Force*, 23.

15   Memo re 2nd Cdn Para Bn, 27 July 1942, DHH File: Org & Mob Jun/Dec 42.

16   Interview, Roy N. Cuff, n.d., Adleman Papers, Box 15, File: 3rd Regiment Interviews.

17   Ibid.

18   War Diary of 2nd Cdn Para Bn (hereafter WD), 6 August 1942, LAC, RG 24, Vol. 15,301.

19   Monthly Report (MR), 2nd Cdn Para Bn, 1–31 August 1942, DHH, 145.3009 (D7), File: Monthly Reports.

20   Ibid.

21   Burhans, *First Special Service Force*, 22.

22   Letter, M-Gen Murchie to Lt-Col McQueen, 4 Aug 1942, DHH File: Org & Mob Jun/Dec 42.

23   WD, 13 Aug 1942.

24   Interim Report, Training Casualties, 15 Aug 1942, Frederick Papers, Box 2.

25   Memo for the Commanding General (CG), Services of Supply, 14 July 1942, Burhans Papers, Box 6, File: Awards, Requests for Officers, Movement Orders.

26   Ibid.

27   Letter, Frederick to Anderson, 17 Aug 1942, Frederick Papers, Box 1, File: FSSF Miscellany.

28   Note for File, Lt-Col Anderson, 17 Aug 1942, DHH File: Org & Mob Jun/Dec 42.

29   Letter, Frederick to Anderson, 17 Aug 1942.

30   Ibid.

31   WD, 25 Aug 1942.

32   MR 2nd Cdn Para Bn, 1–30 Sept 1942, DHH, 145.3009 (D7), File: Monthly Reports.

33   MR 2nd Cdn Para Bn, 1–31 Aug 1942; MR of 2nd Cdn Para Bn, 1–30 Sept 1942.

34   MR 2nd Cdn Para Bn, 1–30 Sept 1942.

35   Ibid.

36   Requisition for Enlisted Personnel, FSSF, 6 July 1942.

37   WD, 30 August 1942.

38   MR 2nd Cdn Para Bn, 1–31 August 1942.

39   Conference between Representatives of Operations Division, War Department General Staff, Brigadier Duncan, and Mr. Geoffrey Pyke, 26 May 1942, NA-CP, RG 165, Entry 21, Stack 390/30/16/4, Box 968, Folder 381 (4-10-42).

40   Memo, McQueen to Stuart, 8 October 1942, DHH File: Org & Mob Jun/Dec 42.

41   Telegram, Frederick to FSSF HQ, 26 Sept 1942, Frederick Papers, Box 1, File: Memoranda, MSS, Map 1942.

42   Letter, Frederick to McQueen, 16 Oct 1942, DHH, 145.3009 (D5), File: Org & Admin, Corresp and Instr, Jul 42–Dec 44.

43   Ibid.

44   Memo, CGS to MND, 26 Oct 1942, DHH File: Org & Mob Jun/Dec 42.

45   Ibid.

46   Ibid.

47   Min of War Cabinet Comm Mtg, 28 Oct 1942, LAC, RG 2, Series B-2, Vol. 24.

48   Pope Diary, 30 October 1942, LAC, MG 27 III F4, Vol. 1.

49   Telegram, Stuart to Pope, 29 Oct 1942, LAC, RG 24, Series C-1, Reel C-5436.

50   Memo, Lt-Gen Joseph T. McNarney to Field Marshal Sir John Dill, 13 Nov 1942, NA-CP, RG 165, Entry 21, Box 968, Stack 390/30/16/4, Folder 320.2 (7-29-42).

51   Ibid.

52   MR of 2nd Cdn Para Bn, 1–30 Nov 1942, DHH, 145.3009 (D7), File: Monthly Reports.

53   Burhans, *First Special Service Force*, 42.

54   FSSF HQ to Commanding General, Army Ground Forces, 24 November 1942, HIA, Robert D. Burhans Papers, Box 1, File: Training; WD, 1–30 November 1942; Monthly Report of 2nd Canadian Parachute Battalion, 1–30 November 1942.

55   Robert T. Frederick, Speech to First Special Service Force Officers, 22 October 1942, HIA, Robert T. Frederick Papers, Box 5, File: Speeches and Writings, 1942–1950.

CHAPTER THREE

# Finding a Mission in 1943

1   Memo, CGS to MND, 20 April 1943, LAC, RG 24, Series C-1, Reel 5481.

2   Letter, Lt-Gen L.J. McNair to Commanding Officer, FSSF, Burhans Papers, Box 1, File: Training.

3   WD, 30 Oct 1942.

4   Memo re Paratroops, 6 Nov 1942, LAC, RG 24, Series C-1, Reel C-5436.

5   Letter, CGS to McQueen, 30 Nov 1942, DHH Org & Mob Jun/Dec 42.

6   MR 2nd Cdn Para Bn, 1–30 Nov 1942; Extract from Board of Discussions of Military Members of Defence Council, 26 Nov 1942, LAC, RG 24, Series C-1, Reel C-5436.

7   MR 2nd Cdn Para Bn, 1–30 Nov 1942.

8   Letter, CGS to McQueen, 9 Dec 1942, DHH File: Org & Mob Jun/Dec 42.

9   Letter, Dir of Staff Duties to DCGS, 15 Dec 1942, DHH File: Org & Mob.

10   Ibid.

11   Memo re Reinforcements, 2nd Cdn Para Bn, 18 Dec 1942, DHH, 112.3S2009 (D255), File: Org & Mob, 1st Cnd Sp Serv Bn, Jun/Dec 42.

12   WD, 10 Dec 1942.

13 WD, 16 January 1943.

14 MR 2nd Cdn Para Bn, 1–28 Feb 1943, DHH, 145.3009 (D7), File: Monthly Reports.

15 Letter, Frederick to DCGS, US Army, 3 Feb 1943, NA-CP, RG 165, Entry 418, Box 830, Stack 390/36/30/6, Folder OPD 322.9.

16 Memo re Employment of FSSF, 8 Feb 1943, Frederick Papers, Box 2.

17 Memo, Dir Staff Duties to CGS, 24 Feb 1943, LAC, RG 24, Series C-1, Reel C-5436.

18 Ibid.

19 WD, 25 Feb 1943.

20 Letter, R.W. Becket to Frederick, 8 Mar 1943, Frederick Papers, Box 3, File: FSSF, History, Corr.

21 Ibid.

22 Telegram, Dir Staff Duties, Ottawa, to Cdn Army Staff, Washington, 3 March 1943, DHH File: Org & Mob, Jan 43/Feb 45.

23 Telegram, CGS, Ottawa, to Cdn Army Staff, Washington, 23 March 1943, DHH File: Org & Mob, Jan 43/Feb 45.

24 Ibid.

25 Memo re Visit to PLOUGH Project by DCGS, 5–6 April 1943, DHH, 112.21009 (D197), Folder 5.

26 Ibid.

27 Ibid.

28 Memo, CGS to Min, 20 April 1943, LAC, RG 24, Series C-1, Reel 5481.

29 Report on Landing Exercises, 25–29 April 1943, Frederick Papers, Box 1, File: FSSF Miscellany.

30 Ibid.

31 Memo re The Plough Force, 18 Aug 1943, NA-CP, RG 165, Entry 421, Stack 390/37/24, Box 156, Folder ABC 320.2 (10-12-42).

32 Ibid.

33 WD, 28 May 1943.

34 Pope Diary, 1 June 1943.

35 Memo re 1st Cnd Sp Serv Bn Reinforcements, 5 June 1943, LAC, RG 24, Series C-1, Reel 5481.

36 Stacey, Six Years of War, 496.

37 Ibid., 497.

38 Ibid., 495.

39 Pope Diary, 24 May 1943.

40 Stacey, Six Years of War, 499.

41 Pope Diary, 12 June 1943.

42 WD, 3–11 July 1943, LAC, RG 24, Vol. 15,301.

43 Report of Activities, 1st Cnd Sp Serv Bn, 10–31 July 1943, DHH, 145.3009 (D7), File: Monthly Reports.

44 Ibid.

45 S-1 Journal, FSSF, 15 Aug 1943, Burhans Papers, Box 1, File: Secret Telegrams, Amchitka, 1943.

46 WD, 16 Aug 1943.

47 S-1 Journal, 17 Aug 1943.

48 Memo, The Plough Force, 18 Aug 1943, NA-CP, RG 165, Entry 421, Stack 390/37/24, Box 156,

Folder ABC 320.2 (10-12-42); "The PLOUGH Force," 112th Meeting of the Combined Chiefs of Staff( CCS), 18 Aug 1943 in Wartime Conferences of the Combined Chiefs of Staff (Wilmington, Del.: Scholarly Resources, 1982).

49 "The PLOUGH Force," Combined Chiefs of Staff, 18 August 1943.

50 WD, 12–28 September 1943.

51 Report of Activities, 1st Canadian Special Service Battalion, 1–27 October 1943, DHH, 145.3009 (D7), File: Monthly Reports.

52 Dziuban, Military Relations, 265; James C. Nixon, Combined Special Operations in World War II (Military Arts and Science master's thesis, U.S. Army Command and General Staff College, 1993), 47.

CHAPTER FOUR

# A "Special" Reinforcements Crisis

1 Telegram, B-Gen A.W. Beament to Lt-Gen K. Stuart, Naples, 15 Jan 1944, LAC, RG 24, Vol. 12,540, File: Org and Admin, 1 Cdn SS Bn.

2 Burhans, First Special Service Force, 88–89.

3 Martin Blumenson, Salerno to Cassino, United States Army in World War II: The Mediterranean Theater of Operations, vol. 3 (Washington, D.C.: Office of the Chief of Military History, Dept of the Army, 1969), 229.

4 Burhans, First Special Service Force, 96.

5 Fifth United States Army, Fifth Army History, vol. 3, The Winter Line (Wilmington, Del.: Scholarly Resources, 1980), 26.

6 Headquarters, Fifth Army, Operations Instruction No. 11, 24 Nov 1943, in Fifth US Army, Fifth Army History, 85.

7 Ibid., 26.

8 Over the next forty-eight hours, II Corps artillery fired 73,746 rounds in support of the attack, while X Corps fired an additional 111,568 rounds during the same period. The total expenditure of ammunition by the two corps equalled 3,191 tons. Fifth U.S. Army, Annex No. 3D – Artillery Expenditures, 100–102.

9 Burhans, First Special Service Force, 96.

10 Ibid., 103.

11 Ibid., 106.

12 Fifth U.S. Army, Fifth Army History, 28.

13 Burhans, First Special Service Force, 113–114.

14 S-3 Journal, 6 Dec 1943, Burhans Papers, Box 13, File: S-3 Journal "Difensa," 1–10 Dec 1943.

15 Ibid.

16 US War Dept, The Fifth Army at the Winter Line, 15 Nov 1943–15 Jan 1944, American Forces in Action Series (Washington, DC: Government Printer, 1945), 28.

17    Commendation, Lt-Gen Mark W. Clark to
      Commanding Officer, FSSF, 10 Dec 1943,
      LAC, RG 24, Vol. 12,540, File: Org and Admin,
      1 Cdn SS Bn.
18    Burhans, *First Special Service Force*, 124.
19    WD, 10 Dec 1943.
20    WD, 14 Dec 1943.
21    Personnel Replacement Requisition, FSSF to II
      Corps, 9 Dec 1943, Burhans Papers, Box 7, File:
      Secret Corr, July 1942–April 1944.
22    Letter, Lt-Gen Mark Clark to Col Frederick, 10 Dec
      1943, Frederick Papers, Box 3, File: FSSF Corr,
      1943.
23    WD, 14 Dec 1943.
24    Report of Activities, 1st Cnd Sp Serv Bn, 16 Dec
      1943–31 Jan 1944, DHH, 145.3009 (D7), File:
      Monthly Reports.
25    Ibid.
26    Burhans, *First Special Service Force*, 154–155.
27    War Diary Annex, Headquarters, Third
      Regiment, Jan 1944, LAC, RG 24, Vol. 15,301.
28    WD, 8–10 Jan 1944.
29    Interview, John R. Dawson, 16 Oct 1963,
      Adleman Papers, Box 13, File: 2nd Regiment
      Interviews.
30    HQ, FSSF, Office of Personnel Officer, 8 Oct 1944,
      Burhans Papers, Box 1, File: Hist File, General.
31    WD, 1 Jan 1944.
32    WD, 14 and 25 Jan 1944.
33    Interview, Jack Akehurst, 15 Nov 1963; Adleman
      Papers, Box 8, File: 1st Regiment Interviews.
34    Letter, Lt-Col T.P. Gilday to B-Gen A.W. Beament,
      15 Jan 1944, DHH, 145.3009 (D3), File: Instructions
      and Directives, 1 Cdn SS Bn.
35    Ibid.
36    Telegram, Beament to Stuart, 15 Jan 1944;
      Telegram, Beament to Stuart, 18 Jan 1944, LAC,
      RG 24, Vol. 12,540, File: Org and Admin, 1 Cdn
      SS Bn.
37    Memo, B-Gen E.G. Weeks to M-Gen P.J. Montague,
      17 Jan 1944, LAC, RG 24, Vol. 12,540, File: Org and
      Admin, 1 Cdn SS Bn.
38    Report of Activities, 16 Dec 1943–31 Jan 1944.
39    Telegram, Montague to Lt-Gen J.C. Murchie,
      18 Jan 1944, LAC, RG 24, Vol. 12,540, File: Org and
      Admin, 1 Cdn SS Bn.
40    Ibid.
41    Memo, B-Gen C.S. Booth to Montague, 24 Jan
      1944, LAC, RG 24, Vol. 12,540, File: Org and
      Admin, 1 Cdn SS Bn.
42    Ibid.
43    WD, 31 Dec 1943.
44    Memo, Booth to Montague, 24 Jan 1944.
45    Memo, Weeks to Booth, 21 Jan 1944, LAC, RG 24,
      Vol. 12,540, File: Org and Admin, 1 Cdn SS Bn.

46    Telegram, Montague to Murchie, 26 Jan 1944,
      LAC, RG 24, Vol. 12,540, File: Rfts File #1.
47    Telegram, Cdn Army Staff, Washington, to
      NDHQ, Ottawa, 28 Jan 1944, LAC, RG 24,
      Series C-1, Reel C-5489.
48    Telegram, Murchie to Stuart, 29 Jan 1944, LAC, RG
      24, Vol. 12,540, File: Org and Admin, 1 Cdn SS Bn.
49    Telegram, Stuart to Murchie, 1 Feb 1944, LAC, RG
      24, Vol. 12,540, File: Org and Admin, 1 Cdn SS Bn.
50    Telegram, Beament to Montague, 29 Jan 1944,
      NAC, RG 24, Vol. 12,540, File: Rfts File #1;
      Telegram, Stuart to Murchie, 1 February 1944.
51    Telegram, Murchie to Stuart, 2 February 1944,
      NAC, RG 24, Vol. 12,540, File: Rfts File #1.
52    Memorandum, Chief of General Staff to the Minister
      of National Defence, 2 February 1944, DHH,
      112.21009 (D195), File: Summary of Correspondence
      on PLOUGH project.
53    Burhans, *The First Special Service Force*, 165.
54    WD, 29 January–2 February 1944.

CHAPTER FIVE

# Punch-Drunk: The Anzio Beachhead

1     Letter, B-Gen Robert T. Frederick to Gen Mark
      Clark, 19 Feb 1944, Burhans Papers, Box 19, File:
      Tables of Org.
2     Blumenson, *Salerno to Cassino*, 359.
3     King, *Rangers*, 39.
4     Activities of the 1st Cnd Sp Serv Bn, 1–29 Feb 1944,
      DHH, 145.3009 (D7), File: Monthly Reports; WD,
      1–7 Feb 1944; Carlo D'Este, *Fatal Decision: Anzio
      and the Battle for Rome* (New York: Harper Collins
      Publishers, 1991), 138–140; Burhans, *First Special
      Service Force*, 166–170.
5     "Anzio Beachhead Operations—February 1944,"
      Burhans Papers, Box 6, File: History FSSF.
6     Ibid.
7     Burhans, *First Special Service Force*, 172.
8     Memo, Lt-Gen Kenneth Stuart to CGS, 9 Feb
      1944, LAC, RG 24, Vol. 12,540, File: Rfts File #1.
9     Telegram, Stuart to Murchie, 11 Feb 1944, LAC, RG
      24, Vol. 12,540, File: Org &Admin, 1 Cdn SS Bn.
10    Memo re: Reinforcements, 1 Cdn SS Bn, 10 Feb
      1944, LAC, RG 24, Vol. 12,540, File: Org & Admin,
      1 Cdn SS Bn.
11    Stacey, *Arms, Men and Governments*, 424.
12    Nicholson, *The Canadians in Italy*, 338.
13    Telegram, Stuart to Murchie, 11 Feb 1944.
14    Memo re Reinforcements, 1 Cdn SS Bn,
      10 Feb 1944.
15    Activities of the 1st Cnd Sp Serv Bn, 1–29 Feb 1944.
16    Ibid.
17    Ibid.

18  "Summary of the Enemy's Actions Opposing this Force, 1–29 Feb 1944," Burhans Papers, Box 6, File: Hist FSSF.
19  WD, 16 Feb 1944.
20  "Summary of the Enemy's Actions," 1–29 Feb 1944; WD, 16 Feb 1944; Burhans, *First Special Service Force*, 179.
21  WD, 18 Feb 1944.
22  Interview, John R. Dawson, 16 Oct 1963, Adleman Papers, Box 13, File: 2nd Regiment Interviews.
23  Interview, J.G. Bourne, 30 Sept 1963, Adleman Papers, Box 12, File: Misc Interviews.
24  Letter, Frederick to CG, US Fifth Army, 19 Feb 1944, Burhans Papers, Box 19, File: Table of Org.
25  Ibid.
26  Ibid.
27  Ibid.
28  "Summary of the Enemy's Actions," 1–29 Feb 1944.
29  Burhans, *First Special Service Force*, 185; "Summary of the Enemy's Actions,", 1–29 Feb 1944.
30  Activities of the 1st Canadian Special Service Battalion, 1–29 February 1944.
31  WD, 29 February 1944.
32  Nicholson, *The Canadians in Italy*, 670-671; Dziuban, *Military Relations Between the United States and Canada*, 265.

## CHAPTER SIX

# Reorganization Under Fire

1  Letter, Weeks to Fifth Army HQ, Naples, 3 April 1944, Frederick Papers, Box 1, File: FSSF Miscellany.
2  Letter, Gen George C. Marshall to Field Marshal Sir John Dill, 16 Feb 1944, NA-CP, RG 165, Entry 418, Box 830, Stack 390/36/30/6, Folder OPD 322.9.
3  Telegram, Stuart to Murchie, 21 Feb 1944, LAC, RG 24, Vol. 12,540, File: Org & Admin, 1 Cdn SS Bn.
4  Ibid.
5  Memo, FSSF Supply Officer to Frederick, 27 Feb 1944, Burhans Papers, Box 7, File: Secret Corr.
6  Letter, US Fifth Army HQ, to CG, FSSF, 8 March 1944, Burhans Papers, Box 19, File: Table of Org.
7  Memo, B-Gen M.H.S. Penhale, CMHQ General Staff, 23 Feb 1944, LAC, RG 24, Vol. 12,540, File: Rfts File #1.
8  Ibid.
9  Letter, Penhale to Stuart, 28 Feb 1944, LAC, RG 24, Vol. 12,540, File: Org & Admin, 1 Cdn SS Bn.
10  WD, 29 Feb 1944.
11  Activities of the 1st Cnd Sp Serv Bn, 1–29 Feb 1944.
12  Telegram, Stuart to Murchie, 4 Mar 1944, DHH File:  Org & Mob, Jan 43/Feb 45.
13  Telegram, Stuart to B-Gen E.G. Weeks, 4 Mar 1944, LAC, RG 24, Vol. 12,540, File: Rfts File #1.
14  Ibid.

15  Letter, US Fifth Army HQ to CG, FSSF, 8 March 1944.
16  Interview Questionnaire, George Sabine, Adleman Papers, Box 8, File: 1st Regiment Interviews.
17  Memo, FSSF Supply Officer to Frederick, 27 Feb 1944, Burhans Papers, Box 7, File: Secret Corr.
18  WD, 21 Mar 1944.
19  FSSF Summary of Ops, 1–30 April 1944, NA-CP, RG 407, Entry 427, Stack 270/64/24/6-7, Box 23,274; WD, 21 Mar 1944.
20  Letter, B-Gen Frederick to Gen Clark, 19 Feb 1944.
21  WD, 28 Mar 1944.
22  WD, 31 Mar 1944.
23  WD, 31 Mar 1944 and 10 April 1944.
24  Letter, Weeks to Fifth Army HQ, 3 April 1944, Frederick Papers, Box 1, File: FSSF Miscellany.
25  Letter, Fifth Army HQ to Weeks, 9 April 1944, Burhans Papers, Box 7, File: Secret Corr.
26  Letter, Lt-Col Wickham to Lt-Col Akehurst, 10 April 1944, Burhans Papers, Box 7, File: Secret Corr.
27  Ibid.
28  Ibid.
29  Interview, K. Wickham, 16 Dec 1963, Adleman Papers, Box 12, File: Interviews: Misc.
30  Interview, George Sabine, n.d., Adleman Papers, Box 8, File: 1st Regiment Interviews.
31  Interview, James R. Metzger, 7 Oct 1963, Adleman Papers, Box 8, File: 1st Regiment Interviews.
32  Sholto Watt, "Crack Mixed Force Is Gradually Becoming American."
33  WD, 27 April 1944.
34  FSSF Summary of Ops, 1–30 April 1944.
35  Ibid.
36  Ibid.
37  Ibid.
38  Activities of the 1st Cnd Sp Serv Bn, 1–30 April 1944, DHH, 145.3009 (D7), File: Monthly Reports.
39  Activities of the 1st Cnd Sp Serv Bn, 1 May–10 June 1944.
40  Ibid.
41  Ibid.
42  Letter, B-Gen Frederick, 22 May 1944, Frederick Papers, Box 1, File: FSSF Miscellany.
43  FSSF G-3 Journal, 23 May 1944, NA-CP, RG 407, Entry 427, Stack 270/64/24/6-7, Box 23,280.
44  Burhans, *First Special Service Force*, 216.
45  William Sheldon, "Battle: 1944, Anzio to Rome," 6, Adleman Papers, Box 8, File: 1st Regiment Interviews.
46  Interview, Thomas Zabski, Adleman Papers, Box 12, File: Misc Interviews.
47  FSSF G-3 Journal, 23 May 1944.
48  Burhans, *First Special Service Force*,  217.
49  FSSF Summary of Ops, May 1944, NA-CP, RG 407, Entry 427, Stack 270/64/24/6-7, Box 23,274.
50  Sheldon, *"Battle"*, 7-8.

51    Interview, John R. Dawson, 16 October 1963.
52    FSSF Summary of Operations, May 1944.
53    FSSF Summary of Operations, June 1944, NA-CP,
      RG 407, Entry 427, Stack 270/64/24/6-7,
      Box 23, 274.
54    Interview, J.G. Bourne, 30 September 1963,
      Adleman Papers, Box 12, File: Misc Interviews.
55    Activities of the First Canadian Special
      Service Battalion, 1 May – 10 June 1944.
56    Ibid.

CHAPTER SEVEN

# Disbandment in Southern France

1     Memo, Lt-Gen Stuart to MND, 7 Oct 1944, LAC,
      RG 24, Vol. 12,540, File: Org & Admin, 1 Cdn SS Bn.
2     WD, 7 June 1944, LAC, RG 24, Vol. 15,301.
3     FSSF HQ, Office of Personnel Officer, 8 Oct 1944,
      Burhans Papers, Box 1, File: Hist File, General.
4     Activities of 1 Cdn SS Bn, 1 May–10 June 1944,
      DHH, 145.3009 (D7), File: Monthly Reports.
5     Letter, Frederick to CG, US Fifth Army, 22 June
      1944, Burhans Papers, Box 7, File: Confidential.
6     Letter, US Fifth Army HQ, to CG, North African
      Theater of Operations, 3 July 1944, Burhans
      Papers, Box 19, File: Table of Org.
7     In June 1944 it was decided that the 1st Cnd Sp
      Serv Bn would be included in the allotment of
      British awards to American troops, but it was not
      until November 1944, however, that the first
      British decorations were received by four Canadian
      members of the Force. Activities of 1st Cnd Sp Serv
      Bn, 11 June–3 July 1944, DHH, 145.3009 (D7), File:
      Monthly Reports; Ibid, 1 Nov 1944–9 Jan 1945.
8     Burhans, First Special Service Force, 249.
9     WD, 23 June 1944.
10    WD, 28 June 1944.
11    WD, 29 June 1944.
12    Ibid.; Letter, Col Walker to B-Gen Weeks, 8 July
      1944, LAC, RG 24, Series C-1, Reel C-5469.
13    WD, 5 July 1944.
14    FSSF Summary of Ops, July 1944, NA-CP, RG 407,
      Entry 427, Stack 270/64/24/6-7, Box 23,274.
15    Memo re. Replacement Training, Lt-Col Wickham,
      24 June 1944, LAC, RG 24, Series C-1, Reel C-5469.
16    Activities of 1 Cdn SS Bn, 11 June–3 July 1944.
17    Ibid., 4–31 July 1944.
18    FSSF Summary of Ops, 1–31 July 1944.
19    Interview, D.M. ["Pat"] O'Neill, n.d., Adleman Papers,
      Box 10, File: Headquarters Interviews.
20    FSSF Summary of Ops, 1–31 July 1944.
21    Memo, US Seventh Army HQ to CG, NATOUSA
      Replacement Command, 22 July 1944, Burhans
      Papers, Box 7, File: Confidential File.
22    Interview, Tom Zabski, n.d., Adleman Papers,
      Box 12, File: Interviews (Misc).
23    WD, 8 July 1944.
24    WD, 10 July 1944.
25    WD, 24 July 1944.
26    FSSF Summary of Ops, 1–31 Aug 1944.
27    Burhans, First Special Service Force, 273.
28    FSSF Summary of Ops, 1–31 Aug 1944.
29    Memo re. Reinforcements, 1 SS Bn, B-Gen Penhale,
      5 Aug 1944, LAC, RG 24, Vol. 12,540, File: Rfts
      File #2.
30    Ibid.
31    Nicholson, The Canadians in Italy, 562.
32    Activities of 1 Cdn SS Bn, 1–30 Sept 1944, DHH,
      145.3009 (D7), File: Monthly Reports.
33    WD, 15 August 1944.
34    WD, 5 Oct and 7 Oct 1944.
35    WD, 20 Sept 1944.
36    WD, 17 Sept 1944.
37    Telegram, Weeks to CMHQ, 16 Sept 1944, LAC, RG
      24, Vol. 12,540, File: Rfts File #2.
38    Telegram, CMHQ to Weeks, 28 September 1944.
39    Letter, Walker to CG, US Seventh Army, 19 Sept
      1944, Burhans Papers, Box 19, File: Table of Org.
40    Ibid.
41    Ibid.
42    WD, 16 Sept 1944.
43    WD, 30 Sept1944.
44    Activities of 1 Cdn SS Bn, 1–30 Sept 1944.
45    Ibid.
46    General Observations on the Visit to Italy of
      Colonel, the Honourable J.L. Ralston, MND, Fall
      1944, LAC, MG 27 III B11, J.L. Ralston Papers
      (hereafter Ralston Papers), File: Fall 1944, General
      Observations and Memos.
47    Memo, Weeks to MND, 3 Oct 1944, LAC, RG 24,
      Vol. 12,540, Org & Admin, 1 Cdn SS Bn.
48    Memo, Stuart to MND, 7 Oct 1944.
49    Diary, Col H.A. Dyde, 12 Oct 1944, Ralston Papers,
      File: Dyde, Col. H.A. Diary.
50    Alfred D. Chandler Jr., ed. The Papers of Dwight
      David Eisenhower, vol. 4, The War Years (Baltimore:
      Johns Hopkins Press, 1970), 2232.
51    Ibid.
52    Ibid.
53    Ibid.
54    Memo, B-Gen L.M. Chelsey to Lt-Gen Murchie,
      13 Oct 1944, LAC, RG 24, Series C-1, Reel C-5481.
55    Ibid.
56    Telegram, Murchie to Ralston, 13 Oct 1944, LAC,
      RG 24, Vol. 12,540, File: Rfts File #2.
57    Memo re Disbandment, Murchie, 21 Oct 1944, LAC,
      RG 24, Series C-1, Reel C-5481.
58    WD, 8 Oct 1944.
59    WD, 10 Oct 1944.

60   WD, 14 Oct 1944.
61   WD, 12 Oct 1944.
62   WD, 24 Oct 1944.
63   WD, 5 Nov 1944.
64   Memo, FSSF Assistant Adj to Col Walker, 13 Nov 1944, DHH, 145.3009 (D3), File: Instrs & Directives, 1st Cnd Sp Serv Bn.
65   Ibid.
66   WD, 14 Nov 1944.
67   Letter, Walker to CG, US Sixth Army Group, 15 Nov 1944, DHH, 145.3009 (D3), File: Instrs and Directives, 1st Cnd Sp Serv Bn.
68   Ibid.
69   Ibid.
70   Ibid.
71   WD, 22 Nov 1944.
72   Memo re. Disbandment, 1 SS Bn, 25 Nov 1944, LAC, RG 24, Vol. 12,540, File: Org & Admin, 1 Cdn SS Bn.
73   Ibid.
74   Memo re Disposition of 1 Cdn SS Bn personnel, Lt-Col Akehurst, 24 Nov 1944, LAC, RG 24, Vol. 12,540, File: Org & Admin, 1 Cdn SS Bn.
75   Ibid.
76   Ibid.
77   Telegram, Major-General Charles Foulkes to CMHQ, 1 December 1944, NAC, RG 24, Vol. 12,540, File: Org & Admin, 1 Cdn Spec Serv Bn.
78   WD, 1–4 December 1944.
79   WD, 5 December 1944.
80   Activities of the First Canadian Special Service Battalion, 1 November 1944 – 9 Januray 1945.
81   Interview, Lewis M. Lindsay, n.d., HIA, Robert H. Adleman Papers, Box 9, File: Forcemen, Recollections.
82   Interview, Harlan Morgan, N.d., HIA, Robert H. Adleman Papers, Box 13, File: 2nd Regiment Interviews.

## CONCLUSION

# More Men, More Guns, No Solutions

1    Letter, Walker to CG, US Sixth Army Group, 15 Nov 1944, DHH, 145.3009 (D3), File: Instrs and Directives, 1st Cnd Sp Serv Bn.
2    Letter, B-Gen Frederick to Gen Clark, 19 Feb 1944, Burhans Papers, Box 19, File: Tables of Org.
3    Letter, B-Gen Frederick to Commanding General, Fifth Army, 22 June 1944, Burhans Papers, Box 7, File: Confidential File.
4    Ibid.
5    Watt, "Crack Mixed Force Is Gradually Becoming American." Written January 1944; delayed by censors to 9 April 1944.
6    Dziuban, *Military Relations*, 267–268.
7    Nixon, *"Combined Special Operations in World War II,"* 52, 64.
8    Dziuban, *Military Relations*, 264.
9    Letter, Dir Staff Duties to DCGS, 15 Dec 1942, DHH File: Org & Mob Jun/Dec 42.
10   Letter, Frederick to Clark, 19 Feb 1944.
11   Telegram, Stuart to Murchie, 21 Feb 1944, LAC, RG 24, Vol. 12,540, File: Org & Admin, 1 Cdn SS Bn.
12   Letter, Frederick to Clark, 19 Feb 1944.
13   Letter, Frederick to CG Fifth Army, 22 June 1944.
14   WD, 10 Oct and 14 Nov 1944, LAC, RG 24, Vol. 15,301.
15   Memo, FSSF Assistant Adj to Col Walker, 13 Nov 1944, DHH, 145.3009 (D3), File: Instrs & Directives, 1st Cnd Sp Serv Bn; WD, 14 Nov 1944.
16   Activities of 1 Cdn SS Bn, 1 Nov 1944–9 Jan 1945, DHH, 145.3009 (D7), File: Monthly Reports.

# BIBLIOGRAPHY

## GOVERNMENT RECORDS

### Canada, Department of National Defence, Directorate of History and Heritage (DHH), Ottawa, Ontario

Correspondence and Instructions re Organization and Administration of 1st Canadian Special Service Battalion (2nd Canadian Parachute Battalion), 16 July 1942 – 20 May 1943.

Instructions and Directives for 1st Canadian Special Service Battalion, June 1943 – December 1944.

Monthly Reports of the 1st Canadian Special Service Battalion, August 1942 – January 1945.

Organization, Administration, Correspondence and Instructions for 1st Canadian Special Service Battalion, June 1942 – December 1944.

Report on the Activities of the 1st Canadian Special Service Battalion, Kiska, 1 August – 30 September 1943.

Report on Visit of DCGS(B) to Plough Project (1st Spec Service Force) Helena, Montana, 5-6 April 1943.

Summary of Correspondence on Plough Project, April 1943.

### Canada. Library and Archives Canada (LAC), Ottawa, Ontario

Records of the Department of National Defence, RG 24

- Employment and Movement - Operations - 1st Special Service Battalion.
- Mobilization and Organization - Plough Project (1st Special Service Battalion).
- Plough Project - 1st Special Service Battalion - Appointments – Generally.
- Plough Project - 1st Special Service Battalion - Command and Senior Appointments.
- Reinforcements Files, 1st Canadian Special Service Battalion.
- War Diary, 2nd Canadian Parachute Battalion (within 1st Special Service Force).

Records of the Privy Council Office, RG 2.

- Minutes of the War Cabinet Committee Meetings, 1942-1944

**United States. National Archives (NA–CP), College Park, Maryland.**

Records of the War Department General and Special Staff, RG 165
- FSSF, Administrative Correspondence
- Records of the Combined Chiefs of Staff
- Reference Collection Relating to Foreign Countries

World War II Operations Reports, 1940-1948, RG 407
- FSSF, Histories, After Action Reports, Periodic Operations Reports, and Orders

## PRIVATE PAPERS

**Library and Archives Canada (LAC), Ottawa, Ontario.**

Maurice Pope Papers
James Layton Ralston Papers
Kenneth Stuart Papers

**Hoover Institution Archives on War, Peace, and Revolution (HIA), Stanford University, California.**

Robert H. Adleman Papers
Robert D. Burhans Papers
Robert T. Frederick Papers

### Government Published Sources

Blumenson, Martin. *Salerno to Cassino. United States Army in World War II: The Mediterranean Theater of Operations.* Vol. 3. Washington, DC: Office of the Chief of Military History, US Army, 1969.

Dziuban, Stanley W. *Military Relations Between the United States and Canada, 1939-1945.* United States Army in World War II. Special Studies. Washington, DC: Office of the Chief of Military History, 1959.

Fifth United States Army. *Fifth Army History.* Vol.3. *The Winter Line.* Wilmington Del.: Scholarly Resources, 1980.

Greenfield, Kent Roberts, et al. *The Organization of Ground Combat Troops.* United States Army in World War II. The Army Ground Forces. Washington, DC: Historical Division, United States Army, 1947.

Nicholson, G.W.L. *The Canadians in Italy, 1943-1945.* Vol. 2 of *Official History of the Canadian Army in the Second World War.* Ottawa: Queen's Printer, 1956.

Stacey, C.P. *Arms, Men and Governments: The War Policies of Canada, 1939-1945.* Ottawa: Queen's Printer, 1970.

————. *The Canadian Army, 1939-1945: An Official Historical Summary.* Ottawa: King's Printer, 1948.

————. *Six Years of War. The Army in Canada, Britain and the Pacific.* Vol. 1 of *Official History of the Canadian Army in the Second World War.* Ottawa: Queen's Printer, 1955.

United States. Department of the Army. Office, Chief of Military History. *The Replacement System in the U.S. Army: An Analytical Study of World War II Experience.* Washington, DC: GPO, 1950.

United States. War Department. *The Fifth Army at the Winter Line, 15 November 1943–15 January 1944.* American Forces in Action Series. Washington, DC: Government Printer, 1945.

*Wartime Conferences of the Combined Chiefs of Staff.* Wilmington Del.: Scholarly Resources, 1982.


## INTERVIEWS

Interviews conducted by Robert H. Adleman and George Walton in 1963. The collection of interviews, along with questionnaires distributed to First Special Service Force veterans, is held by the Hoover Institution Archives on War, Peace, and Revolution at Stanford University, California. Interviews cited in the text are listed below:

| | | |
|---|---|---|
| Jack Akehurst | Lewis M. Lindsay | William Sheldon |
| J.G. Bourne | James R. Metzger | William Story |
| Robert D. Burhans | Harlan Morgan | Kenneth Wickham |
| Roy N. Cuff | D.M. ["Pat"] O'Neill | Thomas Zabski |
| John R. Dawson | George Sabine | |


## BOOKS, ARTICLES AND THESES

Adleman, Robert H., and George Walton. *The Devil's Brigade.* Philadelphia: Chilton Books, 1966.

Beaumont, Roger A. *Joint Military Operations: A Short History.* Westport, Conn.: Greenwood Press, 1993.

————. *Military Elites: Special Fighting Units in the Modern World.* Indianapolis: Bobbs-Merrill, 1974.

Burhans, Robert D. *The First Special Service Force: A War History of the North Americans, 1942-1944.* Washington, DC: Infantry Journal Press, 1947.

Chandler, Alfred D. Jr., ed. *The Papers of Dwight David Eisenhower,* Vol. 4, *The War Years.* Baltimore: Johns Hopkins Press, 1970.

Cohen, E.A. *Commandos and Politicians: Elite Military Units in Modern Democracies.* Harvard: Harvard University Press, 1978.

D'Este, Carlo. *Eisenhower: A Soldier's Life.* New York: Henry Holt, 2002.

———. *Fatal Decision: Anzio and the Battle for Rome.* New York: Harper Collins Publishers, 1991.

Eggleston, Wilfrid. *Scientists at War.* Toronto: Oxford University Press, 1950.

Fergusson, Bernard. *The Watery Maze: The Story of Combined Operations.* London: Collins, 1961.

Granatstein, J.L. "The American Influence on the Canadian Military, 1939–1963." *Canadian Military History* 2, no. 1 (Spring 1993), 63-73.

King, Michael J. *Rangers: Selected Combat Missions in World War II.* Fort Leavenworth: Combat Studies Institute, 1985.

Hogan, David W., Jr. *U.S. Army Special Operations in World War II.* Washington, DC: Center for Military History, 1992.

Hough, Richard Alexander. *Mountbatten.* New York: Random House, 1981.

Lampe, David. *Pyke: The Unknown Genius.* London: Evans Brothers, 1959.

McMichael, Scott R. *A Historical Perspective on Light Infantry.* Fort Leavenworth: Combat Studies Institute, 1987.

Nixon, James C. "*Combined Special Operations in World War II.*" Master's thesis (Military Arts and Science): US Army Command and General Staff College, 1993. Alexandria, Va.: Defense Technical Information Center, 1993.

Pogue, Forrest. *George C. Marshall: Ordeal and Hope, 1939-1942.* New York: Viking Press, 1966.

Springer, Joseph A. *The Black Devil Brigade: The True Story of the First Special Service Force; An Oral History.* Pacifica, Cal.: Pacifica Military History, 2001.

Ross, Robert Todd. *The Supercommandos: First Special Service Force, 1942-1944 : An Illustrated History.* Atglen, Pa.: Schiffer Publishing, 2000.

Shay, Steven E. "*From Braves to Black Devils: The Activation and Battles of the First Special Service Force, 1942-1944.*" Master's thesis: Washington State University, 2000.

Story, William S., ed. *The First Special Service Force: A Commemorative History, July 1942 – January 1945.* Dallas: Taylor Publishing Company, 1995.

Twohig, J.P.O. "Are Commandos Really Necessary?" *Army Quarterly* 57, no. 1 (October 1948), 86-88.

Valentine, Janet G. "*The North Atlantic Triangle and the Formation of the First Special Service Force.*" Master's thesis: University of North Florida, 1995.

Wickham, Kenneth G. *An Adjutant General Remembers.* Fort Harrison, Ind.: Adjutant Generals Corps Regimental Association, 1991.

Yeats, Catherine C. "*The Worst Was Yet to Come: The Genesis and Evolution of the First Special Service Force, 1942-1943.*" Master's thesis: University of Idaho, 1995.

Ziegler, Philip. *Mountbatten: The Official Biography.* London: Collins, 1985.

# INDEX

# ABOUT THE AUTHOR

**JAMES A. WOOD** is a graduate of Wilfrid Laurier University and the University of New Brunswick, where he specialized in military and diplomatic history. He is currently working towards a doctoral degree in Canadian history at Wilfrid Laurier University, where he is the recipient of a doctoral fellowship from the Social Sciences and Humanities Research Council of Canada. He has published articles in *The Journal of Military History*, *The Northern Mariner*, and *Canadian Military History*.

*We Move Only Forward* is his first book.